WOMEN AT PRAYER

A HALAKHIC ANALYSIS OF WOMEN'S PRAYER GROUPS

EXPANDED EDITION

WOMEN AT PRAYER

A HALAKHIC ANALYSIS OF WOMEN'S PRAYER GROUPS

EXPANDED EDITION

Avraham Weiss

KTAV PUBLISHING HOUSE, INC
Hoboken, New Jersey

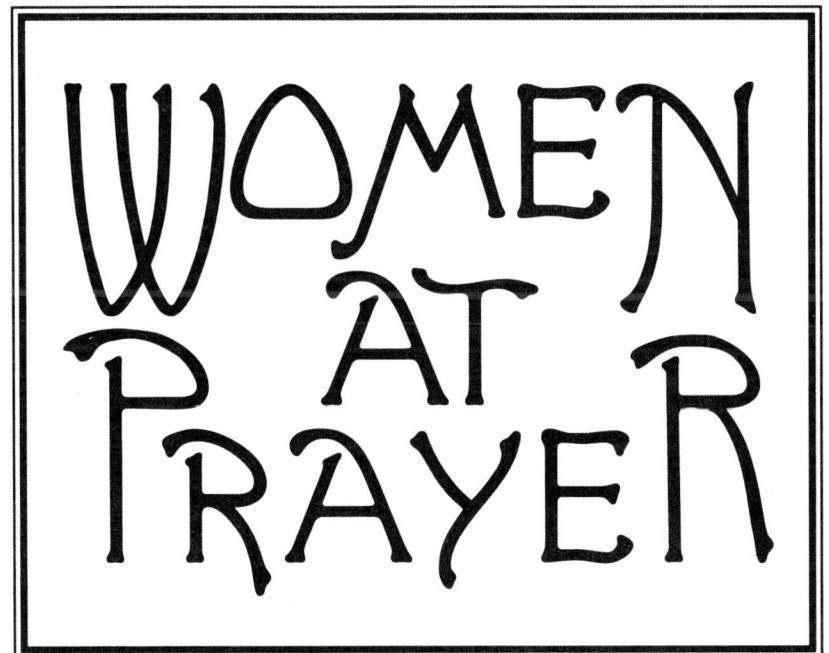

First Edition 1990
Second Edition 1994
Third Edition 2001

Library of Congress Cataloging-in-Publication Data

Weiss, Avraham.
Women at prayer : a halakhic analysis of women's prayer groups /
Avraham Weiss.—Expanded ed.
p. cm.
Includes bibliographical references and index.
ISBN 0-88125-719-2
1. Jewish women—Religious life. 2. Women's prayer groups—Judiasm.
3. Bible, O.T. Esther—Reading. 4. Women—Legal status, laws, etc. 5. Orthodox
Judaism—United States. 6. Women in Judaism. I. Title.

BM726.W45 2001
296.4'5'082—dc21 2001029188

Distributed by KTAV Publishing House, Inc.
900 Jefferson Street
Hoboken, NJ 07030
Fax 201-963-9524
Email KTAV@compuserve.com

For my mother,
Miriam Borenstein Weiss,
of blessed memory

Contents

Preface xi
Introduction xv
Introduction to the Expanded Edition xvii

1. **The Role of Women in Judaism** 1
   The Image of God 1
   Equality and Identity of Roles 3
   The Complementary Tasks 4
      The Only Place 5
      The Secondary Role 6
   The Primary Obligation: The Most Cogent Explanation 7
   The Home Role and Jewish Continuity 10

2. **Women and Private Prayer** 13
   Shemoneh Esreh 13
      Maimonidean Prayer 14
      Nachmanidean Prayer 18
      The Rationale 19
      Rashi and Tosafot 21
   Shema 22
   Birkhot ha-Shaḥar 24
   Pesukei de-Zimra 25
   Birkhot Shema 26
   Blessings Before Shemoneh Esreh 28
   Concluding Prayers 29

3. **The Emergence of Communal Prayer** 33
   The History 33
   The Legal Perspective 37
      Devarim she-bi-Kedushah 37
      Tefillah be-Ẓibbur 39
   Public Torah Reading 41

4. **Women and Communal Prayer** 43
The Exemption of Women from Communal Prayer 43
Women and *Minyan* 44
The Legal Exclusion 45
The Correlation Principle 46
Pirsuma: The Joining of Ten for Publicity 53

5. **Women and Torah Study** 57
The Exemption 57
The Mishnah in Sotah 57
Rambam's View 59
Women and *Talmud Torah* 61
The Obligation 64
"Whoever Does Not Learn Will Not Do" 64
In-Depth Knowledge 64

6. **Women and *Aliyot*** 67
Kevod Ẓibbur 67
The Shame of Ignorance 68
Modesty 70
The Key Definition: Equality of Obligation 71
Private and Public Torah Study 71
Kevod Ẓibbur Defined 75
Women and Public Torah Reading 77
Torah Blessings at Women's *Tefillah* Groups 80

7. **Women and *Sifrei Torah*** 85
The Talmudic Sources 85
"Words of Torah Are Not Susceptible to *Tumah*" 85
Ba'al Keri and *Niddah* 87
The Halakhah 90
The Difficult Rema 90
Tumah and Uncleanliness: A Conceptual Analysis 91
The Rema: A Possible Explanation 93
A Synopsis of Halakhic Sources 94

8. **Additional Issues** 99
An Incomplete Fulfillment of Prayer 99
Kavvanah in Prayer 101

The Appeal to Contemporary Torah Scholars 106
  Rav Yosef Dov Soloveitchik 107
  Rav Moshe Feinstein 108
Imitation of Non-Jewish Practices 112
  Offshoots of the Feminist Movement 112
  While Performing a Mitzvah of the Torah 114
Minhag: A New Practice in Synagogue Custom 115
  Prohibition Based on Novelty 116
  Improper and Insincere 116
  Approbation of Noted Scholars 116
  "We Never Saw" 117
Location: In the Home or the Synagogue? 118
  The Rationale 118
  The Legal Preference 119

Conclusion 123
Women and the Reading of the Megillah 125
Traditional Authorities and Sources 149
Bibliography 157
Index 161

Preface

The proliferation of women's prayer groups (often referred to as women's tefillah groups) has evoked considerable debate in the Jewish community. As will be demonstrated in the pages that follow, however, women's prayer groups are not an aberration of the halakhic (religio-legal) system. They emerge naturally from the wellsprings of the halakhic process and flow from an understanding of the basic principles of Judaism.

In line with this view, the purpose of this study is to analyze the phenomenon of women's prayer groups from a halakhic perspective. First, the status of women in halakhah is reviewed, and a framework is presented within which the legitimacy of women's tefillah groups can be considered. Since women's prayer groups include Torah reading as well as tefillah (prayer), separate sections are devoted to an analysis of the role of women in each of these enterprises, both in the private and the public sphere. How public services have evolved and whether women may touch and/or hold a *Sefer Torah* (Torah Scroll) are questions that are also explored. Only then can specific issues be considered and conclusions reached.

This book has been designed with both learned and less learned readers in mind. To facilitate its usefulness as a guide in learning groups, adult education classes, and private study, the texts of all relevant source materials are quoted at length; and they are systematically analyzed and explicated in a manner that all should be able to understand. To further enhance the book's usefulness, the notes appear at the bottom of each page, so that they can be referred to easily, for they are an integral rather than a tangential element of the work and deserve the attention of all serious readers.

Authors quoted in the study are generally referred to by their traditional appellation—either an acronym or the name of their most famous work. A complete list of such appellations, together with dates and other biographical information, appears at the end of the book.

Wherever possible, the halakhic presentation is rounded off by a conceptual analysis. Halakhah is, after all, the mechanism through which individuals and society strive to reach an ideal plateau. How the halakhah of women's prayer groups and related issues affects the attainment of this ideal deserves careful scrutiny.

Debate between supporters and opponents of women's tefillah groups has often been acrimonious. On occasion, personal attacks have clouded the presentation of arguments. While this study was not written as a response to any rabbi or group of rabbis critical of women's tefillah groups (indeed, much of this work was researched months before the women's prayer groups controversy erupted), it is impossible to discuss the issue without entering the debate on some level. In doing so, every effort is made to discuss the issues in a rational and objective manner.

This study was first presented in a course given at Yeshiva University's Stern College for Women. Many of the arguments were sharpened by the honest questions and probing criticism of my students. The Stern College administration should be applauded too, for authorizing a course on so controversial a topic.

The seventh chapter of this study ("Women and *Sifrei Torah*") was first published in the Summer 1982 edition of *Tradition*. I am thankful to the editors of *Tradition* for granting permission to reprint the article.

Friends of the Hebrew Institute of Riverdale (the *bayit*), where a monthly women's tefillah group has been conducted over the past ten years, deserve acknowledgment. Our women's prayer group program has been supported by extraordinary individuals who have served as presidents of the *bayit:* David Mann, Stanley Langer, Hillel Jaffe, and Bernard Horowitz. No rabbi could be blessed with finer lay leadership. The organizers of the women's service—Ronnie Becher, Cheryl Harris, Nancy Lerea, and Miriam Schacter—and its participants have opened my eyes to the sincere quest of women to become more involved in the experience of tefillah.

Our women's tefillah group is part of a larger vision of Torah, Israel, Outreach, and Activism developed at the Hebrew Institute of Riverdale. Rabbis who helped develop our *bayit* deserve special recognition: Rabbi Ronald Schwarzberg, to whom I am indebted for helping translate so much of our dream into reality; Rabbi Michael Eisenberg, an extraordinary educator; Rabbi Yamin Levy, who touched the lives of many young people; Rabbi Binyamin Hecht and Rabbi Louis Sherby, who carried the great burden of our *bayit* during the months of my convalescing from a serious physical illness; Rabbi Chaim Marder, our associate rabbi, whose sensitivity and warmth have enriched our *bayit*, and who has been of immeasurable assistance to me; and Dr. Eli Kranzler, our *shaliaḥ ẓibbur*, whose voice and soul have touched the lives of hundreds, even thousands.

Dr. Joel B. Wolowelsky, Rabbi Yitzchak Haut and Rabbi Reuven Bulka read parts of the study and made valuable suggestions and criticisms. Mrs. Els Bendheim carefully reviewed the manuscript. The work benefitted greatly from her devoted efforts and keen insights. Ktav Publishing House, including Bernard Scharfstein, Prof. Yaakov Elman, and Robert Milch, have been especially kind and supportive. Their advice and encouragement are most appreciated.

I gratefully acknowledge the efforts of Rabbi Louis Sherby, who translated some of the texts quoted in chapter 5 from the original Hebrew; Zalman Alpert, the periodicals librarian at Yeshiva University's Mendel Gottesman Library, and Robert Milch, who prepared much of the list of traditional authorities and sources; Rabbis Tzvi Flaum and Ephraim Kanarfogel, who read parts of the manuscript; Dr. Dov Frimer, Rabbi Shmuel Boylan, Rabbi Shalom Carmy, Rabbi Yitzchak Ginsberg, and Stanley Langer, who critiqued chapter 7 before it was published in *Tradition*; Rabbi Kenneth Hain, rabbi par excellence and treasured friend; Rabbi Heshy Reichman, my *ḥavrutah* and dear *ḥaver*; and Dr. Gabriel Moran, chairman of the Department of Religion and Religious Studies at New York University, who encouraged me to write.

I am thankful to Michael Horen, who designed the cover; Elliot Schwartz, who offered logistical advice; Michael Spingarn and Sue Prince, my dedicated secretary, who helped in the typing and computer preparation of the book; and Jerome and Ellen Stern for graciously allowing me and my family the use of their idyllic home in Yemin Moshe, Jerusalem this past summer. It was the most beautiful of places in which to write and reflect.

During the course of my rabbinical career, I have been influenced by great teachers, including the distinguished scholars Rabbi Norman Lamm, president of Yeshiva University; Rabbi Emanuel Rackman, chancellor of Bar-Ilan University; Rabbi Shlomo Riskin, chief rabbi of Efrat; and Rabbi Saul Berman, spiritual leader of Lincoln Square Synagogue. Their erudition and ability to translate the theory of Torah into life serve as a role model example for all. I am one of the thousands whose life has been touched by the brilliance of the rebbe of rebbes, Rav Yosef Dov Soloveitchik, *shelita* and the writings of Rav Avraham Yitzḥak ha-Cohen Kook, *zikhrono livrakha*, the two great luminaries of our generation.

Much of the material in this work was gleaned from basic sources and was derived from the insights of teachers, friends, and students. While acknowledging individuals who have influenced me, as well as their works, I assume complete responsibility for all aspects of this study. Indeed, some of the rabbis I have mentioned may disagree with portions of this analysis and its conclusion. All of them, however, have had a major influence upon me.

My family, including my sisters, Tova Reich and Sarah Tov, and my brothers, Rabbi Mordechai Weiss and Dr. David Weiss, have always encouraged me with their support and ongoing concern. To my wife, Toby Hilsenrad Weiss, I shall always be grateful for her friendship and love over the years, and, in particular, for her steadfastness as she helped carry me through a recent grave physical setback. Our children, Dena, Elana, and Dov, have been a constant source of joy and inspiration. May they continue to grow in their commitment to Torah, *Am Yisrael*, and *Medinat Yisrael*.

My father, Rabbi Moshe Weiss, a man of great courage, has by example taught me to stand up for principles, however unpopular. My sensitive and brilliant mother, Miriam Borenstein Weiss, of blessed memory, to whom this study is dedicated, taught me, through her ideas and deeds, the central place that women have in halakhah. May this work bring joy to her departed soul.

Jerusalem, 5749/1989

Introduction

In recent years, women committed to the halakhic process have expressed interest in becoming more actively involved in the Jewish religious experience. Part of this quest has manifested itself in the development of women's prayer groups. These services have grown significantly and are now being held in many communities.[1]

The introduction of these groups has precipitated much controversy; the issue has been vigorously debated in many forums and newspaper articles. Pressure to discuss the matter openly reached a crescendo when a former president of the Rabbinical Council of America suggested in his farewell address that the RCA develop a commission to investigate the role of women in the synagogue. Issues to be debated would have included the setting of halakhic guidelines for women's tefillah groups.[2] His successor rejected the proposal. In a debate with this writer, he claimed that women's prayer groups were a passing fad, a non-issue.[3]

Subsequent to the debate, the new president of the RCA approached five rabbis on the faculty of Yeshiva University's Rabbi Isaac Elchanan Theological Seminary for an opinion on the issue. In a brief statement, they concluded that "separate *hakafot* for women on Simḥat Torah, and separate gatherings *'minyanim'* of

---

1. In the New York area alone, women's tefillah groups are now being held monthly in Brooklyn, Great Neck, Riverdale, Washington Heights, the West Side, and the East Side, as well as in Teaneck, New Jersey.

2. Rabbi Gilbert Klaperman, Presidential Address, May 30, 1984 in Lancaster, Pa. He spoke of "the needs of women to find some form of rewarding participation in the synagogue. I leave to my successor the urgent request to create such a commission which would deal with at least the following: membership for women on synagogue boards, women's *hakafot*, women's *davening* groups, Torah study, *Bat Mitzvahs*, etc. Again this is to establish guidelines that need not be mandatorily imposed on synagogues but will provide a halakhically valid guide for those who want and/or need it."

3. Rabbi Louis Bernstein succeeded Rabbi Klaperman as president of the RCA. The debate was held at the Hebrew Institute of Riverdale on November 14, 1984. The tape of the debate is available through the Hebrew Institute.

women for prayer, for reading of the Torah and for reading of the Megillah are prohibited according to Jewish law."[4]

At a meeting held two months later, the RCA's executive committee concluded that the statement did not represent the position of the RCA. The query leading to the statement was to be viewed as one submitted by an individual rabbi, not by the RCA as an organization.[5]

The purpose of this study is to analyze women's tefillah groups from a halakhic perspective. If these services have halakhic validity, the right of women to be part of such an experience becomes clear, as does the responsibility of rabbis to allow for this option. At the least, it is hoped that this study will place the issue on the halakhic agenda as one that should be seriously discussed and debated in a spirit of mutual respect and understanding.

---

4. The statement (dated 19 Kislev 5745/December 13, 1984) was accompanied by a longer amplification of its content, written by Rabbi Abba Bronspigel (dated Erev Ḥanukkah 5745/December 18, 1984).

The statement and amplification have been published. See Rabbi Alpert, et al., "Teshuvah be-Inyan Nashim be-Hakafot, ve-khu," and "Minyanim Meyuḥadim le-Nashim."

Rabbi Hershel Schachter, one of the five signatories of the statement, has written an article on the issue, "Ze'i Lakh be-Ikvei ha-Ẓon." Rabbi Schachter further expanded on his position in "Be-Inyanei Beit Kneṣset."

5. The meeting was held on February 27, 1985.

Introduction to the Expanded Edition

Since the publication of Women at Prayer in 1990, a number of developments have taken place relative to women's prayer groups that have allowed me to further reflect on my thinking concerning this issue.

First, following the book, some halakhic criticism emerged that focused on the blessings recited before and after the reading of the Torah. While remaining convinced that, from a technical perspective, these blessings may be recited under the conditions outlined in chapter six, I have come to recognize the legitimacy of some of the concerns voiced by those who oppose these blessings. Indeed, this issue has been so divisive that it has, for many, undercut the enterprise of women's tefillah groups altogether. For this reason alone, it is understandable that some women's prayer groups have excluded these blessings from their tefila. It is possible that the non-recitation of these blessings would make women prayer groups more widely acceptable and lower the bitterness of debate.

Some groups have introduced different texts prior to, and after the reading of, the Torah instead of the berakhot. This suggestion not only addresses our previous concern, it is also in sync with sentiments I've heard from several women who are eager to shape women's prayer groups with the uniqueness that reflects their particular form of spiritual striving. Innovative texts before and after the reading of the Torah allows women to further develop women's prayer groups, allowing for a deeper spiritual experience.

In any event, there is no doubt that if a woman's prayer group takes place on Shabbat minha service, the opening blessing asher bahar should not be recited. One may not discuss Torah until this berakhah is said, and there is no reason to avoid such Torah discussions all day in order to say the berakhah.

A second area of development, concerns the view of Rav Yosef Dov

Halevi Soloveitchik zt"l. In a recent article in *Tradition* by Rabbis Aryeh and Dov Frimer, they concluded that while the Rav did not criticise these groups from a technical halakhic perspective, he had serious public policy concerns about them. The Rav himself, always encouraged me and my colleagues in the rabbinate to pasken for our respective communities on these matters, for he realized that it is the individual Rav who has the responsibility to decide what is best for his community, as he often knows what is best for his constituency. This was the position of Rav Moshe Feinstein, as his grandson, Rabbi Mordechai Tendler, confirmed to me about two years ago. In any event, as Rav Aaron Soloveitchik has pointed out, public policy can be fluid, and what was a bad policy years ago might now be beneficial, or the contrary. The policy must be evaluated in current terms, not those of decades ago.

With this in mind, it ought also be noted that some of the Rav's hesitation to accept women's prayer groups was based on the fact that these groups may be a first step in moving toward egalitarian practices of non-Orthodox movements. From that perspective, what the Rav thought to be an issue years ago may not be of any concern to him today. After twenty years of women's prayer groups, it is clear that these groups are not a slippery slope leading to an embrace of non-Orthodox practices.

The Frimers' study on the Rav's position reinforces my conviction, as outlined in this book, that the Rav felt that there was no halakhic barrier that would prevent women from engaging in women's prayer groups. As I have argued in the book, public policy considerations should encourage them in our current communities.

The third development is one that comes from personal observation. While women's prayer groups have added much to the synagogues in which they are housed, there are also down sides. They, like the hashkama minyan, can sometimes decentralize communal worship and take away from the feeling of b'rov am hadrat melekh. Notwithstanding this concern, over the years, I have become further convinced that the participants in women's tefillah are sincere beyond question in their quest for a meaningful halakhic prayer experience. In this way, they have truly become my teachers.

In this, the third edition of *Women at Prayer,* I have included a chapter on Women Reading the Megillah, first published in the *Torah U-Madda Journal,* which I had the honor to research together with my son Rabbi Dov Weiss-a genuine talmud hakham. I am grateful to Rabbi Jacob J. Schacter, editor of the Torah U-Madda

Journal for permitting the article to be republished here. Many thanks to Bernard Scharfstein of KTAV, a wonderful friend for his support of this book.

The sources from the chapter on Women and Reading of the Megillah are not included in the Traditional Authorities and Sources as well as the Bibliography found at the end of the book.

I am grateful that *Women at Prayer* has exceeded all predictions. After five thousand copies in the first two editions, the need for this third edition gives testimony to the importance of this issue in contemporary times. Despite the success, I have not taken any remuneration for this project. My reward has been the dissemination of the ideas surrounding women's prayer groups.

Most important, it is my hope that the debate concerning women's prayer groups be conducted with civility, and above all, respect for the views of others, especially those with whom we disagree. Only in this framework can we bring credit to God and His Torah.

Chapter One

The Role of Women in Judaism

THE IMAGE OF GOD

An analysis of the biblical verses dealing with the creation of Adam and Eve yields important insights concerning the nature of man and woman. In describing the creation of Adam, the Torah first states: "And God created Adam in His image, in the image of God created He him, male and female created He them" (Genesis 1:27). This description of Adam's creation differs in major ways from the story of the emergence of man and woman as described in the second chapter of Genesis. There, the Torah states that Adam came into being first, with Eve created from his rib (Genesis 2:21–23). One can think of these different accounts as Genesis One and Genesis Two.

Many suggestions have been made to resolve the apparent contradiction between the two narratives of the beginning of human life. Rashi suggests that Genesis One is a general story of creation in which the reader is told that male and female were created on the sixth day. Genesis Two then details how and in what sequence Adam and Eve came into being.[1] Midrash Aggadah, the homiletical exposition of the Torah dating from the talmudic period, records that Adam and Eve were originally created with "two faces," and the rib narrative concerns the bifurcation of Adam into two distinct beings, male and female.[2]

There is another possibility. Genesis Two may be seen as the story of how the human being was first formed; it is an "external" and quantitative description of the mechanical process of creation. Genesis One, on the other hand, deals with the essence of humanity; it

---

1. Rashi to Genesis 1:27, s.v. *zakhar u-nekevah bara otam.*
2. Quoted in Rashi, ibid. See Ketubbot 8a.

is "internal" and qualitative, concentrating on the value of the human persona.[3]

What makes the human being superior to the rest of creation is that every person is created in the image of God. The image of God (*ẓelem Elohim*) goes well beyond the ability to think, speak, and choose,[4] but reflects the inherent potential of the human being to emulate God, to transcend limitations and reach nobly to attain Godly heights. *Ẓelem Elohim* is not the monopoly of one gender; it is the common heritage of all humankind. Genesis One, which emphasizes the inestimable value of human beings, states, "male and female created He them" (Genesis 1:27). This underscores the fundamental principle that male and female are of equal importance, neither one greater than the other.

The same principle is enunciated in the Mishnah: "For this reason was Adam created alone . . . for the sake of peace among people, that one might not say to his fellow, 'My father was greater than yours.' "[5] We descend from one being. We share a common grandparent. We emerge from the same source. In short, we are all equal.[6]

---

3. Rav Joseph B. Soloveitchik, in "The Lonely Man of Faith," suggests that Adam of Genesis One portrays majestic and creative characteristics of the human being, characteristics that give the person the potential to accomplish virtually everything he/she desires. Genesis One, therefore, describes Adam as created in the "image of God" (Genesis 1:27), commanded *ve-khivshuha*, "[to] subdue it [the earth]" (Genesis 1:28). Therefore male and female are created together (Genesis 1:27). Indeed, Adam requires a work partner to collaborate with him in controlling the world.

While Adam in Genesis One is concerned with *how* to conquer the world, in Genesis Two he deals with the existential questions of "*Why?* For what purpose?" Adam in Genesis Two senses his own finiteness. He is, therefore, created from "dust of the ground" (Genesis 2:7), mandated "to work and protect it [the earth]" (Genesis 2:15) and is created alone. Recognizing Adam's sense of existential loneliness (Genesis 2:18), God creates Eve. Together, Adam and Eve give each other the comfort and love they desperately need. Unlike Adam of Genesis One, Adam of Genesis Two is concerned with inner value rather than outer accomplishments, with being more, rather than having more.

In the end, Adam One and Adam Two reflect different aspects of the human being. The goal is to merge these aspects into one whole personality.

4. See Rabbi Isidore Epstein, *The Faith of Judaism*, pp. 209–228.

5. Mishnah Sanhedrin 4:5 or Sanhedrin 37a.

Translation of talmudic texts follows, with minor changes, *The Soncino Talmud*, edited by Dr. I. Epstein (London: Soncino Press, 1952). The bracketed words are notes found in the Soncino translation.

6. Rav Aharon Soloveichik argues otherwise ("The Attitude of Judaism Toward the Woman," in *Major Addresses Delivered at Midcontinent Conclave and National Leadership Conference*, Union of Orthodox Jewish Congregations [November 27 through November 30, 1969], pp. 21–32). Drawing upon the chronological sequence of creation, which proceeds from the simpler to the more complex, he concludes that

EQUALITY AND IDENTITY OF ROLES

The equality of men and women does not mean, however, that the two genders are identical. Describing the creation of Eve, the Torah states: "And the Lord God said, it is not good that Adam is alone, let Me make for him an *ezer ke-negdo*" (Genesis 2:18). *Ezer ke-negdo* literally means "helper against him," a contradiction in terms. In his commentary on the Torah, Rashi contends that the phrase alludes to two potential relationships: "If he is meritorious, she will be a help; if he is not meritorious, [she will be] against him to fight."[7] While this thought expresses a truth about marital and other relationships, it nonetheless breaks the flow of the text and cannot be considered the literal rendering of this phrase.

A more direct approach, one closer to the *peshat* (the literal meaning of the text) is to interpret *ke-negdo* as "next to" or "opposite." In effect, God says, "It is not good that Adam is alone; I will create a help (*ezer*) to stand near him (*ke-negdo*), to share life experiences with him on a practical and existential level." From the Torah's perspective, men and women have complementary roles as

---

women are innately superior to men and hence were created last.

> It appears from Genesis, that whatever is superior was created later. . . . First light was created and with it other forms of energy. Then the inorganic world; then the organic world. And in the organic world, vegetative life came first and then animal life. And again, in the animal kingdom, the lower species came first and then the higher species. The human being was created after all animals. But in the human species, the male gender came first and then the female gender. This proves the proposition that the woman has innate spiritual superiority as compared with man. (p. 27)

Basing himself on this principle, Rav Soloveichik explains why men are mandated to perform more mitzvot (commandments) than women.

> There is an abundance of energy (*kibbush*) in the male gender which, if not tempered and controlled properly, might be released in a very destructive manner. Almighty God in His Infinite Wisdom, therefore imposed upon the male gender the obligatory *mitzvot* created by a time element and the obligation of constantly being engaged in the study of Torah so that man's psyche will always be preoccupied with spiritual and intellectual endeavors, thereby counteracting man's disposition toward abusive *kibbush*.
>
> . . . Man has to struggle in order to be good, compassionate, tolerant and noble. A woman's personality was molded in such a way that she is naturally disposed towards compassion and consideration. Woman's character was molded by God in accordance with the eschatological goals that Almighty God reserved for the world. (pp. 29–30)

The goal of mitzvot is to refine character. Women, according to Rav Soloveichik, are obligated to perform fewer mitzvot because they intrinsically possess "inner spiritual superiority."

7. Rashi to Genesis 2:18, s.v. *ezer ke-negdo*.

Note that the halakhic term for "betrothal," *erusin*, also has a double meaning. It is related to the Greek word *eros*, descriptive of passionate love, and the Hebrew word *eres*, which means "poison." Such is the power of a deep relationship. The greater the potential to love, the greater the possibility to hate the very same person.

they relate to each other and to the larger Jewish community. As individuals, we find it difficult to survive; together, we can overcome challenges. As individuals, we endure; together, our lives become more purposeful. Redemption is no longer elusive; it is within our grasp. Ecclesiastes (*Kohelet*) vividly describes this sharing of responsibilities and destiny: "The two are better than the one because they have a good reward for their labor. For if they fall, the one will lift up his fellow; but woe to him that is alone when he falls, and has not another to help out" (Ecclesiastes 4:9–10).[8]

THE COMPLEMENTARY TASKS

The complementary tasks of men and women are reflected in the private and public realms of Jewish experience. The respective roles of men and women in these realms are the subject of dispute.

---

8. Rav Soloveitchik, in "The Lonely Man of Faith," understands *ezer ke-negdo* in a similar manner.

> "It is not good for man to be lonely" (Genesis 2:18). . . . The connotation of these words in the context of the world-view of Adam the first [Adam as found in Genesis One] even if they had been addressed to him, would have been related not to loneliness, an existential in-depth experience, but to aloneness, a practical surface-experience. Adam the first, representing the natural community, would translate this pronouncement into pragmatic categories, referring not to existence as such, but to productive work. If pressed for an interpretation of the pronouncement, he would paraphrase it: "It is not good for man to work (not to be) alone."
>
> The words "I shall make him a helpmate [*ezer ke-negdo*]" would refer in accordance with his social philosophy, to a functional partner to whom it would be assigned to collaborate with and assist Adam the first in his undertakings, schemes and projects. Eve vis-à-vis Adam the first would be a work partner, not an existential co-participant. Man alone cannot succeed, says Adam the first, because a successful life is possible only within a communal framework. (p. 22)

Here Rav Soloveitchik views *ezer ke-negdo* as an antidote to being alone. Aloneness is a physical state, the reality of being by oneself. With "a functional partner," "a work partner," one is no longer alone.

Loneliness, unlike *aloneness*, is a metaphysical state. One can be in a crowd, share a room with someone, and yet be lonely. Rav Soloveitchik's understanding of *ezer ke-negdo* extends to the existential loneliness of Adam the second (Adam as found in Genesis Two). He writes: "At this crucial point, if Adam is to bring his quest for redemption to full realization, he must initiate action leading to the discovery of a companion who, even though as unique and singular as he, will master the art of communicating and, with him, form a community" (p. 26).

The phrase *ezer ke-negdo* may also relate to the dynamic tension in a husband-wife relationship. On the one hand, husband and wife are friends, sharing each other's destiny and "being" (*ezer*). As close as they are, however, they still maintain their own independence and individuality, leaving each other room to grow and realize their unique potential (*ke-negdo*). See Rav Joseph B. Soloveitchik, "The Community," p. 8.

The Only Place

Sefer Abudarham ha-Shalem contends that the home is *virtually the only place* in which women may function. He bases his opinion on the talmudic axiom that positive commandments whose performance is limited to a specific time (*mitzvot aseh she-ha-zeman geramah*) are binding only on men, whereas positive commandments not limited to a specific time of performance are binding on both women and men.[9] *Sefer Abudarham* claims that since women are preoccupied with obligations to their husbands, they are relieved of any positive time-bound commandments which could dctract from these responsibilities. In his words:

> And the reason women are exempt from positive time-bound commandments is because a woman is obligated to fulfill the needs of her husband. Were she mandated to perform the positive commandments fixed by time, it is possible that while performing this mitzvah her

9. See Kiddushin 29a.

Rabbi Saul J. Berman analyzes Rambam's listing of positive commandments fixed by time from which women are exempt. Rabbi Berman's analysis reveals that the number of commandments which are exceptions to this rule is greater than the number following the rule. See his "The Status of Women in Halakhic Judaism."

Rambam, in the conclusion of his *Book of Commandments*, Positive Commandments, indicates that women are exempt from *eight* positive commandments fixed by time: reciting the Shema (commandment no. 10), wearing the tefillin shel rosh (no. 12), the tefillin shel yad (no. 13), and ẓiẓit (no. 14), counting the omer (no. 161), "dwelling" in the sukkah (no. 168), taking the lulav (no. 169), and hearing the shofar (no. 170).

The Talmud and commentaries, loc. cit., however, identify *ten* positive commandments fixed by time that women are obligated to perform. They are: reciting Kiddush (Berakhot 20b), fasting on Yom Kippur (Sukkah 28a–b), eating matzah on the first night of Passover (Kiddushin 34a), being joyous on a holiday—*simḥat he-ḥag* (Kiddushin 34a), *Hakhel* (Kiddushin 34a), hearing the Megillah on Purim (Megillah 4a), drinking four cups of wine during the Seder (Pesaḥim 108a–b), reciting Hallel during the Seder (Sukkah 38a, Pesaḥim 108a), lighting Ḥanukkah candles (Shabbat 23a), and sacrificing and eating the *Korban Pesaḥ* (Pesaḥim 91b).

Rav Aharon Soloveichik (see above, n. 6) maintains that women are exempt from some positive commandments fixed by time since they are intrinsically aware—by virtue of their innate spiritual superiority—of the message these mitzvot convey.

Similarly, Rabbi Emanuel Rackman (*One Man's Judaism*, p. 330) and Rabbi Norman Lamm (*A Hedge of Roses*, pp. 68–78) suggest that a woman's menstrual cycle and her observance of the *niddah* laws invests her with an awareness of the sanctity of time. Hence, women are not obligated to observe many of the positive commandments fixed by time. Men, on the other hand, learn the importance of time by fulfilling the time-bound mitzvah.

As indicated, this idea is problematical, since the rule that women are exempt from positive commandments fixed by time is far from iron-clad. In reality, there are more mitzvot that are exceptions to the rule than mitzvot that follow the rule.

> husband will insist that she fulfill the mitzvah of listening to him. . . . Therefore, the Creator relieved her of performing these mitzvot, so that she would be at peace with her husband.[10]

This argument could be extended to other obligations facing women. Since women are responsible for the welfare of their children and family, they are exempt from positive commandments fixed by time because of the principle of *ha-osek be-mitzvah patur min ha-mitzvah*, "if one is occupied with a mitzvah, he/she is exempt from other mitzvot."

The Secondary Role

In contrast, *Akedat Yiẓḥak* suggests that a woman's family role is *secondary* to her responsibility in the public realm. Commenting on why Jacob was angry with Rachel after she demanded children of him (Genesis 31:1–2), he states that women have two roles based upon the names given to the first woman at creation: Woman (*Ishah*) and Eve (*Ḥavah*).

> The first [name] teaches that woman was taken from man, stressing that like him you may understand and advance in the intellectual and moral field. . . . The second alludes to the power of childbearing and rearing children, as is indicated by the name Eve—the mother of all living. A woman deprived of the power of childbearing will be deprived of the *secondary purpose* [emphasis added] and be left with the ability to do evil or good like the man who is barren. . . . Jacob was therefore angry with Rachel when she said, "Give me children or else I die" [Genesis 30:1], in order to reprimand her and make her understand this all-important principle that she was not dead as far as their joint purpose in life because she was childless, just the same as it would be, in his case, if he would have been childless.[11]

The contemporary scholar Neḥama Leibowitz comments on this view:

---

10. *Sefer Abudarham ha-Shalem, Seder Tefillot shel Ḥol, Ha-sha'ar ha-Shelishi, Birkhot ha-Mitzvot.* This position may be based on the principle *kol kevudah vat melekh penimah*, "the king's daughter is all glorious within" (Psalms 45:14).

11. *Akedat Yiẓḥak* to Genesis 30:1–2.

Translation is from Aryeh Newman's English translation of Neḥama Leibowitz, *Studies in the Book of Genesis*, p. 334.

> Jacob's anger is here explained as being directed at Rachel's forgetting the true and chief purpose of her existence which, according to the *Akedat Yiẓḥak* is no different from that of her partner, the man's. She, in her yearnings for a child saw her whole world circumscribed by the second purpose of woman's existence (according to the *Akedat Yiẓḥak* "the *secondary* purpose"!) to become a mother. Without it her life was not worth living. "Or else I die" [Genesis 30:1]. This was a treasonable repudiation of her function, a flight from her destiny and purpose, shirking the duties imposed on her, not in virtue of her being a woman, but in virtue of her being a human being.[12]

THE PRIMARY OBLIGATION: THE MOST COGENT EXPLANATION

The most cogent explanation of the respective roles of men and women is as follows: Women are *primarily* obligated to fulfill laws pertaining to private Jewish ritual; men are obligated to see to it that the public performance of Jewish ritual is carried out.[13] This does not mean that women cannot participate in the religio-legal or societal aspects of the public domain, or that men have no role to play in the more private arena of Jewish life. Women, for example, are required to hear the public reading of the Megillah;[14] while men

---

12. Ibid., p. 335.

13. This position differs from that of Abudarham, who limits the role of women to the home, and that of *Akedat Yiẓḥak*, who maintains that the role of women in the home is secondary to their responsibilities in the public realm.

The concept of a preferred but not mandatory role for women is developed by Rabbi Berman, "The Status of Women in Halakhic Judaism," pp. 16–18. Rabbi Berman first lists and then analyzes the exemptions and obligations of women in regard to positive commandments bound by time (see above, n. 9). Noting that the exemptions involve mitzvot whose performance is encouraged or limited to the public domain, while the obligations involve mitzvot which with few exceptions (hakhel, where the Torah specifically mandates that women hear the reading; and Megillah, where the rabbis do the same) are performed at home, Rabbi Berman writes:

> The underlying motive of exemption would then be neither the attempt to unjustly deprive women of the opportunity to achieve religious fulfillment, nor the proposition that women are inherently more religiously sensitive. Rather, exemption would be a tool used by the Torah to achieve a particular social goal, namely to assure that no legal obligation would interfere with the selection by Jewish women of a role which was centered almost exclusively in the home. However, it is vital to emphasize that even with these exemptions, the wife-mother-homemaker role is not the mandated, or exclusively proper role, though it is clearly the preferred and therefore protected role.

14. See Megillah 4a; Tosefta Megillah 2:4; Tosafot to Megillah 4a, s.v. *nashim ḥayavot be-mikra Megillah;* Arakhin 2b–3a; Tosafot to Arakhin 3a, s.v. *la'atuei nashim; Shulḥan Arukh,* Oraḥ Ḥayyim 689:2. For a discussion of this issue, see below, chap. 4.

are commanded to be fruitful and multiply.[15] Within their respective roles, there is some cross-over, sometimes required, sometimes optional. Nonetheless, the *major* roles of men and women remain virtually intact.

Although their primary role is home-centered, women may delegate others to perform home chores. The Mishnah states:

> The following are the kinds of work that a woman must perform for her husband: grinding corn, baking bread, washing clothes, cooking, suckling her child, making ready his bed, and working in wool. If she brought him one bondwoman (or the sum that would purchase one) she need not do any grinding or baking or washing. [If she brought] two bondwomen (or their value), she need not even cook or suckle her child. If three, she need neither make ready his bed nor work in wool. If four, she may lounge in an easy chair.[16]

While the Mishnah lists home chores as a woman's responsibility, it concludes that she may opt out of these commitments by finding a replacement.

The Mishnah then concludes:

> Rabbi Eliezer said: Even if she brought him [her husband] a hundred bondwomen, he may (or, according to another interpretation, should) compel her to work in wool; for boredom leads to wanton behavior.
>
> Rabbi Simeon ben Gamaliel said: Even if a man forbade his wife under a vow to do any work, he must divorce her and give her a

---

15. See Mishnah Yevamot 6:6 or Yevamot 61b; Yevamot 65b.

The element of danger in childbearing is probably the reason why women are not required to "be fruitful and multiply." See *Meshekh Ḥokhmah*, parashat *Noaḥ*, s.v. *peru* (Genesis 9:7): "It is not going too far to say that the Torah exempts women from 'be fruitful and multiply,' but obligates men, because the laws of God and 'His ways are ways of pleasantness, and all His paths are peace.' The Torah does not burden a Jew to do what he is incapable of doing. . . . Therefore, the Torah only commands that we fast for one day [not two consecutive days], . . . [and that] women whose lives are endangered through pregnancy and birth, . . . are not mandated to be fruitful and multiply."

Although the physical danger to women has decreased in modern times, the reasoning of *Meshekh Ḥokhmah* illustrates the great sensitivity that the Torah displays towards the welfare of women.

Ḥiddushei Ran to Kiddushin 41a, s.v. *mitzvah bo yoter mibisheluḥo*, states: "Even though she is not personally commanded concerning procreation, she performs a meritorious act (mitzvah) because she thereby assists her husband in the fulfillment of his religious duty [of 'be fruitful and multiply']."

16. Mishnah Ketubbot 5:5 or Ketubbot 59b.

> *ketubbah* (thus enabling her to engage in work again), for boredom leads to emotional disturbance.[17]

For Rabbi Eliezer, work is necessary, preventing boredom that could lead to wanton behavior. It would appear that if a woman were working in the public realm and thus avoided boredom, she could not be forced to "work in wool." Similarly, for Rabbi Simeon ben Gamaliel, if the vow did not refer to the public realm, the husband need not divorce his wife since she would not remain bored.[18]

Rambam codifies the Mishnah in this way:

> We find that a woman must perform five types of work for her husband. She weaves, washes his face, hands and feet, and pours the cup, and prepares his bed, and stands and serves before him. And the [types of] work that some women do and some do not do are six: She grinds, and cooks, and bakes, and washes, and nurses, and gives food to his animal.[19]

Here Rambam distinguishes between the more intimate activities a wife must do for her husband, and the less intimate type of work for which she may seek out a suitable replacement. Elsewhere Rambam states that the work a wife does for her husband is in exchange for her sustenance.

> The sages have further enacted that a wife's earnings are chargeable against her maintenance. . . . Therefore, if the wife says, "I want neither maintenance nor work," her wish must be respected and she may not be coerced. On the other hand, if the husband says, "I will neither support you nor take any of your earnings," no attention need be paid to him, perchance her earnings will not suffice for her support.[20]

---

17. Ibid.

18. Ketubbot 61b distinguishes between the reasoning of Rabbi Eliezer and Rabbi Simeon ben Gamaliel. In the words of the Talmud: "The practical difference between them [is the case of a woman] who plays with little cubs [or 'wooden cubs,' counters in a game] or [is addicted to] checkers. [A woman who spends her time in this manner may be exposed to the temptation of permissive behavior but is in no danger of emotional disturbance since she keeps herself occupied.]"

19. Rambam, *Code*, Laws of Marriage 21:7.

The English translations of quotations from Rambam's *Code* are based on the Moses Hyamson translation (New York: Feldheim, 1981) and the Yale University Press translation (New Haven: Yale University Press, 1972).

20. Laws of Marriage 12:4. See Ketubbot 58b.

Tur Shulḥan Arukh concludes that husband and wife may enter into a prenuptial agreement in which the husband is relieved of almost all obligations to sustain his wife and she relinquishes virtually all responsibility to perform household tasks.[21]

After citing these sources, Rabbi Saul Berman concludes:

> Thus the law ends up mandating for women, neither marriage, nor procreation, nor specific household duties. Jewish law does not then define with any precision whatsoever, a "proper" or "necessary" role for Jewish women. While not demanding adherence to one particular role, it is nevertheless clear that since for most of our history, our continuation as a people depended upon the voluntary selection by women of the role of wife-mother-homemaker, the law would, and did, encourage the exercise of that choice.[22]

THE HOME ROLE AND JEWISH CONTINUITY

The home role that women are encouraged, although not compelled, to fulfill is viewed as critical for Jewish survival. Judaism is home-centered. Its fundamental rituals—Shabbat, kashrut (dietary laws), taharat ha-mishpaḥah (family purity), and tefillah (prayer)—are home-oriented. Of course, these laws do have elements of public observance. Nonetheless, commitment to these rituals emerges from the home.

The Shabbat experience, for example, includes Kiddush, zemirot, the blessing of children, and Torah learning—aspects of Shabbat observance which are bound to the home. The dietary laws, while an all-encompassing life-style, center around food preparation within one's own kitchen or dining room. Family purity, while requiring a visit to the mikvah, governs conjugal relationships. Prayer, while possible within a communal framework, can also be fulfilled in a private setting.

The home has always been viewed within Judaism as the key source of Jewish continuity. With it, Judaism flourishes; without it, Judaism withers. The deflection of importance from home to synagogue is probably a result of Christian influence. When Chris-

---

21. *Tur Shulḥan Arukh*, Even Ha-Ezer 80. See *Kesef Mishneh* to Rambam, *Code*, Laws of Marriage 21:10, s.v. *kol ishah she-timneh me-la'asot melakha*.

22. Rabbi Berman, "The Status of Women in Halakhic Judaism," p. 16.

tianity became church-centered, Judaism became synagogue-centered.[23]

As important as the synagogue has become, the transmission of Jewish values continues to take place primarily within the home. Jewish belief and practice are best taught and refined there. A reinforcement of these basic values is crucial for Jewish continuity.

23. For an example of Jews emulating Christian practice, see Rabbi Norman Lamm, "Separate Pews in the Synagogue." According to Rabbi Lamm: "[The practice of mixed seating in the synagogue is a] case of religious mimicry. The alien model in this case is Christianity; worse yet, the specifically pagan root of Christianity. . . . Mixed seating thus represents a desire by Jews to Christianize their synagogues by imitating the practices of contemporary Christian churches. . . . Lest the reader still remain skeptical of our thesis that mixed seating represents a pagan-Christianization of the synagogue, he ought to consider the origin of mixed pews in the synagogue itself. Reform in Europe did not know of mixed seating. It was first introduced in America by Isaac Mayer Wise, in about 1825, when he borrowed a Baptist church for his Reform services in Albany, N.Y., and found the mixed pews of the church so to his liking that he decided to retain this feature for his temple." (pp. 161–163)

Chapter Two

Women and Private Prayer

It is precisely because women are encouraged to fulfill the role of wife-mother-homemaker that all authorities deem them to be obligated with respect to prayer that is private or home-centered. The degree of obligation, however, is the subject of considerable debate. According to some authorities, women are minimally mandated to pray once a day, at any time, using any format. Other authorities maintain that women should pray a significant portion of the standard morning and afternoon service. Still others encourage and even require women to pray three times daily.

Our analysis of these positions begins with a presentation of women's obligation in regard to the primary unit of prayer, the Shemoneh Esreh ("Eighteen Benedictions").[1] The Shemoneh Esreh is central to the service. Other prayers prepare and embellish upon its fundamental concepts. Once we have determined whether women are required to recite the Shemoneh Esreh, their obligation in connection with other parts of the prayer service will fall more easily into place.

SHEMONEH ESREH

The issue of women and the Shemoneh Esreh is in turn linked to the origin, development, framework, and ultimate obligation of prayer itself. Quoting the verse "and you shall serve Him with all your heart" (Deuteronomy 11:13) the Talmud declares: "What is considered a service of the heart? You must say that this is prayer."[2]

1. In Jewish religio-legal sources, the term *tefillah* ("prayer") is usually synonymous with Shemoneh Esreh. Shemoneh Esreh is so central to the prayer service that it alone is called *tefillah*.
2. Ta'anit 2a.

Maimonidean Prayer

Basing himself on this talmudic argument, Rambam states:

> It is a positive commandment to pray every day, as it says "And you shall serve the Lord your God" (Exodus 23:25). From tradition, we have learned that "service" is prayer, as it says "And to serve Him with all your heart" (Deuteronomy 11:13).[3] The sages commented, "What is the service of the heart? Prayer." The number of [daily] prayers does not stem from the Torah, and the formula of prayer does not emanate from the Torah, and there is no standard time of prayer [established in] the Torah.[4]

Rambam here suggests that prayer is biblical in origin. However, since biblical prayer has no fixed time, it falls into the category of commandments not circumscribed by time, which are obligatory upon women.[5]

> And therefore [writes Rambam], women and *avadim*[6] are obligated to pray, since it is a commandment which is not fixed by time. . . . One who was fluent would offer up many prayers and supplications. If one was slow of speech, he would pray as he could and whenever he pleased. . . . There would be those who would pray once a day, and others who would pray many times a day. . . . This was the uniform practice from the time of Moses our teacher until Ezra.[7]

---

3. The *Kesef Mishneh* on Rambam, *Code*, Laws of Prayer 1:1, s.v. *mitzvat aseh le-hitpallel*, asks why Rambam quotes "and you shall serve the Lord, your God" (Exodus 23:25) as the source of the biblical obligation to pray, and not "and you shall serve Him with all your heart" (Deuteronomy 11:13). He suggests that the verse from Deuteronomy may be understood as offering good advice rather than requiring daily prayer, or it may refer to the "service" of learning Torah as well as the "service" of prayer.

4. Rambam, *Code*, Laws of Prayer 1:1.

5. See Kiddushin 29a.

There are exceptions to this rule. See the conclusion of Rambam's *Book of Commandments*, positive commandments, where he lists these exceptions. They include studying Torah (commandment no. 11), acquiring a scroll of the Torah (no. 18), male priests blessing Israel (no. 26), be fruitful and multiply (no. 212), and the bridegroom devoting himself for one year to his bride (no. 214).

6. I have not followed the common practice of translating *avadim* as "slaves." The concept of slavery as understood in contemporary times is foreign to Jewish thought, and "slaves," therefore, would be a misleading and inappropriate English rendering.

There are several terms in the Torah that have no suitable English equivalent. Such terms should not be translated. Leaving them in the original Hebrew makes the reader understand that a more detailed analysis of the word is necessary. See below, chap. 7, where the term *tumah* is not translated for this reason.

7. Rambam, *Code*, Laws of Prayer 1:2–3.

Rambam's rationale may be that prayer is fundamentally a function of praising God, wherein the limited and finite person acknowledges the gifts of life bestowed upon him/her by the unlimited and infinite source of all creation. Its mode is intellectual, and its motif makes it incumbent to express gratitude to God every day.

After the destruction of the First Temple and the consequent exile and dispersion of Jews to Babylonia and Persia, Rambam continues, Jews found it difficult to pray spontaneously. Living among people who did not speak Hebrew, a new generation of Jews arose who no longer had the ability to use Hebrew as a means of articulating their inner feelings to the Almighty. Responding to this loss of language proficiency, Ezra and the Great Assembly introduced a precisely formulated prayer. This consisted of three opening blessings of praise, a middle portion of requests detailing human needs, and a final three blessings of thanks to God.

In the words of Rambam:

> When the people of Israel went into exile in the days of the wicked Nebuchadnezzar, they mingled with the Persians, Greeks, and other nations. In those foreign countries, children were born to them whose language was confused. Everyone's speech was a mixture of many tongues. No one was able, when he spoke, to express his thoughts adequately in any one language. . . . Consequently, when anyone of them prayed in Hebrew, he was unable adequately to express his needs or recount the praises of God, without mixing Hebrew with other languages. When Ezra and his Council realized this condition, they ordained the Eighteen Benedictions (Shemoneh Esreh) in their present order. . . . The object aimed at was that these prayers should be in an orderly form in everyone's mouth, that all should learn them, and thus the prayer of those who were not expert in speech would be as perfect as that of those who had command of a pure [Hebrew] style. For the same reason, they arranged [in a fixed form] all the blessings and prayers for all Jews so that the substance of every blessing should be familiar and current in the mouth of one who is not expert in speech.[8]

With the introduction of the standardized Shemoneh Esreh, Rambam maintains, all Jews, regardless of background and ability to express themselves, were made equal in the fraternity of prayer: the well-spoken and the least educated recited the same prayers.

Rambam may also be suggesting that with the appearance of the

8. Ibid. 1:4.

standardized Shemoneh Esreh, the dispersed Jews were united through a structured formula of prayer.[9]

Finally, Rambam states that Ezra designed the prayer service to correspond to the standard sacrificial service offered in the Temple. In the words of Rambam: "Thus, too, they ordained that the services of prayer should be equal in number to the sacrifices."[10]

This position follows the view of Rabbi Joshua ben Levi in the Talmud that prayer corresponds to the sacrificial service.[11] In following this view, Rambam might be suggesting that after the destruction of the First Temple, the rabbis sought to promote religious procedures which would link Jews living after the First Temple era with those who had lived during the time of the Temple. Elements of the Temple service were therefore repeated in some form, in order to bind Jews to their glorious past.

Hence, what was originally a biblical obligation to pray once daily, in any format and at any time, eventually became the rabbinically ordained obligation to recite the Shemoneh Esreh at three specific times, using a special formula of prayer. It follows that from the rabbinical perspective Shemoneh Esreh is a positive commandment dictated by time from which women should be exempt. However, the original biblical commandment obligating women to pray once daily remains operative. The rabbis, by introducing set prayer three times daily, did not relieve women of their prior biblical obligation. It remained intact. *Magen Avraham* concludes:

> Following [Rambam's] reasoning, most women are not accustomed to pray in the standard fashion [by reciting the regular *tefillah* with consistency], because immediately upon washing their hands after rising in the morning, they recite some form of request and have thereby fulfilled their biblical obligation. And perhaps the rabbis did not obligate them to do more than this.[12]

---

9. See Rabbi Shlomo Riskin, "Structure and Spontaneity in Prayer," pp. 328–329, where a similar understanding of Rambam is noted.

10. Rambam, *Code*, Laws of Prayer 1:5.

11. Berakhot 26b. There the Talmud quotes Rabbi Joshua ben Levi's statement that the three daily services recited during the morning, afternoon, and evening hours parallel the Temple's standard morning offering, the afternoon offering, and "the limbs [of the burnt-offerings] and the fat [of the other offerings] which were not consumed [on the altar] by the evening [and] could be brought for the whole of the night."

12. See *Magen Avraham* to *Shulḥan Arukh*, Oraḥ Ḥayyim 106:2. Although this is

Alternatively, it may be argued that since the biblical obligation is applicable to women, the rabbinical mandate which extends from and expands on the biblical source relates equally to them.[13] In practical terms, this would mean that women should recite the Shemoneh Esreh twice, and perhaps three times, daily.[14]

Rabbi Joseph Karo's statement in the *Shulḥan Arukh*, "Women

---

quoted as the general custom of women, *Magen Avraham* concludes that most authorities side with Ramban (cited later in this chapter) and not Rambam.

The talmudic text discussing women's *tefillah* obligation is in Berakhot 20b. Commenting on the mishnah which states that women are required to recite the *tefillah*, the Gemara states: "[They are obligated] because this [prayer is a supplication for Divine] mercy (*de-raḥamei ninhu*). You might think that because it is written in connection therewith, "[I pray] evening and morning and at noonday" (Psalms 55:18), it is like a positive precept fixed by time [from which women are exempt]. We are, therefore, told (*ka mashma lan*) [that this is not so]."

Arukh ha-Shulḥan, Oraḥ Ḥayyim 106:5, understands Rambam's text of the Gemara to begin with the word *peshita*, "is it not obvious?" This would imply that daily prayer is of biblical origin and has no set period during the day. Hence, the Gemara says, *peshita*, "obviously" women are obligated, since prayer falls into the category of positive commandments not limited by time. Why is there any need to mention the obligation in the Mishnah? *Ka mashma lan*, "because this tells us" that the biblical requirement that women must pray once daily remains operative. The rabbis, by introducing set times, did not relieve women of their prior biblical obligation, which remains intact.

Rambam's text of Berakhot 20b, according to *Arukh ha-Shulḥan*, does not begin or conclude with the phrase *de-raḥamei ninhu*. This follows our analysis of Rambam, that prayer is not a function of mercy (*raḥamim*) but rather of praising God (*hoda'ah*).

Note, however, *Megillat Esther* to Rambam, *Book of Commandments*, positive commandment 5, s.v. *nireh li* (end). He maintains that the basic motif of prayer for Rambam is *raḥamim* (asking for mercy), which is deemed powerful enough to overrule the exemption of women from prayer based upon its being a positive commandment fixed by time. See Rav Yosef Dov Soloveitchik's analysis of Rambam later in this chapter.

13. This second view of Rambam understands the conclusion of the talmudic text (Berakhot 20b, quoted in n. 12) differently. *Ka mashma lan*, we are told that the rabbis did not exempt women from praying twice or three times daily, as they were included in the original biblical obligation to pray once daily, using any format. If "biblical prayer" was obligatory for them, so too was "rabbinical prayer." Meiri to Berakhot 20b seems to express a similar understanding of Rambam.

Arukh ha-Shulḥan can also be understood to support this interpretation of Rambam.

14. See Berakhot 27b–28a for a discussion of whether Ma'ariv (the evening service) is *reshut* (optional) or *ḥovah* (obligatory). Rambam, *Code*, Laws of Prayer 1:6, states that men have now accepted Ma'ariv as an obligation.

Rema, *Shulḥan Arukh*, Oraḥ Ḥayyim 299:10, notes that women who do not recite the separation (Havdalah) paragraph in the Saturday evening (Ma'ariv) service should recite a special formula, *ha-mavdil bein kodesh le-ḥol*, "who has separated between the holy and profane," before beginning their weekly activities. *Magen Avraham*,

. . . are obligated in prayer because it is a positive commandment not fixed by time," may be understood as following either of these interpretations of Rambam.[15]

Nachmanidean Prayer

Ramban differs in his understanding of prayer. For Ramban, the biblical source for prayer is the verse: "And when you go to war in your land against the adversary that oppresses you, then you shall sound an alarm with the trumpets; and you shall be remembered before the Lord your God, and you shall be saved before your enemies" (Numbers 10:9).

Ramban states:

> It is a mitzvah to plead fervently with God through prayer and *teru'ah* [shofar blasts] whenever the community is faced with great distress . . . for it is a mitzvah to affirm in moments of distress our belief that the Holy One listens to prayers and intervenes to grant aid.[16]

---

ibid., no. 15, and *Ba'er Heitev*, ibid., no. 12, conclude from Rema's comment that Ma'ariv has remained optional for women and thus Rema assumed they did not pray.

Note *Mishnah Berurah*, ibid., no. 37, who, in explaining Rema's position, states that most women were not accustomed to pray on Saturday evenings, implying that it was their custom to pray Ma'ariv on other evenings. *Mishnah Berurah* to Oraḥ Ḥayyim 106:4, quoting Ramban, seems to agree, however, that Ma'ariv is optional for women every night. See *Sha'ar ha-Ẓion*, to *Shulḥan Arukh*, Oraḥ Hayyim 299:49.

Note *Kaf ha-Ḥayyim* to *Shulḥan Arukh*, Oraḥ Ḥayyim 299:62, who writes: "Nonetheless, the custom today is that women versed in *tefillah* pray morning, afternoon, and night. And they should conduct themselves on Shabbat as they do during the week." The last statement stresses that women should pray on Saturday evenings, in the same way that they pray on other weekday evenings.

Even if Ma'ariv is optional for women, it is important to note the comment of Tosafot to Berakhot 26a, s.v. *ta'ah ve-lo hitpallel*. Tosafot reasons that the evening service is only optional if it is in conflict with another mitzvah that must be performed during the evening time period. However, where there is no conflict, the Ma'ariv service falls into the obligatory category. Hence, in most situations, Ma'ariv is obligatory.

15. *Shulḥan Arukh*, Oraḥ Ḥayyim 106:1. Rif to Berakhot 20b (in Rif 11b), may also be understood in both ways.

(Note Ran to Rif on Berakhot 20b, s.v. *tefillah u-mezuzah*. He states that even though prayer now has set times, nonetheless, since in theory it would be appropriate to pray at every moment, prayer is viewed as a positive commandment which is not fixed by time and women are therefore obligated to pray. Ran then includes the reasoning of *raḥamim*.)

A careful reading of *Magen Avraham*, Oraḥ Ḥayyim 106:2 indicates his uncertainty as to the proper interpretation of Rambam. When suggesting that according to Rambam women need only pray once daily, he writes: "And perhaps (*ve-efshar*) the rabbis did not obligate them to do more than this [pray once daily]." Note the term *perhaps*. Perhaps only once daily, but perhaps two or three times daily.

16. Ramban's commentary to Rambam's *Book of Commandments*, positive commandment 5.

In Ramban's view, biblical prayer is petitional and is offered in times of distress. It is essentially a supplicatory cry, wherein the finite and frightened human being seeks out God's help in his hour of need. There is, according to Ramban, no biblical obligation to pray every day, as one may not feel compelled to petition God every day. Rather one approaches God, using one's own format, only when personally motivated to do so. Prayer, for Ramban, is a function of *raḥamim* in which one asks God to be merciful and supportive during moments of concern and necessity.

Ramban agrees that in the time of Ezra and the Great Assembly the rabbis composed the Shemoneh Esreh, requiring Jews to use the specific format of the Amidah thrice daily. For Ramban, however, the obligation to pray daily is rabbinical and not biblical.[17] Since the first obligation to pray is a positive time-oriented commandment, women should not be required to pray at all. However, according to Ramban, the basic motif of prayer is *raḥamim.* This theme is deemed powerful enough to overrule the exemption of women from prayer based upon its being a positive commandment fixed by time.[18] Thus, according to Ramban, women are required to pray the Shemoneh Esreh every morning and afternoon.[19]

The Rationale

Rav Yosef Dov Soloveitchik reconciles the views of Rambam and Ramban by maintaining that both see prayer as meaningful only if it derives from a sense of *ẓarah.*

For Ramban, *ẓarah* "is an external crisis which arises independently of man. It emerges out of the environment and usually appears suddenly." The "surface *ẓarah*" of Ramban arises only at particular moments.

Rambam regards "daily life itself as being existentially in straits, inducing in the sensitive person feelings of despair, a brooding sense of life's meaninglessness, absurdity, lack of fulfillment. It is a

---

17. See ibid., where he quotes Berakhot 21a and Sukkah 38a in support of his position that prayer is rabbinical. *Megillat Esther* to Rambam, *Book of Commandments*, positive commandment 5, s.v. *nireh li*, responds by claiming that the text of the prayers is rabbinical, but the origin of prayer is biblical.

18. *Arukh ha-Shulḥan* to Oraḥ Ḥayyim 106:5–6.

19. Ramban does not accept the reading *peshita* in Berakhot 20b on women's obligation in *tefillah* (see above, n. 12, for text). He does have the text *deraḥmei ninhu*. See *Arukh ha-Shulḥan* to Oraḥ Ḥayyim 106:6 and *Mishnah Berurah* to Oraḥ Ḥayyim 106:4.

persistent *ẓarah*, which exists *bekhol yom*, daily. The word *ẓarah* connotes more than external trouble; it suggests an emotional and intellectual condition in which man sees himself as hopelessly trapped in a vast, impersonal universe, desolate, without hope."[20]

The Rav's understanding of Maimonidean prayer as relating to life's "depth crisis" may not be very different from the understanding of Rambam as presented here: that prayer is a function of praising God. Limited man/woman, overwhelmed by the forces and tension of life, feels in constant crisis, and in gratitude to God for his/her very survival prays daily.

There is yet another interpretation of the Ramban-Rambam controversy.[21] Ramban may be following the view of Rabbi Yose bar Ḥanina, who claims that the prayer service was instituted by the Patriarchs (*Avot*).[22] It can be suggested that the characteristics of each of the three *Avot* motivated them to pray at different times. Abraham, who introduced a new faith commitment to the world, prayed at dawn, the beginning of the new day. Isaac, the meditator who evaluated and then transmitted Abraham's novel ideas, was passive, content to follow in his father's footsteps. He was taken to Moriah to be offered as a sacrifice, had a wife chosen for him, and reopened the wells which his father had discovered. He was a man who contemplated rather than initiated. Therefore he prayed in the afternoon, as the sun set, an especially suitable time for contemplative thought. Jacob, Isaac's son, was the loneliest of the biblical figures. Hated by his brother, he was separated from his parents for twenty-two years. His beloved wife, Rachel, died young; his favorite son, Joseph, disappeared and was believed to be dead. Appropriately, Jacob prayed at night, a time when one is often overcome by fear and a sense of groping loneliness.

For Ramban, prayer is spontaneous, the cry or song of individuals who feel motivated by some experience to communicate with God. Prayer, Ramban suggests, corresponds to the *Avot,* who prayed when they felt the personal need to reach out to God. They did so at times which best reflected their inner feelings and aspirations.

Rambam, who follows the view of Rabbi Joshua ben Levi, believes that prayer corresponds to the sacrificial service.[23] For Rambam,

20. Quoted from Rabbi Abraham R. Besdin, *Reflections of the Rav*, pp. 79–82.
21. See Rabbi Shlomo Riskin, *Home Studies in Prayer*, lesson no. 1.
22. See Berakhot 26b.
23. See ibid. Rambam, *Code*, Laws of Prayer 1:5.

prayer is fundamentally a structured form of dialogue with God and, therefore, corresponds to the daily obligatory sacrifices.

The Jerusalem Talmud offers another observation: "And from where do we derive the three prayers? Rabbi Samuel ben Naḥmani says: They correspond to the three times that the day visibly changes over [God's] creatures."[24]

This position can be reconciled with the positions of both Rabbi Joshua ben Levi (followed by Rambam) and Rabbi Yose b. Ḥanina (followed by Ramban), as it involves elements of structure (the natural cycle repeating itself morning, afternoon, and night consistently) and spontaneity (the feelings of the *Avot* that different times of the day were most suitable for their own personal needs to pray).

In the end the Talmud concludes: "the Patriarchs instituted the *tefillah* and the rabbis found a basis for them in the offerings."[25] Structure and spontaneity must merge to form a single unit.[26]

Rashi and Tosafot

Rashi is of a different opinion. According to Rashi, the exemption of women from all precepts for which there is a fixed time applies only to biblical law. No such rule exists vis-à-vis rabbinical ordinances.[27] Rashi maintains that since *tefillah* is a postbiblical institution, reciting the Shemoneh Esreh remains obligatory for women despite the fact that it is a positive commandment fixed by time.[28]

---

24. Yerushalmi Berakhot 4:1.

25. Berakhot 26b.

26. *Shulḥan Arukh*, Oraḥ Ḥayyim 119:1 states that one may include personal prayers in each of the central petitional blessings (*bakashot*) of the Shemoneh Esreh. See Avodah Zarah 8a.

Rabbi Riskin, "Structure and Spontaneity in Prayer," pp. 328–332, explains the views of Rabbi Joshua ben Levi and Rabbi Yose b. Rebi Ḥanina as they relate to elements of structure and spontaneity. Quoting the talmudic passage which merges both views, Rabbi Riskin concludes that "the Prayer Book was not meant to exhaust but, rather, to inspire prayer." (p. 331)

27. See Rashi to Berakhot 20b, s.v. *hakhi garsinan*, and the elaboration of Rashi's view in Tosafot to Berakhot 20b, s.v. *bi-tefillah peshita*.

28. Rashi agrees with Ramban that daily prayer is rabbinical in origin. However, Rashi, unlike Ramban, does not depend on the principle of *raḥamim* to explain why women are required to perform the positive time-oriented mitzvah of *tefillah*, since the exemption of women from positive time-fixed commandments does not apply to rabbinic ordinances.

Rashi's text of Berakhot 20b (which discusses women's obligation in regard to *tefillah*, see above, n. 12) does not include *peshita*. According to Maharsha to Berakhot 20b, Rashi's text includes two words, *de-raḥamei ninhu*, that explain why the rabbis instituted the prayer service in the first place.

Tosafot dissents, maintaining that the exemption of women from positive time fixed precepts is applicable to rabbinic ordinances.[29] Nonetheless, Tosafot would follow the view of Ramban that *tefillah* is rabbinically obligatory for women because of *raḥamim*.[30]

Arukh ha-Shulḥan concludes that according to Rashi and Tosafot, it is incumbent on women to pray the Shemoneh Esreh three times daily.

> And behold, this is certain—that according to Rashi, women are obligated to recite the *tefillah* three times a day, just as men are, since according to Rashi there is no difference between a time-oriented and a non-time-oriented rabbinical commandment. Tosafot would agree. . . . Since it is a prayer of mercy, the rabbis obligated them even in regard to a commandment set by time. Consequently they are obligated to perform this mitzvah the same as any man.[31]

After summarizing the views of Rambam and Ramban and alluding to Rashi, *Mishnah Berurah* states that Ramban is correct, "for it is the position of the majority of halakhic authorities. . . . Therefore women should be reminded to pray the Shemoneh Esreh."[32]

SHEMA

The second crucial prayer of the morning and evening services is the Shema. In Tractate Berakhot, the Mishnah declares that women

---

29. Tosafot to Berakhot, s.v. *bi-tefillah peshita*. Tosafot deduces from Sukkah 38a that women are exempt from the recitation of Hallel, which is rabbinic in nature, since it is a positive commandment fixed by time.

30. Tosafot unlike Ramban believes that prayer, even in times of distress, is rabbinical, not biblical, in origin. See *Arukh ha-Shulḥan* to Oraḥ Ḥayyim 106:6.

Tosafot to Berakhot 20b, s.v. *bi-tefillah peshita*, has the talmudic text *peshita* (when discussing the obligation of women in regard to *tefillah*, see n. 12). This is difficult. According to Tosafot, it is not self-evident that women are obligated to pray, since Tosafot claims that prayer is rabbinical in origin and bound by time.

Tosafot ha-Rosh (to Berakhot 20b, s.v. *ḥayyavin be-tefillah peshita*, found in *Sefer Berakhah Meshuleshet al Masekhet Berakhot* [New York: Hotza'at Ohr, 5707]), suggests that *peshita* is found in our talmudic text only because the term is consistently used at the beginning of each of the other discussions on this *daf* (page). Tosafot concludes the talmudic text with *de-raḥmei ninhu*.

31. *Arukh ha-Shulḥan* to Oraḥ Ḥayyim 106:7. See above, n. 14, which discusses whether Ma'ariv is obligatory or optional.

32. *Mishnah Berurah* to Oraḥ Ḥayyim 106:4. The allusion to Rashi's position is found in the statement: "and even though it is a positive commandment ordained by the rabbis fixed by time, and women are exempt from positive commandments fixed by time, even if they are rabbinical."

are exempt from reciting the Shema.[33] The Talmud asks whether this exemption is not self-evident. After all, women are exempt from commandments whose performance is linked to set times, and the Shema is one of these mitzvot, as is indicated by the phrase "When you lie down and when you rise up" (Deuteronomy 6:7). The Talmud responds with the following argument: The recitation of the Shema includes a declaration of absolute belief in the perfect unity of God; since this belief is so central to Judaism, it might be argued that the exemption of women from positive commandments fixed by time does not apply to the Shema; "we are therefore told that this is not so."[34]

Rif[35] Rambam,[36] and Rosh[37] all conclude that the Shema is a positive commandment fixed by time and therefore women are exempt from reciting it. *Shulḥan Arukh* agrees, but says that women should be taught to accept the yoke of the Kingdom of Heaven."[38] Rema adds that women should at least (*"lefaḥot"*) read the first verse, which is the principal sentence of the Shema.[39]

What *Shulḥan Arukh* meant when he stated that women should be taught to accept the yoke of the Kingdom of Heaven is a subject of dispute. *Naḥalat Ẓevi* maintains that he was referring to their reciting the entire first paragraph of Shema. Rema, as noted above, comments that the first sentence is enough. *Levush* claims that *Shulḥan Arukh* had the first sentence in mind for daily recital, and this is in fact what Rema explains.[40] *Magen Gibborim* maintains that the intent of *Shulḥan Arukh* is that it is proper for women to be taught to recite all three portions of Shema.[41]

What emerges from this analysis is that with the passage of time the mishnaic exemption of women was significantly modified. As a means of expressing their commitment to God, women ought to recite the first sentence and even the first paragraph of the Shema, and perhaps all three paragraphs.

Later authorities concur. *Mishnah Berurah* states: "And it is proper that women accept the yoke of the Kingdom of Heaven, in

---

33. Mishnah Berakhot 3:3, Berakhot 20a.
34. Berakhot 20b.
35. Rif to Berakhot 20a–b (in Rif, 11b).
36. Rambam, *Code*, Laws of Keri'at Shema 4:1.
37. Rosh to Berakhot 20b, s.v. *keri'at shema u-tefillin*.
38. *Shulḥan Arukh*, Oraḥ Ḥayyim 70:1.
39. Rema, loc. cit.
40. *Mishnah Berurah* to Oraḥ Ḥayyim 70:5, quotes both these views.
41. *Magen Gibborim, Elef ha-Magen* on *Tur* and *Shulḥan Arukh*, Oraḥ Ḥayyim 70:3.

other words, that they should at least (*al kol panim*) recite the Hear, O Israel."[42] Here *Mishnah Berurah* uses the phrase *al kol panim* even as Rema uses the term *lefaḥot*. Clearly women are strongly encouraged to recite the complete Shema.

Arukh ha-Shulḥan extols women who recite Keri'at Shema: ". . . and our women recite Keri'at Shema, and may they be blessed for this act."[43]

Rabbi David Auerbach in *Halikhot Beitah* concludes: "And the custom has already spread that women read the three portions [of Shema]."[44]

BIRKHOT HA-SHAḤAR

While a careful analysis of the development and ultimate obligation of women in connection with other parts of the prayer service is beyond the scope of this chapter, a cursory glimpse at the conclusions reached by some of our authorities is in order.

Arukh ha-Shulḥan maintains that the Birkhot ha-Shaḥar (morning blessings) are equally applicable to women and men, and therefore women are required to recite them.[45] The key message of the morning blessings is the daily gift of physical reinvigoration and spiritual revitalization, concerning which women have as much to be grateful for as men. *Mishnah Berurah* states that while it is best that the morning blessings be recited during the first four hours of the day and certainly by midday, nonetheless they can be recited post-facto after the morning time period, even during the night hours.[46] Post-facto, these blessings have no specific time boundaries, and therefore they should be said by women. "It appears," writes *Mishnah Berurah*, "that women recite the Birkhot ha-Shaḥar like men."[47]

Authorities strongly encourage or oblige women to recite the morning Torah blessings (Birkhot ha-Torah), which are central to the Birkhot ha-Shaḥar. *Shulḥan Arukh* records this halakhah simply but firmly: "Women recite the Torah blessings."[48] The association

42. *Mishnah Berurah* to Oraḥ Ḥayyim 106:4.
43. *Arukh ha-Shulḥan*, Oraḥ Ḥayyim 70:1.
44. Rabbi David Auerbach, *Halikhot Beitah*, p. 27, halakhah 1.
45. *Arukh ha-Shulḥan*, Oraḥ Ḥayyim 70:1.
46. See *Mishnah Berurah* to Oraḥ Ḥayyim 52:10 and *Biur Halakhah* to Oraḥ Ḥayyim 52, s.v. *kol ha-berakhot*.
47. *Mishnah Berurah* to Oraḥ Ḥayyim 70:2.
48. *Shulḥan Arukh*, Oraḥ Ḥayyim 47:14.

between the Torah blessings and the Birkhot ha-Shaḥar is clear. As we acknowledge God for the renewal of body and soul, of life itself, we declare that through Torah we can sanctify our every endeavor and ennoble our existence.

Opinions differ as to how the specific obligation is derived. *Ba'er Heitev* states that women are required to recite the blessings because they are required to study Torah laws which apply to them.[49] *Sefer Emek Berakhah* argues that the blessings relate to the Torah itself (not to learning Torah). Therefore, even if women are exempt from *Talmud Torah* (an issue which will be discussed in a later chapter), they still recite the Torah blessings.[50] *Magen Avraham* suggests that the blessings are connected to the portion dealing with the sacrificial service or with the Shemoneh Esreh. Since women recite these prayers they must also say the Torah blessings.[51] The Vilna Gaon states that women can recite blessings even when performing commandments they are exempt from. Exemption does not imply exclusion, and if women choose to perform the mitzvah, they should recite a blessing. Hence, even if women are exempt from *Talmud Torah*, they may recite the Torah blessings.[52]

PESUKEI DE-ZIMRA

While the Birkhot ha-Shaḥar stress the re-creation of man and woman on both the physical and spiritual level, Pesukei de-Zimra, the psalms recited immediately after Birkhot ha-Shaḥar, emphasize God's greatness for having renewed the splendor and glory of nature. The term *zimra* is derived from the word *zemer*, "to sing." Through these prayers one sings God's praises as the Creator of the beautiful and magnificent world of nature. Adopting this concept, *Arukh ha-Shulḥan* strongly suggests that these psalms should be recited by women, though without obligation: "Women are not obligated to say Barukh she-Amar and Yishtabbaḥ, but they may do so. And why should women not be permitted to offer praises to the Lord as Miriam and all the women of Israel did at the splitting of the sea?"[53]

---

49. *Ba'er Heitev* to *Shulḥan Arukh*, Oraḥ Ḥayyim 47:14.

50. *Sefer Emek Berakhah* (beginning of the laws of Torah blessings).

51. *Magen Avraham* to *Shulḥan Arukh*, Oraḥ Ḥayyim 47:14, quoting the *Beit Yosef* in the name of *Ha-Agur*. (*Magen Avraham*, ibid., also notes that women recite the blessings because they are required to study Torah laws which apply to them. See Rema, Yoreh De'ah 246:6.) Note *Ba'er Heitev* to *Shulḥan Arukh*, Oraḥ Ḥayyim 47:14. See also below, n. 67 regarding a woman's obligation to recite Korbanot.

52. *Be'ur ha-Gra* to *Shulḥan Arukh*, Oraḥ Ḥayyim 47, s.v. *nashim*, quotes Tosafot to Rosh Hashanah 33a, s.v. *ha*.

53. *Arukh ha-Shulḥan*, Oraḥ Ḥayyim 70:1.

There is a second position. *Zimra* may be derived from the word *zomer*, "to prune." Just as one prunes a tree to prepare it for future growth, so, too, do these psalms serve as preparatory prayers, setting the mood and arousing the sensitivities so that one may have complete *kavvanah* (pure intent) when reciting the basic *tefillot* beginning with Barekhu.[54] Indeed, *Mishnah Berurah* quotes Rabbi Akiva Eger, who maintains that Pesukei de-Zimra were introduced only because of the ensuing Shemoneh Esreh. Therefore, concludes *Mishnah Berurah*, as women are obligated to recite the Shemoneh Esreh, so, too, are they obligated to recite Pesukei de-Zimra.[55]

BIRKHOT SHEMA

The function of the blessings prior to the Shema (Birkhot Shema) is mainly to set the proper mood for the recitation of the Shema. The first of these blessings, both in the morning and the evening service (Yoẓer ha-Me'orot and Ha-Ma'ariv Aravim, respectively), speaks of God as the Master of nature, while the second (Ahavat Olam, Ahavah Rabbah) speaks of God who revealed the Torah. Having contemplated God as Creator and Revealer, one can properly proceed to recite Shema, in which the Unity of God (Shema) and His giving of mitzvot (Ve-Hayah and the portion of *ẓiẓit*) are expressed.

In addition, the three paragraphs of Shema may parallel the themes of its preceding and ensuing blessings. Shema corresponds to Yoẓer ha-Me'orot, as both deal with the unity of God as Creator of the world. Ve-Hayah and Ahavah Rabbah relate to the theme of Divine revelation. The portion of *ẓiẓit* ("I am the Lord your God, who took you out of the land of Egypt") and the blessing of Ge'ulah (the paragraph following Shema) speak of the process of redemption.[56]

Birkhot Shema and the Shema itself also revolve around the theme

---

54. *Menorat ha-Ma'or* of Rabbi Isaac Aboab offers this understanding of Pesukei de-Zimra.

55. *Mishnah Berurah* to Oraḥ Ḥayyim 70:2 quoting *Rav Akiva Eger* to Oraḥ Ḥayyim 52.

56. Another way of viewing the paragraphs of Shema is that they correspond to the three basic principles of faith as developed in the *Sefer ha-Ikkarim* 1:11: the existence of God (Shema), reward and punishment (Ve-Hayah), and Divine revelation (the portion of *ẓiẓit*, which many interpret as referring to a commitment to the 613 commandments, the numerical value of the word *ẓiẓit* plus the eight threads and five knots in the fringes). See Rashi to Numbers 15:39, s.v. *u-zekhartem et kol mitzvot Hashem*.

of God's transcendence and immanence.[57] In the first *berakhah* God is spoken of as *Melekh*, the King of kings who with His infinite power created the world. God, in this blessing, is described as separate, apart, transcendent. The second *berakhah* speaks of God as the "Father of mercy" (*av ha-raḥaman*) who remains intimately involved with His people. He is a God who is close, concerned, and immanent. The *berakhah* rejects the theory of deism, which maintains that God created the world and then withdrew. God remains involved, concerned with every creature. Appropriately, the second blessing begins and ends with the word *ahavah* ("love"), descriptive of a God who loves His people.

The Shema suitably follows these blessings. In the first sentence we proclaim: *Shema Yisrael*, "Hear, O Israel," *Hashem*, "the Lord," a title descriptive of a God of mercy and love, *Elokeinu*, "our God," a term defining God's infinite power and titanic strength, *Hashem eḥad*, "the Lord [with both characteristics] is One." There is only one perfect God, the absolute Unity who possesses the traits of transcendence and immanence. The blessings appropriately introduce the Shema itself.

It follows, therefore, that since women are exempt from Shema, they are equally exempt from the blessings prior to Shema. Furthermore, just as the reciting of Shema is fixed by time, so too are the blessings of Shema linked to a specific time period. Almost all authorities, however, maintain that women certainly have the right to recite these blessings and encourage them to do so. Indeed, *Arukh ha-Shulḥan* writes: "women may recite the blessing of the Keri'at Shema and the Shema itself. . . . And our women do this, and may they be blessed."[58] When we recall that women should fulfill their

---

57. For an analysis of God's transcendence, immanence, and unity, see Rabbi Epstein, *The Faith of Judaism*, pp. 134–168; Dr. Aron Barth, *The Modern Jew Faces Eternal Problems*, pp. 29–33.

58. *Arukh ha-Shulḥan*, Oraḥ Ḥayyim 70:1. See also *Mishnah Berurah* to Oraḥ Ḥayyim 70:2.

See Rambam, *Code*, Laws of Prayer 7:17; he states that the Kedushah of the first *berakhah* before Shema must be said with a minyan. For Rambam this Kedushah she-be-Yoẓer cannot be said by women. Rosh (quoted in *Tur Shulḥan Arukh*, Oraḥ Ḥayyim 59) disagrees. Since Kedushah she-be-Yoẓer is a *sippur devarim*, the *telling* of how the ministering angels (*malakhim*) sanctify God and not a personal sanctification process, [it] may be said without a minyan. *Beit Yosef* to *Tur Shulḥan Arukh*, Oraḥ Ḥayyim 59, s.v. *Kedushah she-be-Yoẓer* notes that Rambam's son indicated that his father later altered his opinion and concluded that even an individual may recite Kedushah she-be-Yoẓer.

See *Responsa Yabi'a Omer* 2:6 that women from Sephardic communities should not recite the blessings of Shema. This is probably based on the view of Rambam,

daily obligation of accepting the "yoke" of God's Kingdom by at least reciting the first sentence or paragraph of Shema (and perhaps all three paragraphs), we can clearly understand why women have the right to recite these preparatory blessings and the reason they are encouraged to do so.

BLESSINGS BEFORE SHEMONEH ESREH

Whether the blessing of Ge'ulah (redemption) before Shemoneh Esreh is incumbent on women depends upon the reason it is recited. *Magen Avraham* concludes that women are obligated to recite the blessing because it deals with remembering the Egyptian exodus, a recitation which is not fixed by time.[59] *Peri Megadim* maintains that the requirement of mentioning the exodus in the evening is of rabbinical origin, while the daytime one is a biblical commandment. From this perspective, the day and evening mitzvot to remember the exodus are fundamentally different and are each fixed by time. Women would, therefore, be exempt from reciting these blessings.[60] *Sha'agat Aryeh* adds that the duty of mentioning the exodus during the day is independent of the obligation to do so at night (even if the latter obligation is biblical); hence the blessing is circumscribed by time, and women would be exempt from its recitation.[61]

There is another possibility. The blessing of Ge'ulah, reaffirms one's belief in a God who has the power to redeem and help His people. At that point, one is properly prepared to begin the Shemoneh Esreh, in which each individual petitions God for personal and communal needs. A God who redeems His people has the power to fulfill anyone's requests. This may explain why the blessing of Ge'ulah must precede the Shemoneh Esreh without any interruption.[62] It follows that since women are obligated to recite Shemoneh Esreh, so, too, are they obligated to recite the blessing of Ge'ulah.[63]

The central message of the morning service is, therefore, renewal

---

Code, Laws of Ẓiẓit 3:9, that although women may fulfill mitzvot they are exempt from doing, they should not recite blessings on these mitzvot, as the term *ve-ẓivanu* ("and You have commanded us") in the *berakhah* does not apply to them. Rabbi Auerbach in *Halikhot Beitah*, p. 32, n. 11, points out that many authorities disagree with *Yabi'a Omer*, as the Keri'at Shema blessings do not include the term *ve-ẓivanu*.

59. *Magen Avraham*, quoted in *Mishnah Berurah* to Oraḥ Ḥayyim 70:2.

60. *Peri Megadim*, quoted by *Mishnah Berurah* 70:2.

61. *Sha'agat Aryeh*, quoted in *Mishnah Berurah* to Oraḥ Ḥayyim 70:2.

62. See Berakhot 4b, where the Talmud speaks of the juxtaposition of the Ge'ulah blessing with the Shemoneh Esreh.

63. *Magen Avraham* to *Shulḥan Arukh*, Oraḥ Ḥayyim 70:1.

(*hithadshut*). Birkhot ha-Shahar stresses the renewal of body and soul, Pesukei de-Zimra emphasizes the renewal of nature, and the blessings of Shema focus on the renewal and redemption of Israel as a people. The service reaches its crescendo with the Shemoneh Esreh, where one supplicates God for personal and communal needs. It is followed by the concluding prayers of hope for the ultimate redemption.

CONCLUDING PRAYERS

Women are strongly encouraged to recite the concluding prayers of Ashrei,[64] La-Menazze'ah, U-Va le-Zion,[65] Aleinu,[66] and the Shir shel Yom.[67] These prayers are an appropriate conclusion to the service, for they deal with the hope for the messianic redemption, an aspiration that is equally applicable to women and men.

In Ashrei, for example, we long for the time when all people will be

---

64. See *Shibbolei ha-Leket*, siman 44, in the name of Rashi, who indicates that people remained in synagogue to study Torah after services. They therefore added Ashrei, "Happy are those who dwell in your house," which they understood to mean, "happy are they who tarry in synagogue to learn Torah." Since women did not study Torah in the synagogue, they are exempt from reciting Ashrei.

Arukh ha-Shulhan, Orah Hayyim 132:1, quotes Berakhot 4b, which says that one should recite Ashrei three times daily to ensure a place in the world to come, a status that both women and men yearn for equally. In Orah Hayyim 132:2, *Arukh ha-Shulhan* adds that Ashrei parallels the Shema and Shemoneh Esreh. In Shema and Shemoneh Esreh we ask God to sustain us spiritually, while in Ashrei we ask for physical sustenance. It follows, therefore, that just as women recite Shema and Shemoneh Esreh, so should they recite Ashrei. From both these perspectives, Ashrei should also be said by women during the Minhah service.

65. Rashi to Sotah 49a, s.v. *akedushah de-sidra*, suggests that *U-Va le-Zion* was introduced to give all of Israel the chance to study Torah on some level daily. Since women are exempt from *Talmud Torah*, they are also exempt from U-Va le-Zion. However, as women may, and in virtually all areas must, study Torah (see below, chap. 5), it is proper for them to recite *U-Va le-Zion*. See *Arukh ha-Shulhan*, Orah Hayyim 132:3–7, where it is argued that *La-Menazze'ah* and *U-Va le-Zion* relate to God's response to the needs and pain of His people, a theme equally applicable to women and men.

66. *Levush* to Orah Hayyim 133:1 states that Aleinu is recited in order to conclude the service with praise of God. In this way, we begin and end *tefillah* with *hoda'ah* (praise).

Indeed, *Arukh ha-Shulhan*, Orah Hayyim 133:1 and *Mishnah Berurah*, Orah Hayyim 132:7 quote R. Isaac Luria, who states that Aleinu should be said at the conclusion of each service. As women are obligated to pray twice and according to some authorities three times daily, they should recite Aleinu after each *tefillah*.

Responsa Mahazeh Eliyahu, siman 10, links Aleinu to Shemoneh Esreh. Since women are obligated to recite the Shemoneh Esreh, they should also recite Aleinu.

67. *Responsa Mahazeh Eliyahu*, no. 10, quoting *Massekhet Soferim* 18:1, relates

provided for ("You open your hand and satisfy the desire of every living being," Psalms 145:16); in La-Menaẓẓe'aḥ we express our desire for universal peace ("Some [rely] upon chariots and some upon horses, but as for us, upon the name of the Lord our God we call," Psalms 20:8); in U-Va le-Ẓion we yearn for the coming of the redeemer ("The redeemer shall come to Zion") and the hope that the Messiah will soon arrive ("and to inherit the goodness and blessing of the messianic day"); in Aleinu we express our hope for a time when the whole "world will be perfected under the reign of the Almighty"; and in the daily psalm (Shir Shel Yom) chanted by the levites, we long for the time when the Temple will be rebuilt.[68]

Women are also urged to recite the Hallel[69] and the Musaf service.[70]

* * *

The Talmud considers the prayers of Hannah, the mother of Samuel the prophet, as a model for the optimal prayer experience.[71] The choice of a woman as a role model in prayer is significant. It reflects the basic truth that women, like men, can reach the highest levels of dialogue with God. Both women and men possess the inner Godly spark through which one can rendezvous with the Infinite

---

the Shir Shel Yom to Korbanot. Since women have no portion in Korbanot, so are they exempt from reciting the Shir. See however, Taz to *Shulḥan Arukh*, Oraḥ Ḥayyim 47:10, *Magen Avraham*, ibid., 47:14, *Ba'er Heitev*, ibid., sec. 14, and *Bi'ur Halakhah*, ibid., s.v. *nashim*, who maintain that women must recite the portion of Korbanot. It follows, according to these opinions, that women should recite the Shir.

68. Many prayers and Jewish ritual experiences conclude with an expression of the hope for messianic redemption (e.g., the Sabbath, the Passover Seder, and the Grace after Meals).

69. Women are exempt from Hallel because it is a positive commandment fixed by time. See *Bi'ur Halakhah* to *Shulḥan Arukh*, Oraḥ Ḥayyim 422, s.v. Hallel, end, who concludes that although women are exempt from Hallel, they may recite Hallel with a *berakhah*. However, women from Sephardic communities recite Hallel without a *berakhah*. See Rabbi Auerbach in *Halikhot Beitah*, siman 8, sec. 2, p. 54.

70. Rabbi Akiva Eger in his *Haggahot* to *Shulḥan Arukh*, Oraḥ Ḥayyim 106, quotes Ramban in *Responsa Besamim Rosh*, no. 89, that although women are exempt from Musaf, "they have already accustomed themselves to recite all prayers and have obligated themselves to perform all the mitzvot."

Mishnah Berurah to *Shulḥan Arukh*, Oraḥ Ḥayyim 106:4, quotes Ẓlaḥ as maintaining that women are exempt from Musaf, while *Magen Gibborim* concludes that they are obligated.

It could be argued that women are required to observe the holidays, and therefore, they are similarly required to recite the Musaf service, since Musaf was introduced because of the sanctity of the holidays. See Rabbi Auerbach, *Halikhot Beitah*, p. 41, n. 8.

71. Berakhot 30b–31a.

God. In halakhic terms, this intrinsic strength is translated into the position recorded in this chapter, that women are obligated or strongly encouraged to pray the morning, afternoon, and evening services.[72]

72. For a review of the obligations of women with regard to private prayer, see Rabbi Menachem M. Kasdan, "Are Women Obligated to Pray?" See also Rabbi Auerbach, *Halikhot Beitah*.

Chapter Three

The Emergence of Communal Prayer

THE HISTORY

In addition to private prayer there emerged within our history a tradition of communal prayer. It is difficult to pinpoint precisely when this tradition began. Although daily public services appear to have commenced during or immediately after the Babylonian exile (586 B.C.E.), there are indications that on certain occasions Jews prayed in communal groups in the biblical period.

The Talmud, for example, states:

> Rabbi Simeon ben Lakish said: "And Jacob called unto his sons, and said: Gather yourselves that I may tell you [that which shall befall you in the end of days]" (Genesis 49:1). Jacob wished to reveal to his sons the end of the days [the final universal redemption], whereupon the Shekhinah departed from him. Said he, "Perhaps, Heaven forfend, there is one unfit among my children," . . . [But] his sons answered him, "Hear, O Israel, the Lord our God, the Lord is One" (Deuteronomy 6:4). [In plain words, addressing Jacob by his other name, Israel, the sons said:] "Just as there is only One in thy heart, so there is only One in our heart." In that moment our father Jacob opened [his mouth] and exclaimed: "Blessed be the name of His glorious kingdom forever and ever."[1]

In recording this dialogue, Targum Yerushalmi has Jacob respond, *Yehai shemeh rabba mevarakh le-almei almin*, "May His

1. Pesaḥim 56a. Rambam, *Code*, Laws of Keri'at Shema 1:4, interprets Jacob's fears as concerning the denial of the unity of God by one of his sons; he does not mention that Jacob wished to reveal the end of days. See *Kesef Mishneh* to Rambam, *Code*, Laws of Keri'at Shema 1:4, s.v. *ha-koreh Keri'at Shema*.

great name be blessed forever."[2] Although Jacob's reaction may simply have been an expression of personal exhilaration about his sons' commitment to a basic principle of Jewish faith, the phrase *Yehai shemeh* is associated with public services. Indeed, Jacob recites *Yehai shemeh* in the presence of his sons, who constitute a public quorum.

Public prayer was also part and parcel of the mitzvah of *Hakhel* ("assemble"), which is of biblical origin. On the first day of the intermediate days of Sukkot, when the last year of the seven-year sabbatical cycle had ended and a new year had started, the king would read various parts of the Torah to the assembled.

> And Moses commanded them, saying: "At the end of [every] seven years, in the set time of the year of release, in the feast of Tabernacles: When all Israel is come to appear before the Lord thy God in the place which He shall choose, thou shalt read this before all Israel in their hearing: Assemble the people, the men, the women, and the children, and thy stranger that is within thy gates that they may hear, and that they may learn, and fear the Lord your God, and observe to do all the words of this Law." (Deuteronomy 31:10–12)[3]

The king who read the Torah recited the same blessings that we recite before and after reading the Torah. He would then add seven more benedictions. The first three are blessings found in the holiday Shemoneh Esreh: Reẓeh ("be pleased"), Modim ("we are thankful") and Atah Veḥartanu ("You chose us from all the peoples") until Mekadesh Yisrael ve-Hazmanim ("sanctifies Israel and the seasons").[4]

King Solomon's dedicatory prayer when the First Temple was

---

2. Targum Yerushalmi to Genesis 49:1. Ibid. to Deuteronomy 6:4 presents a similar response. See Targum Jonathan ben Uzziel to Deuteronomy 6:4, where the response of Jacob is as recorded in Pesaḥim 56a, "Blessed be the name of His glorious kingdom forever and ever."

3. See Sotah 41a; Ḥagigah 3a; Yerushalmi Ḥagigah 1:1; Rambam, *Code*, Laws of Ḥagigah 3:1–7; idem, *Book of Commandments*, positive commandment 16; *Sefer Mitzvot Gadol*, positive commandment 230; *Sefer ha-Ḥinnukh*, commandment 612.

According to Rambam, *Code*, Laws of Ḥagigah 3:3, the reading by the king consisted of the following portions of Deuteronomy: Deut. 1:1–6:9, 11:13–21, 14:22–28:69.

For an analysis of *Hakhel*, see Rabbi Menachem Kasdan's "Hakhel."

4. See Maimonides, *Code*, Laws of Ḥagigah 3:4, and *Sefer ha-Ḥinnukh*, commandment 612, for a history of the seven blessings. The fourth blessing concerns the Temple, the fifth relates to the chosenness and redemption of Israel, the sixth deals with the priests, and the last is a prayer that Israel's needs be heeded.

completed (1 Kings 8:22–53) indicates that Jews were then praying in large assemblies when the need arose. There King Solomon proclaimed that God would help the people of Israel in their times of distress if they offered sincere prayers to Him.

> And You shall turn toward Your servant's prayer and to his supplication, O Lord my God; to hearken to the song and to the prayer that Your servant is praying before You today. That Your eyes may be open toward this house night and day, toward the place which You said, "My Name will be there"; to listen to the prayer that Your servant will pray toward this place. And You shall listen to the supplication of Your servant and of Your people Israel that they will pray toward this place; and You shall hear in heaven, Your abode, and You shall hear and forgive. (1 Kings 8:28–30)[5]

While these verses could refer to the prayers of individuals, the simplest interpretation is that they deal with communities in need, who physically turn toward Israel, Jerusalem, and the Temple, as part of a collective, in prayer.[6]

Synagogues were in existence in the Babylonian period. The Talmud relates that Rabbi Isaac, in discussing the verse "Yet I have been to them as a little sanctuary" (Ezekiel 11:16), stated: "This refers to the synagogue and house of learning in Babylon."[7]

It appears that those returning from the Babylonian exile "brought with them to Israel the custom of establishing synagogues wherever they settled."[8] By the beginning of the Second Common-

---

5. Translation is from *Judaica Books of the Prophets, Kings I* (New York: Judaica Press, 1980), pp. 92–93. For an analysis of the structure of King Solomon's dedication prayer, see *Soncino Books of the Bible, Kings I and II* (London: Soncino Press, 1950), 1 Kings 8:22, p. 60.

> Solomon's dedicatory prayer consisting of a series of short prayers for the general fulfillment of God's promise (23–26), His constant presence in the Temple and His acceptance of all prayers (27–30), Divine punishment for a false oath (31f.), help when the people repent after a defeat in battle (33f.), rain in times of drought (35f.), help in the event of other calamities (37–40), answering the prayers of a stranger (41–43), success in a war commanded by Him (44f.), mercy and forgiveness in captivity (46–51) and, finally, His readiness to receive the supplications of both King and people (52f.).

6. See Berakhot 30a, where verses from the dedicatory prayer of Solomon are understood to have reference to one's obligation to turn towards Israel, or, if in Israel, towards Jerusalem, or, if in Jerusalem, towards the Temple while praying.

7. Megillah 29a.

8. Abraham Kon, *Prayer*, p. 82. See ibid., pp. 76–111, for an overview of the place of the synagogue in Jewish history.

wealth, hundreds of synagogues were in existence in Jerusalem. The Talmud states:

> Rabbi Phinehas . . . on the authority of Rabbi Hoshaiah . . . stated . . . that there were 394 courts of law [each consisting of twenty-three judges] in Jerusalem, and an equal number of synagogues, houses of study [for Mishnah and Talmud], and schools [for children].[9]

And at the Holy Temple in Jerusalem, prayer accompanied the offering of the daily communal sacrifices. In the words of the Mishnah:

> The appointed one said to them [the priests], "Pronounce one blessing." [There is a difference of opinion as to whether this was "Who Fashionest Light" (Yoẓer ha-Me'orot) or "Great Love" (Ahavah Rabbah).[10] This and the succeeding prayers were said in the Chamber of Hewn Stone (*Lishkat ha-Gazit*).] And they did so.
>
> Then they recited the Aseret ha-Dibbrot [commonly translated "Ten Commandments"],[11] and the first, second, and third sections of the Shema.
>
> And they blessed the people[12] with three benedictions [since they had no time to say all eighteen benedictions, i.e., the entire Shemoneh

9. Ketubbot 105a.

Yerushalmi Ketubbot 13:1 states in the name of Rabbi Phinehas on the authority of Rabbi Hoshaiah that there were 460 synagogues in Jerusalem at that time.

Yerushalmi Megillah 3:1 quotes Rabbi Phinehas on the authority of Rav Hoshaiah that there were 480 synagogues in Jerusalem then. *Korban ha-Edah*, ibid., s.v. "480 synagogues were in Jerusalem," concludes that there were 481 courts in Jerusalem, basing his calculation on Isaiah 1:21, *meleti mishpat ẓedek*, "full of judgment and righteousness." He interprets "judgment" to refer to synagogues, and the numerical value of *meleti* is 481, the additional synagogue being the Holy Temple.

10. See Berakhot 11b–12a for the differing opinions.

Rambam in his commentary to Mishnah Tamid 5:1 (s.v. *amar lahem ha-memuneh*), follows the opinion in Berakhot 11b, that Ahavat Olam (the equivalent of Ahavah Rabbah) was said first, and Yoẓer ha-Me'orot was recited after sunrise.

11. Aseret ha-Dibbrot is more properly translated as the "ten statements." Aseret ha-Dibbrot may include fewer than ten commandments. Others maintain that many more commandments than ten are alluded to. See Sa'adia Gaon in his *Azharot* which are published in his siddur. There he states that the 613 commandments are implicit in the Aseret ha-Dibbrot.

The Aseret ha-Dibbrot were not included in prayer services outside of the *Mikdash* (Temple) so that no one would conclude (as the heretics did) that the Aseret ha-Dibbrot were the only valid part of the Torah. See Berakhot 12a.

12. Rashi understands "and they blessed the people" to mean "and they said these blessings *with* the people." See Rashi to Berakhot 11b, s.v. *u-veirkhu et ha-am*.

> Esreh], namely, "True and Firm" [Emet ve-Yaẓiv, the blessing following the Shema], Avodah (Reẓeh), and the Priestly Benediction.[13]

After the destruction of the Second Temple, public services were firmly in place. The Talmud declares that Elijah told Rabbi Yose:

> Whenever Israel enters [its] synagogues and houses of study and responds: "May His great name be blessed!" the Holy One, blessed be He, shakes His head and says: "Happy is the King who is praised in this house!"[14]

Clearly, by the time of R. Yose, a student of Rabbi Akiva, prayer in synagogue was well established.[15]

THE LEGAL PERSPECTIVE

Devarim she-bi-Kedushah

As public prayer services developed, there also emerged a rabbinical obligation to recite or hear *devarim she-bi-kedushah* (Kaddish, Kedushah, Barekhu, etc.) in an assembly of ten people.[16] The basic source of this obligation is found in the Talmud Bavli.

---

13. Mishnah Tamid 5:1, Tamid 32b.

Tosafot to Berakhot 11b, s.v. *u-birkat kohanim*, states that the priests recited the Priestly Benediction without actually blessing the people (*dukhan*). The *dukhan* took place after the *haktarat eimurim* (the burning of those portions of sacrifices offered on the altar).

Rambam in his commentary to Mishnah Tamid 5:1, s.v. *amar lahem ha-memuneh*, states that the people recited Emet ve-Yaẓiv, Reẓeh, Modim and Sim Shalom, prayers which deal with the welfare of Israel, and afterwards the priests blessed the people without reciting the *dukhan*. He concludes that all these prayers were said in the *Lishkat ha-Gazit*, except for the regular Priestly Benediction (*dukhan*), which was said after the morning standard offering, on the steps of the hall.

14. Berakhot 3a.

15. Rabbi Yose in the Mishnah and baraita is invariably Rabbi Yose ben Ḥalafta, a student of Rabbi Akiva who flourished in the fourth generation of tannaim (135–165 C.E.).

16. See *Mishnah Berurah*, Oraḥ Ḥayyim 55:2, 5, 6, who states that Kaddish, Kedushah, Barekhu, the public reading of the Torah, the Priestly Benediction, the repetition of the Shemoneh Esreh, and the recitation of the Haftarah all fall into the category of *devarim she-bi-kedushah*, prayers and blessings which sanctify the name of God.

Tur Shulḥan Arukh, Oraḥ Ḥayyim 565, cites Rav Nathan, who maintains that the thirteen attributes of God (the *yud gimmel middot*), recited as part of the prayer service, fall into the category of *devarim she-bi-kedushah*. *Tur* disagrees, likening it to one who reads from the Torah. *Shulḥan Arukh*, Oraḥ Ḥayyim 565:5, concludes that an individual may read the *yud gimmel middot* as long as it is not recited as a prayer. *Magen Avraham*, ibid., adds that the *yud gimmel middot* should be sung with the appropriate cantillation.

> R. Adda b. Abaha said: Whence do we know that a man praying by himself does not say the Sanctification [*devarim she-bi-kedushah*]? Because it says: "I will be hallowed *among* (*tokh*) the children of Israel (*Bnei Yisrael*)" (Leviticus 22:32); for any manifestation of sanctification not less than ten are required. How is this derived? Rabinai, the brother of R. Ḥiyya bar Abba, taught: We draw an analogy between two occurrences of the word *among*. It is written here, "I will be hallowed *among* the children of Israel," and it is written elsewhere, "Separate yourselves from *among* this congregation (*edah*)" (Numbers 16:21). Just as in that case ten are implied [the "congregation" referred to being the ten spies, Joshua and Caleb being excluded], so here ten are implied.[17]

Alternatively, the Talmud Yerushalmi states:

> Said R. Simon: it is written here *among* ["I will be hallowed *among* the children of Israel (*Bnei Yisrael*)" (Leviticus 22:32), and it is written elsewhere, "And the sons of Israel (*Bnei Yisrael*) came to buy *among* those that came" (Genesis 42:5). Just as *among* in the Jacob story refers to ten [ten of the twelve brothers came, since Joseph was already in Egypt and Benjamin had remained with his father], so too *among* refers here to ten. ["I will be hallowed *among* the children of Israel."][18]

Although both the Talmud Bavli and the Talmud Yerushalmi cite biblical verses as the source of obligation, virtually all authorities point out that the deductions are *asmakhta be-alma*, inferred from the biblical text, and therefore the mandate to recite *devarim she-bi-kedushah* in the presence of "ten" is rabbinical.[19] This position follows logically. Since prayer according to virtually all authorities is

---

17. Berakhot 21b. See Megillah 23b and Sanhedrin 74b for a similar text.

Interestingly, *Keli Yakar* suggests that had Moses sent women spies, their report would have been favorable and the people of Israel would have been permitted to enter the land of Israel immediately.

18. Yerushalmi Berakhot 7:3. The Yerushalmi may prefer relating the term *Bnei Yisrael* to Genesis 42:5, where it is associated with the ten sons of Jacob for the first time. The term *Bnei Yisrael* is found earlier in Genesis 32:33, where it pertains to the future nation of Israel who will be forbidden to consume the *gid-ha-nasheh*, the sciatic nerve. See *Torah Temimah* to Genesis 42:5, no. 2.

19. Ran to Megillah 23b, s.v. *ve'ein nos'in* (in Ran commentary to Rif, 13b, and Rambam in *Perush ha-Mishnayot* to Megillah 4:3. Rif and Rambam have chapters 3 and 4 of Megillah in reversed order. Their third chapter, *ha-kore omed*, is our fourth, and vice versa.) See also *Keren Orah* to Sotah 38, s.v. *ve'od ashuv*, and *Yad Eliyahu*, siman 6, who support this position.

rabbinical in origin, *devarim she-bi-kedushah* can only be rabbinical.[20]

Rabbi Menaḥem ben Solomon Meiri maintains that the recitation of *devarim she-bi-kedushah* before ten is derived from the verse "Bless God in congregations [*be-makhelot*]" (Psalms 68:27),[21] since "congregation" is never less than ten.[22]

Tefillah be-Ẓibbur

Independent of *devarim she-bi-kedushah* is the halakhah of *tefillah be-ẓibbur*, communal prayer in an assembly of ten. While the concept of *devarim she-bi-kedushah* pertains to the recitation of Kaddish, Kedushah, and Barekhu during the prayer service, *tefillah be-ẓibbur* pertains to the recitation of non-*devarim she-bi-kedushah* prayers, specifically the silent Shemoneh Esreh, in the company of ten.

There is a presumption that prayer has greater efficacy when offered. in a communal setting, as part of *tefillah be-ẓibbur*. The advantages of *tefillah be-ẓibbur* are illustrated in the Talmud.

> Rabbi Nathan says: How do we know that the Holy One, blessed be He, does not despise the prayer of the congregation? For it is said: "Behold, God does not despise the mighty" (Job 36:5) [the numerous people that pray to him]. . . . The Holy One, blessed be He, says: If a man occupies himself with the study of the Torah and with works of charity and *prays with the congregation*, I account it to him as if he had redeemed Me and My children from among the nations of the world.[23]

Rambam codifies this talmudic portion in precise terms.

> The prayer of the community is always heard. Even if there are sinners amongst the community, God does not reject the prayers of the multitude. Therefore, one should associate himself with the congregation. He should not pray individually as long as he can pray with the community.[24]

---

20. See *Keren Orah*, loc. cit. For a fine review of the source of obligation of *devarim she-bi-kedushah*, see Rabbi Yitzchak Ya'akov Fuchs, *Ha-Tefillah be-Ẓibbur*, pp. 27–29.
21. See Meiri, *Beit ha-Beḥirah* to Berakhot 47b.
22. See Rashi to Ketubot 7b, s.v. *be-makhelot*.
23. Berakhot 8a. For an analysis of the preference for the synagogue as a place of prayer, see below, chap. 8, end.
24. Rambam, *Code*, Laws of Prayer 8:1.

Rabbi Judah Halevi notes that public prayer allows individuals within the community to compensate for each other's weaknesses. No person is perfect. As part of a collective whole, however, one's deficiencies can be offset by the strength of other participants in the prayer experience.

> Common prayer has many advantages. . . . An individual rarely accomplishes his prayer without slips and errors. It has been laid down, therefore, that the individual recites the prayers of a community, and if possible in a community of not less than ten persons, so that one makes up for the forgetfulness or error of the other. In this way [a complete prayer is gained, read with wholly pure devotion. Its blessings rest on everyone] each receiving his portion.[25]

Whether *tefillah be-ẓibbur* is obligatory as a rabbinical decree or not is the subject of considerable debate. Rabbi Yitzchak Ya'akov Fuchs, in *Ha-Tefillah be-Ẓibbur*, traces the history of this controversy.[26]

> Once R. Eliezer entered a synagogue and not finding there ten he liberated his *eved* [commonly translated "slave"] and used him to complete the ten. . . . But how could he do so, seeing that Rav Judah has said: If one liberates his *eved* he transgresses a positive precept, since it says, "they shall be your bondmen for ever" (Leviticus 25:46)? If it is for a religious purpose, it is different. But can a religious act be carried out by means of a transgression? A religious act which affects a whole company [as in the case of R. Eliezer] is different—*mitzvah derabbim shani.*[27]

Rashi and Rosh understand the talmudic response of *mitzvah derabbim shani*, "a religious act which affects a whole company is different," to refer to the rabbinical obligation of sanctifying God's name in public, i.e., reciting *devarim she-bi-kedushah.*[28] Rabbi Fuchs concludes that since

> Rashi and Rosh did not explain *mitzvah de-rabbim* to refer to *tefillah be-ẓibbur*, this proves that *tefillah be-ẓibbur* is not a rabbinical com-

---

25. Judah Halevi, *Book of Kuzari* 3:19, translated by Hartwig Hirschfeld (New York: Pardes Publishing House, 1946), pp. 137–138.
26. Rabbi Fuchs, *Ha-Tefillah be-Ẓibbur*, pp. 30–37.
27. Berakhot 47b.
28. Rashi to Berakhot 47b, s.v. *mitzvah de-rabbim*. Rosh to Berakhot 47b.

mandment but rather an advantageous and good practice *(me'ulah ve-hanhagah tovah)*, and only the rabbinical obligation of *devarim she-bi-kedushah* is a mitzvah.[29]

Tosafot, however, who explains *mitzvah de-rabbim* as referring to *tefillah de-rabbanan*, would maintain that *tefillah be-ẓibbur* is an obligation of rabbinical origin.[30]

PUBLIC TORAH READING

Aside from public prayer there developed the obligation to hear a communal reading of the Torah. The Talmud records that Moses introduced communal Torah reading, by rabbinical decree. Quoting the enactment of Ezra "that the Law be read [publicly] on Mondays and Thursdays," the Talmud states:

> But was this ordained by Ezra? Was this not ordained before him? For it was taught: "And they went three days in the wilderness and found no water" (Exodus 15:22), upon which those who expounded verses metaphorically said: Water means nothing but Torah, as it says: "Ho, everyone that thirsteth come ye for water" (Isaiah 55:1). It thus means that as they went three days without Torah they immediately became exhausted. The *prophets among them* thereupon rose and enacted that they should publicly read the Law on the *Sabbath*, make a break on Sunday, read again on Monday, make a break again on Tuesday and Wednesday, read again on Thursday, and then make a break on Friday so that they should not be kept for three days without Torah. [Why then was it necessary for Ezra to enact this?] Originally, it was ordained that one man should read three verses or that three men should together read three verses, corresponding to Priests, Levites, and Israelites [in which groups the people were classed]. Then Ezra came and ordained that three men should be called up to read, and that ten verses should be read, corresponding to ten *batlanim* [the ten persons released from all obligations and thus having leisure to attend to public duties and to form the necessary quorum for synagogue services].[31]

Rambam understands the Sabbath mentioned in the Gemara to refer to Shabbat morning and "the prophets among them" to refer

29. Rabbi Fuchs, *Ha-Tefillah be-Ẓibbur*, p. 31.
30. Tosafot to Berakhot 47b, s.v. *mitzvah de-rabbin shani*. See also Ramban's appendix to his commentary on Gittin 38b, where he too concludes that *tefillah be-ẓibbur* is rabbinically obligatory.
31. Bava Kamma 82a. See Mishnah Megillah 1:3 and Megillah 21b for information on the ten *batlanim*.

to Moses. The obligation to read the Torah on Shabbat afternoon was introduced by Ezra. In his words:

> Moses our teacher[32] enacted that Jews should read the Torah communally on Shabbat and on Monday and Thursday mornings, so that no one should be kept for three days without hearing Torah. And Ezra enacted that they should read the Torah on Shabbat afternoons on account of shopkeepers [who during the weekdays have no time to hear the reading of the Law.][33] And he also established that three men should read no less than ten sentences on Monday and Thursday mornings.[34]

The Talmud Yerushalmi adds:

> Moses decreed that Jews read from the Torah on Shabbat, holidays, the new moon, and the intermediate days. . . . Ezra enacted that Jews should read from the Torah on Mondays, Thursdays, and Shabbat afternoons.[35]

* * *

From the Jewish perspective there has always been a dialectic between the needs of the individual and the community. That balance is reflected in the prayer experience. Prayer includes moments when we approach God as individuals, and still other moments when we speak to God as part of a collective whole. And, independent of praying alone, i.e., physically by oneself, there emerged in our history the mandate to join the congregation in communal prayer. The obligation of women with respect to the private encounter has already been outlined, their obligation in regard to the public experience of prayer must yet be analyzed.

---

32. See *Kesef Mishneh* to Rambam, *Code*, Laws of Prayer 12:1, s.v. *Mosheh Rabbenu.*

33. See Bava Kamma 82a. Quoting the enactment of Ezra "that the Law be read [publicly] in the Minḥah service on Sabbath," the Talmud states: "on account of shopkeepers [who during the weekdays have no time to hear the reading of the Law]." See Rashi to Bava Kamma 82a, s.v. *mishum yoshvei kranot,* "on account of shopkeepers."

34. Rambam, *Code,* Laws of Prayer 12:1.

35. Yerushalmi Megillah 4:1. The statement that Ezra enacted communal Torah reading on Mondays and Thursdays refers to his decree that three men be called up to read ten verses. The original enactment of reading the Torah on Monday and Thursday mornings was introduced by Moses, as recorded in Bava Kamma 82a.

See Rif to Megillah (in Rif 13a), quoting the Yerushalmi Megillah 4:1. Ezra was the first to introduce Torah reading on Shabbat afternoon. Once Ezra decreed that three men reading ten sentences were needed on Monday and Thursday mornings, he legislated the same requirements for Shabbat afternoon.

Chapter Four

Women and Communal Prayer

THE EXEMPTION OF WOMEN FROM COMMUNAL PRAYER

While women are required to pray privately, they are not required to join communal prayer, that is, *devarim she-bi-kedushah* or *tefillah be-ẓibbur.*

The legal framework exempting women from *devarim she-bi-kedushah* is implicit in the passages quoted in the Talmud as the basis of the *devarim she-bi-kedushah* obligation.[1] Its key source, "And I will be sanctified among *B'nai Yisrael*" (Leviticus 22:32), is defined as an assemblage of ten men.[2]

The exemption of women from *tefillah be-ẓibbur* may also be implicit in the talmudic text which establishes its basis,[3] and is

1. Berakhot 21b; Megillah 23b; Sanhedrin 74b; Yerushalmi Berakhot 7:3, quoted in chap. 3.

2. *Levush* to Oraḥ Ḥayyim 55:4. Although his comment relates to excluding women from being counted for a minyan, it would similarly apply to the exemption of women from *devarim she-bi-kedushah.* The other relevant verses refer to the ten *male* spies, "Separate yourselves from among this congregation [*edah*]" (Numbers 16:21), and the *sons* of Jacob, "And the sons of Israel came to buy among those that came" (Genesis 42:5).

According to Meiri, *Beit ha-Beḥirah* to Berakhot 47b, the source for *devarim she-bi-kedushah* before ten is the verse "In a congregation (*be-makhelot*) they blessed God" (Psalms 68:27). Meiri notes that the term *kahal* excludes women. See also *Gilyonei ha-Shas* to Berakhot 45a, who understands the term *kahal* to exclude women.

3. Berakhot 47b, quoted above, chap. 3. There we are told that Rabbi Eliezer freed his *eved* to "complete the ten." If women are obligated to participate in *tefillah be-ẓibbur,* why didn't his wife participate and help make up the ten? See *Responsa Toledot Ya'akov,* Oraḥ Ḥayyim, siman 5.

found in the responsa literature.[4] Indeed, the Vilna Gaon advised women not to attend *tefillah be-ẓibbur.*[5]

Beyond this legal framework, the conceptual rationale for not obligating women to take part in public prayer flows from our analysis of the status of women in halakhah. Private prayer is obligatory for women because it can easily be fulfilled in the home, the place where women carry out their primary responsibilities. On the other hand, an obligation to participate in public prayer would make it difficult, and in some cases impossible, for women to fulfill their preferred home role. Jewish law does not make public prayer a duty for women because it wishes to protect their home role. It does so by building a kind of protective shield around the home in order to make it optimally possible for women to efficiently function as homemakers if they so wish.[6]

WOMEN AND MINYAN

Jewish law requires a quorum of ten (a minyan) in select areas of Jewish ritual—including public prayer.[7] Who can be counted in the minyan is the subject of considerable discussion.[8] The question as it relates to our study can be formulated as follows: Although women

---

4. For example, *Responsa Ẓiẓ Eliezer* 9:11; *Responsa Shevut Ya'akov*, Oraḥ Ḥayyim 3:54; *Responsa Teshuvah me-Ahavah* 2:229.

5. *Iggeret ha-Gra Livnei Beito*, commonly known as *Alim Literufah*. The Vilna Gaon wrote this letter to his family while on his way to Israel, a trip he never completed. In his words: "It is better that our daughter not attend the synagogue, for there she sees nice clothes, and covets and speaks about them at home. Inevitably this will lead to harmful speech and other undesirable things." Translation by Rabbi Elazar Robinson (Staten Island, N.Y.: Avraham Zelik Shafransky Torah Award Fund, 5736/1976).

6. See Rabbi Saul J. Berman, "The Status of Women in Halakhic Judaism," p. 17.

7. Mishnah Megillah 4:3 records several areas of halakhah in which a quorum of ten is required.

> When less than ten are present we do not repeat the Shema and its attendant blessings in an abbreviated form; nor does one appoint a ḥazzan (to lead communal prayer, i.e., Kaddish, Kedushah, Barekhu and the repetition of Shemoneh Esreh); nor do the priests bless the congregation; nor do we read the Torah in public; nor read the Haftarah from the Prophets; nor are funeral halts made; nor is the blessing for mourners said; nor is the mourners consolation (after the funeral) or the nuptial blessings said; nor is the name (of God) mentioned in the invitation to say grace (said by one of those present after the meal to the rest of the company).

Other areas of halakhah which require ten are discussed in the course of this chapter.

8. For a fine discussion of this issue, see Rabbi Aryeh Avraham Frimer, "Ma'amad ha-Isha be-Halakhah—Nashim u-Minyan." Rabbi Frimer's paper has now been published in English in revised form: "Women and Minyan."

are *exempt* from communal prayer, are they *excluded* from being counted towards the ten required for a "prayer minyan"?

The Legal Exclusion

There are several religio-legal sources that clearly restrict participation in a minyan to men alone. The exclusion may be based on the talmudic statement *ve-ha me'ah nashei kitrei gavrei damyan*, "a hundred women are compared [from this legal perspective] to two men."[9]

Rashi understands this phrase to refer exclusively to the obligation of *zimmun*, the quorum needed to introduce the Grace After Meals. In his words: "They are not obligated to participate in *zimmun*, but if they wish they may."[10]

Tosafot, on the other hand, associates the phrase with *le-inyan kibbutz tefillah, u-le-inyan kol davar she-be-ahsarah*, indicating that women are not counted as part of a minyan for "public prayer and *everything* that requires ten."[11] From the perspective of Tosafot, women are excluded, *in all circumstances*, from being counted into a minyan for prayer, or for that matter, for any other purpose that "requires ten" according to Jewish law.

The rationale of Tosafot may be the position of *Sefer Abudarham* as enunciated in the first chapter of this study.[12] Men "carry out" public responsibilities; women's role is private. For *Sefer Abudarham*, the home is *virtually the only place* in which women may function. Men can, therefore, be counted into a minyan; women cannot.[13]

Shulḥan Arukh codifies this position. In his words, "*Kaddish* is

---

9. Berakhot 45b.

10. Rashi, ibid., s.v. *de'afilo me'ah kitrei damyan.*

11. Tosafot, ibid., s.v. *ve-ha me'ah nashei kitrei gavrei damyan.*

12. *Sefer Aburdarham, Seder Tefillot shel Ḥol, Ha-Sha'ar ha-Shelishi*, Birkhot ha-Mitzvot. This position may be based on the principle *Kol kevudah vat melekh penimah*, "the king's daughter is all glorious within" (Psalms 45:14). See above, chap. 1, n. 10.

13. Rabbi Frimer ("Women and Minyan" p. 62) mentions several other explanations in support of this position. In his words:

> *Sefer ha-Masbir* suggests that *Ḥazal* simply followed the Torah's lead which refrained from counting women in any of the various censuses. (*Ḥiddushei Batra* on *Sefer ha-Masbir*, Berakhot 45b, 334).
>
> R. Yosef Engel maintains that the concept of community is dependent on inheritance and possession of the Land of Israel, for land is what ultimately binds individuals together into a community. Since women did not participate in the inheritance of the Land, they do not constitute a community. (*Gilyonei ha-Shas*, Berakhot 45a)

not said with less than ten adult free males . . . And the same is true for *Kedushah* and *Barekhu*."[14]

The Correlation Principle

Beyond the legal exclusion of women from being counted for a minyan,[15] there emerged a school of thought which defines a min-

---

14. *Shulḥan Arukh*, Oraḥ Ḥayyim 55:1. See also *Shulḥan Arukh ha-Rav*, Oraḥ Ḥayyim 55:2.

Mishnah Berurah, ibid., nos. 2, 5, 6, adds Keri'at ha-Torah, the Priestly Benediction, the repetition of the Shemoneh Esreh, and the Haftarah to the *devarim she-bi-kedushah* category.

The exclusion of women from being counted into a minyan for prayer applies not only to *devarim she-bi-kedushah* but to *tefillah be-ẓibbur*. (See chapter 3, where the distinction between these categories is developed. Their definitions and sources of obligation are outlined there.)

It can be argued that the very sources which exempt women from public prayer would exclude women from being counted in a minyan for prayer.

The verses from which we deduce that ten are required for *devarim she-bi-kedushah* refer to ten adult males. As women are exempt from *devarim she-bi-kedushah* so too they are excluded from *minyan*. See *Levush* to Oraḥ Ḥayyim 55:4, Meiri to Berakhot 47b and *Gilyonei ha-Shas* to Berakhot 45a.

Responsa Toledot Ya'akov, Oraḥ Ḥayyim, siman 5, notes that the source of *tefillah be-ẓibbur*, Berakhot 47b, also seems to exclude women from minyan. There we are told that Rabbi Eliezer freed his *eved* to "complete the ten." If women can be counted in a minyan, why couldn't his wife be included?

Note, however, Rabbi Frimer ("Ma'amad ha-Isha be-Halakhah," p. 75, n. 43, and "Women and Minyan," p. 72, n. 28), who records the "unusual position" of *Yad Eliyahu*, vol. 1, pesakim 7. *Yad Eliyahu* suggests that "even though women are not included in the *minyan*, they are counted, if there are ten men present, in order to meet the requirement that the congregation include ten persons who have not yet prayed so that the prayers obtain the special status of a *tefillah be-ẓibbur*."

15. *Mordekhai* to Berakhot 48a quotes but does not accept the position of Rabbenu Simḥah that women may be counted toward a minyan. See Rabbi J. David Bleich, "Survey of Recent Halakhic Periodical Literature: Women in a *Minyan?* " He proves that Rabbenu Simḥah's position is that "a woman may be co-opted as the tenth person"; in other words, Rabbenu Simḥah "sanctions only the inclusion of a single woman" into a *minyan*.

As Rabbi Bleich points out, Rabbenu Simḥah's position has bearing on the controversy of whether nine men and a minor can form a minyan. In Rabbi Bleich's words:

> *Rosh* on B. T. *Berakhot* 48a [suggests] . . . that the authorities who permit inclusion of a minor maintain that in actuality it is the Divine Presence which is included as the tenth member of the *minyan*. [See, however, *Ba'al ha-Ma'or, Berakhot* 48a.] Attention may be drawn to the Biblical narrative concerning Abraham's supplication on behalf of Sodom and Gomorrah. Abraham at first prayed that those cities be spared if fifty righteous inhabitants be found. *Rashi* explains that in actuality five cities were marked for destruction and Abraham prayed that the cities be spared if ten righteous persons—a *minyan*—could be found in each. Subsequently Abraham prayed that the cities be spared even in the event that only forty-five righteous persons could be found. *Rashi* (Genesis 18:28) comments that Abraham recognized that a *minyan* must be found for each city but beseeched of the

yan as a group of ten people united by a common obligation. This mode of definition may be referred to as the correlation principle. The union of these ten people normally takes place in a public setting, the realm in which halakhah does not obligate women. Thus the exclusion of women from minyan is due to their lack of obligation; it is not discriminatory.

From this perspective, there is no *absolute declaration* that women are ineligible for minyan. Participants in minyan must share a mutual obligation. If women share the obligation equally, they are counted; if not, they are excluded. Indeed, in matters concerning a minyan, Meiri points out: "There are those who say that in cases where women are equally obligated as men, they are counted toward the ten."[16]

While this view would effectively exclude women from a minyan constituted for prayer, as they are not obligated to participate in public prayer,[17] it leaves open the possibility that in other areas of halakhah where minyan is necessary, women could be counted if

---

Almighty that He include Himself in that number. This would explain why those authorities who sanction inclusion of a minor as the tenth person require that he hold a written scroll of one of the books of the Pentateuch in his hand. In reality it is the Divine Presence which is symbolized by the scroll of the Law which is included. The presence of a minor is required by virtue of rabbinic decree which regards him as being already a quasi-member of the *minyan* because the minor will one day share the religious obligations of the rest of the *minyan*.

Rabbenu Simḥah maintains that not only a minor but even a woman may be co-opted as the tenth person. According to Rabbenu Simchah a *minyan* must consist of nine persons obligated to public worship while the tenth individual may be a participant who does not share an equal obligation. Both minors and women are included in this category. Citation of Rabbenu Simchah does not justify the conclusion that women may be counted equally with men since 1) his view is rejected by *Mordekhai* [See *Be'er ha-Golah, Orach Chaim* 55:4]; 2) most latter-day authorities, including *P'ri Megadim, Chayyei Adam* and *Arukh ha-Shulchan* maintain that even a minor may not be included in a *minyan;* 3) he sanctions only the inclusion of a single woman. On the basis of the above sources one can no more contend that a *minyan* may be comprised of ten women than that it may be comprised of ten minors. (pp. 114–115)

16. Meiri to Megillah 5a.

Rabbi Frimer, "Ma'amad ha-Isha be-Halakhah-Nashim u-Minyan" suggests that this may be the position of Rashi recorded above. For Rashi, the absolute exclusion relates only to *zimmun.* (Rashi to Berakhot 45b, *de-afilu me'ah kitrei gavrei da-myan.*) In all other areas, it would depend on the correlation principle. If women are equally obligated, they count toward the minyan; if not, they don't.

17. Some have suggested that women are not counted toward the minyan because they are not obligated in regard to every aspect of the service (the entire Shema, the blessings which precede Shema, etc.) Not sharing the same *level of obligation* in prayer, they are excluded from the minyan. Women's responsibility in private prayer, however, is virtually equal to that of men. Moreover, a minyan is a function of public prayer, not private prayer. The exclusion of women from the minyan is therefore related to the optional nature of their participation in public prayer.

they had the same level of obligation as their male counterparts. And, for that matter, it suggests that men who for some reason do not have the usual obligation are not counted. Several halakhic proofs can be noted in support of this idea.

• An *onen*, for example, is exempt from all positive commandments. (From the moment of death until interment, each member of the immediate family of the deceased is considered an *onen.*)[18] The exemption is a vehicle through which maximal respect may be given to the deceased by freeing the bereaved to arrange an appropriate funeral and burial. Alternatively, halakhah understands that the *onen* is unnerved, transfixed, and in mental shock. In such a state he/she is deemed unable to fulfill any of the mitzvot. It is a way of dealing in the most sensitive manner with the needs of the *onen* during a time of emotional trauma.

According to many authorities a male *onen* may not be counted into the quorum of public prayer.[19] Not being under any obligation with respect to public prayer, he cannot be counted as one of the minyan. His exclusion does not express a bias against mourners, but is consistent with the position that if one is not required to participate in public prayer, one may not be counted toward the minyan.

• The nature of women's obligation in regard to the reading of the Megillah (Book of Esther) on Purim is the subject of debate. The Talmud states that women are required to *read* the Megillah.[20] Despite the fact that reading the Megillah is a positive commandment fixed by time, Esther's role in the Purim miracle overrides the exemption of women from positive commandments limited by

18. *Shulḥan Arukh*, Yoreh De'ah 341. Only the closest relatives (father, mother, brother, sister, son, daughter, spouse) are considered halakhic mourners. For a fine analysis of *onen* and the laws of mourning, see Rabbi Maurice Lamm's *The Jewish Way of Death and Mourning*, where a conceptual analysis of *onen* is offered (pp. 21–26). See also Rav Joseph B. Soloveitchik, "A Eulogy for the Talner Rabbi."

19. *Kenesset ha-Gedolah* to Oraḥ Ḥayyim 55; *Ba'er Heitev* to Oraḥ Ḥayyim 55:7; *Mishnah Berurah* to Oraḥ Ḥayyim 55:24; and *Pitḥei Teshuvah* to Yoreh De'ah 341:14.

Mishnah Berurah, ibid., maintains that if the deceased is in another city and is being cared for, the *onen* can be counted in a minyan. *Peri Ḥadash*, quoted in *Ba'er Heitev*, loc. cit., seems to suggest that even if the deceased is in the same city but is being attended to, the *onen* may be counted in a minyan.

20. Megillah 4a: "Rabbi Joshua ben Levi says: Women are obligated to read Megillah, for they were [included] in that miracle." See also Arakhin 2b–3a. "All are fit to read the scroll. What [does 'all'] include? It is meant to include women, in accord with the view of Rabbi Joshua ben Levi; for Rabbi Joshua ben Levi said: Women are obliged to read the Megillah scroll because they, too, had a part in that miracle."

time.[21] From a Tosefta it may be deduced that women are only required to *hear* the Megillah read.[22]

Basing themselves on these texts, authorities disagree as to whether women are obliged to *read*[23] or only to *listen*[24] to the Megillah. If the halakhic responsibility of women is to read the Megillah, they would be on the same level of obligation as men and can therefore read the Megillah for them.[25] If, however, a woman's responsibility is only to listen to the Megillah, they are not on the same level of obligation as men, and cannot fulfill their male counterparts' *ḥiyyuv* (obligation).[26]

---

21. Rashi to Megillah 4a, s.v. *she'af hein hayu be-oto ha-nes*, suggests that women were involved in the Purim miracle in the sense that Haman had decreed the murder of women as well as men (Esther 3:13). Tosafot to Megillah 4a, s.v. *she'af hein hayu be-oto ha-nes*, cites two positions: that of Rashbam, who states that the Purim miracle was brought about because of the merit of Esther and the women of that time, and the view of Rashi, with which Tosafot concurs.

Rashi and Rashbam to Pesaḥim 108b, s.v. *she'af hein hayu be-oto ha-nes*, explain *she'af* to mean that the Purim miracle occurred through righteous women, including Esther. Tosafot to ibid., s.v. *hayu be-oto ha-nes*, citing a passage in the Yerushalmi, states that women were also included in Haman's decree of extinction.

22. Tosefta Megillah 2:4. See Tosafot to Megillah 4a, s.v. *nashim ḥayyavot be-mikra Megillah*.

23. Rashi to Arakhin 3a, s.v. *la'atuyei nashim;* Ran to Megillah 2, end, s.v. *ha-kol kasheirin likrot ha-Megillah;* Rambam, *Code*, Laws of Megillah 1:1; *Or Zaru'a* 2:368.

24. *Behag* as quoted in Tosafot to Megillah 4a, s.v. *nashim ḥayyavot be-mikra Megillah*, and in Tosafot to Arakhin 3a, s.v. *la'atuyei nashim*.

25. Rashi to Arakhin 3a, s.v. *la'atuyei nashim;* Ran to Megillah 2, end, *ha-kol kesherin likrot ha-Megillah;* first opinion in *Shulḥan Arukh*, Oraḥ Ḥayyim 689:2.

26. *Behag*, quoted in Tosafot to Megillah 4a, s.v. *nashim ḥayyavot be-mikrah Megillah; Yesh Omrim* in *Shulḥan Arukh*, Oraḥ Ḥayyim 689:2. See *Be'er ha-Golah* there.

Some suggest that *Yesh Omrim* maintains that women are obligated to read Megillah. They cannot, however, fulfill the obligation of their male counterparts because of *kevod ẓibbur*. See *Mishnah Berurah*, ibid., no. 7. For a definition of *kevod ẓibbur*, see below, chap. 6.

In general, women "are *moẓiot*" men (i.e., can fulfill the obligation for them) if they share the same level of obligation. For example, since women and men are equally obligated to light Ḥanukkah candles, a woman may light the Ḥanukkah candles for a man. See *Shulḥan Arukh*, Oraḥ Ḥayyim 675:3, and Taz, ibid., 675:4, s.v. *she'af hi ḥayyevet*.

The same is true of Kiddush. Since women are obligated to recite Kiddush, they may recite Kiddush for their male counterparts. See *Shulḥan Arukh*, Oraḥ Ḥayyim 271:2, and Taz, ibid., s.v. *u-moẓi'ot*. Some suggest that even if women have the same level of obligation as men, they should still not recite Kiddush for men, as it would imply that the men present are unable to recite Kiddush. See *Magen Avraham* to *Shulḥan Arukh*, Oraḥ Ḥayyim 271:2, s.v. *umoẓi'ot*, and Rashal quoted in Taz, ibid.

Whether a woman may recite Havdalah for a man depends upon whether Havdalah is considered the last act of Shabbat or the first act of the week. If Havdalah is part of Shabbat, it follows that since women and men are equally obligated to observe

Aside from this general issue, there emerged the question of whether the reading of the Megillah is preferable with, and perhaps even requires, a minyan.[27] It is certainly preferable that the Megillah be read in a public setting rather than privately. The ruling that "the greater the multitudes, the greater the honor and glory for God" applies.[28]

Assuming that women are obligated to *read* the Megillah and that a minyan is necessary or at least preferable, the question is whether women may be counted toward the minyan. Rema leaves the question unresolved,[29] but Ran and Meiri respond in the affirmative. In the words of Ran: "How is it possible that women can fulfill the obligation of men to read the Megillah, and not be counted with

---

Shabbat, women may say Havdalah for men. However, if Havdalah pertains to the obligations linked to the rest of the week, women would be exempt (since it is a positive commandment fixed by time), although not excluded from Havdalah. They would, therefore, be unable to say Havdalah for men, since they are not obligated in its recitation. See *Shulḥan Arukh*, Oraḥ Ḥayyim 296:8, and *Mishnah Berurah*, ibid, n.34.

Women are of course obligated to observe Shabbat, although it is a positive commandment fixed by time, because the positive aspects of Shabbat (*zakhor*) are inextricably linked to the negative commandments (*shamor*). Since women are obligated in regard to *shamor*, they are similarly obligated in regard to *zakhor*. See Berakhot 20b.

27. See Megillah 5a: "Rav said: On the actual day of Purim, the Megillah may be read even by an individual, but on the alternative days [lit., not in its proper time; see Mishnah Megillah 1:1] it should be read only in a company of ten. Rav Assi, however, said: Whether on the actual day or on the alternative days, it should be read only in a company of ten. In an actual case, Rav gave weight to the opinion of Rav Assi [and put himself out to assemble ten persons]."

Rif to Megillah 5a concludes: "Even though Rav gave weight to the view of R. Assi, we follow the view of Rav, because Rav Yoḥanan follows this position." On the day of Purim, one may read the Megillah individually, although it is preferable that it be read with a minyan. On alternative days it should only be read in a company of ten. Rabbenu Tam (quoted in *Tur Shulḥan Arukh*, Oraḥ Ḥayyim 690, end) states that one need not pursue a minyan to read the Megillah (even *le-khatḥillah*, optimally). Apparently, this applies to the fourteenth (or fifteenth). On the alternative days a minyan is needed.

However, *Behag* (quoted in *Tur*, loc. cit.) concludes that the Megillah must be read before ten people. *Baḥ* to ibid., s.v. *u-Behag*, states that *Behag* follows the view of Rav Assi that ten are required at all times, even *b'-de-avad*.

Shulḥan Arukh, Oraḥ Ḥayyim 690:18 concludes: "On the fourteenth or fifteenth day [the fifteenth is the proper time to read the Megillah in a city surrounded by walls from the time of Joshua], one must seek out ten [before whom the Megillah should be read], and if ten were not found, an individual may [nevertheless] read the Megillah."

28. *Mishnah Berurah* to *Shulḥan Arukh*, Oraḥ Ḥayyim 690:62; *Arukh ha-Shulḥan*, Oraḥ Ḥayyim 690:25.

29. Rema, *Shulḥan Arukh*, Oraḥ Ḥayyim 690:18.

them as part of the [Megillah] minyan; certainly they can be counted."[30]

The inclusion of women in this minyan has nothing to do with sensational feminist quests. It is a consequence of the status of women in halakhah. If women have the same obligation as men in regard to the public reading of the Megillah, they have the right to be counted into the *Megillah minyan.*

---

30. Ran to Megillah, chap. 2, end, s.v. *ha-kol kesherim likrot ha-Megillah;* Meiri to Berakhot 47b.

Rabbi Bleich ("Survey of Recent Halakhic Periodical Literature: Women in a Minyan?," p. 116) notes that Rema, *Shulḥan Arukh,* Oraḥ Ḥayyim 690:18, raises the question of counting women as part of the ten for a Megillah reading in the name of *Haggahot Asheri,* Megillah, chap. 1. The latter states that it is unclear whether the requirement of ten people to hear the Megillah is a function of the rules regarding a minyan or a separate halakhah of *pirsuma,* publicizing the Purim miracle. This, in fact, is the basis of Rema's query. If the ten mentioned in regard to the Megillah function as a minyan, women may not be counted; if the ten assemble to publicize the miracle, women may be counted. From this perspective, Rabbi Bleich argues that Rema clearly disagrees with Ran, and concludes that counting women is precluded by the rules regarding minyan, but they may be counted as part of the ten to publicize the miracle.

In reality, *Haggahot Asheri,* Megillah, chap. 1, asks whether minors may be counted toward the ten for Megillah reading. If the requirement of ten people is a function of the rules of minyan, non-adults may not be counted. On the other hand, if the essential issue is the publicizing of the Purim miracle, even a minor can be counted. Extending the query of *Haggahot Asheri* to the question of whether women can be counted toward the ten for Megillah reading may be excessive. The case of women is fundamentally different, since they, unlike minors, are under an obligation regarding the Megillah. From both considerations of the *Haggahot Asheri* (minyan and *pirsuma*), it can be argued that women may be counted towards the ten for the Megillah reading.

Magen Avraham (*Shulḥan Arukh,* Oraḥ Ḥayyim 690:24) makes this point and notes that *Haggahot Asheri* raises the question regarding minors. *Levushei Serad* to *Magen Avraham,* ibid., states: "The source as quoted [in Rema] as being *Haggahot Asheri* is incorrect. The *Haggahot Asheri* only speaks about minors, but concerning women [being counted toward the ten for Megillah reading] there is a dispute in *Tur Shulḥan Arukh* [chap. 689]."

Indeed, Rema could maintain that the requirement of ten people to hear the Megillah is a function of the rules regarding a minyan.

Rema may leave the question of including women in the Megillah minyan unresolved and dependent on the degree of obligation that women have in respect to the Megillah. If women's obligation is on the same level as that of men, they are counted into the minyan. If not, they may not be part of the minyan.

Rema may also be read as maintaining that women are on the same level of Megillah obligation as men, and can, in principle, be counted as part of a Megillah minyan, but in practice are not because including them in a minyan might create a situation of *periẓut* (immodesty). This, in fact, may be the essence of Rema's question as to whether women can be counted as part of the ten for Megillah reading.

Ran to Megillah, chap. 2, end, s.v. *ha-kol,* seems to relate the question of women in the Megillah minyan to *periẓut* and concludes that since the text of the Megillah and its blessings is the same whether it is read in public or private (unlike Birkat ha-

- Minyan is also associated with *Kiddush ha-Shem* (martyrdom; literally, "sanctification of God's name"). The Talmud states that one should allow oneself to be killed rather than commit the sin of idolatry, incest (which includes adultery), or murder.[31] In certain situations, even in a time free from religious persecution, the obligation to die rather than transgress may be expanded to include virtually every precept, even minor ones. This all-encompassing *Kiddush ha-Shem* mandate applies only when one is in the presence of ten people, a minyan.

The Talmud states:

Mazon), there is no *perizut*. For Ran, however, women's participation in the ten is a function of minyan.

Ba'al ha-Ittur, cited in *Tur Shulḥan Arukh*, Oraḥ Ḥayyim 689, seems to adopt the reverse position. See *Baḥ*, ibid., s.v. *u-B"H katav*, who understands *Ba'al ha-Ittur* as follows: "Even though a woman can fulfill a man's obligation in reading the Megillah, nonetheless, they are *ab initio* (*le-khathillah*) not counted towards the ten because of *prizutah*."

According to *Ba'al ha-Ittur*, women can be counted *b'-de-avad* (post-factum) towards the ten in Megillah. This is implicit in the words of *Ba'al ha-Ittur* as found in *Tur*, ibid.

It is also possible that the requirement of ten for the Megillah reading is *pirsuma* and not minyan. The Rema's uncertainty may again be related to the question of *perizut*. If the inclusion of women is considered as leading to *perizut*, women may not be counted toward the ten. If there is no issue of *perizut*, they may be counted. (See *Responsa Rav Pe'alim*, pt. 2, Oraḥ Ḥayyim 62.)

31. Sanhedrin 74a. Rav Aharon Soloveichik in one of his *hashkafah* classes given in the fall of 1962 pointed out that the ultimate *Kiddush ha-Shem* is living for God. "You shall therefore keep My statutes, and Mine ordinances, which if a 'man' do, he shall live by them: I am the Lord" (Leviticus 18:5).

Rav Soloveichik noted that Rambam, *Code*, Laws of the Fundamentals of Torah 5:1–2, first mentions those times when one is to transgress a law rather than die (5:1), and only afterwards records the cases of idolatry, immorality, and idol worship in which one is to die rather than transgress the law (5:2). In the words of Rambam:

> All the members of the house of Israel are commanded to sanctify the great Name of God, as it is said, "But I will be hallowed among the children of Israel" (Leviticus 22:32). . . . How are these precepts to be applied? Should an idolater arise and coerce a Israelite to violate any one of the commandments mentioned in the Torah under the threat that otherwise he would put him to death, the Israelite is to commit the transgression rather than suffer death; for concerning the commandments it is said, "which a man do them, he shall live by them" (Leviticus 18:5): "Live by them, and not die by them." And if he suffered death rather than commit a transgression, he himself is to blame for his death.
>
> This rule applies to all the commandments, except the prohibitions of idolatry, immorality, and murder. With regard to these: if an Israelite should be told "transgress one of them or else you will be put to death," he should suffer death rather than transgress.

The order of presentation of these *halakhot* indicates that for Rambam the highest level of *Kiddush ha-Shem*, the one mentioned first, is to "live for God." Only while living can one be involved in the daily ongoing commitment to Torah.

Rav Soloveichik further pointed out that Rambam chose Joseph as an example par excellence of *Kiddush ha-Shem* (ibid., 5:10). Joseph, a lone Jew in Egypt, had the inner strength to maintain his identity and *live* according to Jewish principles.

> When R. Dimi came, he said: . . . If there is a royal decree [forbidding the practice of Judaism], one must incur martyrdom rather than transgress even a minor precept. When Rabin came, he said in R. Yoḥanan's name: Even without a royal decree it was only permitted in private; but in public one must be martyred even for a minor precept rather than violate it. . . . And how many make it public? R. Jacob said in R. Yoḥanan's name: The minimum for publicly is ten.[32]

The obvious question is, Who can be counted into the *Kiddush ha-Shem* minyan? *Gilyonei ha-Shas* and *Margaliyyot ha-Yam* state that women can be counted among the ten.[33] Since the mitzvah of *Kiddush ha-Shem* is incumbent on women, they may be counted for the minyan as well.[34]

The upshot, as it relates to counting women into a minyan for prayer, is clear. Women are not obligated to take part in communal prayer; hence they cannot be counted in the prayer minyan. *Shulḥan Arukh's* statement that "Kaddish is not said with less than ten adult free males . . . and the same is true for Kedushah and Barekhu,"[35] may be based on the correlation principle.

Pirsuma: The Joining of Ten for Publicity

Rabbi Aryeh Frimer outlines a third approach to minyan. He writes:

> It is necessary to differentiate between two types of *minyanim*. Normally, the sages required ten male adults as a prerequisite for the performance of particular rituals, generally communal in nature. However, in certain cases, the *minyan* is not intrinsic to the performance

32. Sanhedrin 74a–b.

The Talmud, Sanhedrin 74b, distinguishes between a demand to violate a law as a matter of religious persecution and a demand to violate the law to satisfy the persecutor's personal pleasure. See Rambam, *Code*, Laws of Fundamentals of Torah 5:2; *Shulḥan Arukh*, Yoreh De'ah 157:1.

Rambam, *Code*, Laws of Fundamentals of Torah 5:4, further points out that "where one is enjoined to suffer death rather than transgress and commits a transgression and so escapes death, he has profaned the name of God. . . . Still, as the transgression was committed under duress, he is not punished with stripes and, needless to add, he is not sentenced by a court to be put to death, even if, under duress, he committed murder."

33. *Gilyonei ha-Shas* to Sanhedrin 74b; *Margaliyyot ha-Yam* to Sanhedrin 74b, no. 27.

34. See *Minḥat Ḥinnukh* no. 296, who disagrees with the position of *Gilyonei ha-Shas* and *Margaliyyot ha-Yam*. Perhaps *Minḥat Ḥinnukh* subscribes to the position of Tosafot that women are in all cases excluded from minyan.

35. Rabbi Joseph Karo, *Shulḥan Arukh*, Oraḥ Ḥayyim 55:1. See above, n. 14.

> of the *mitzvah*, for the obligation is essentially the individual's. Rather the *minyan* is needed only to give "publicity" to the performance. In such a case, women are counted even if their obligation is not equivalent to that of men.[36]

In support of this observation, Rabbi Frimer notes various examples, amongst them the view of *Sefer ha-Berit*, who states "that since the *minyan* recommended for circumcision is in order to publicize the *milah*, women are included."[37]

Still, in most cases of minyan needed for publicity (*pirsuma* minyan) the correlation between equality of obligation and the right to be counted among the ten is evident. For example:

• A slaughterer is declared untrustworthy if he is seen desecrating the Sabbath publicly (before ten people).[38] Some authorities suggest that this law applies whether the desecration takes place before ten men or ten women.[39] Since women are obligated to observe Shabbat, they can be counted among the ten.

• If someone wronged another person, asked his/her pardon, and was refused, he/she can fulfill his/her obligation to express contrition to the person he/she hurt by appearing before ten people to declare that he/she has sought forgiveness.[40] Here again, if this takes place before ten women it is considered valid.[41] Since women, like men, are obligated to ask forgiveness, they can constitute a group of ten for this purpose.

• According to some authorities, the Ḥanukkah candles kindled

---

36. Rabbi Frimer, "Women and Minyan," p. 63.

37. Ibid., p. 63. See *Sefer ha-Berit*, Yoreh De'ah 265:6, 79–80.

38. *Shulḥan Arukh*, Yoreh De'ah 2:5.

39. *Ba'er Heitev* to *Shulḥan Arukh*, Yoreh De'ah 2:15, concludes that women are not counted among the ten.

Responsa Rav Pe'alim, pt. 2, Oraḥ Ḥayyim 62, suggests that women are counted among the ten. *Rav Pe'alim* limits his decision to a desecration which takes place before ten women. He does not allow women to be counted together with men to make up the ten, because of the issue of *periẓut*.

Rabbi Auerbach, in *Halikhot Beitah*, p. 71, n. 9, states that if "before ten women it is considered public, so too before a minyan of men and women together. *Priẓutah* becomes an issue when men and women are united to read a *sefer* or recite blessings. This does not apply to [the act of] random seeing, as when one sees the Sabbath being desecrated."

40. Rema, *Shulḥan Arukh*, Oraḥ Ḥayyim 606:1.

41. *Responsa Rav Pe'alim*, pt. 2, Oraḥ Ḥayyim 62, claims that it is preferable to ask forgiveness before ten men, but if one does so before ten women, it is acceptable.

It would appear that if there is no problem of *periẓut*, women can be counted among the ten.

in synagogue should be lit in the presence of ten people.[42] Since women are required to kindle the Ḥanukkah lights, they can be counted as the group of ten.[43]

The case of counting women into the minyan recommended for circumcision may also operate on the correlation principle. Rabbi Frimer notes that the *Koret ha-Berit* "states that women are included because they are considered to be circumcised."[44]

Whether or not the *pirsuma* minyan operates in accordance with the correlation principle, one thing remains clear: it has little bearing on counting women into a minyan constituted for prayer. Public prayer is the fulfillment of a particular ritual requirement, it is not carried out for "publicity" purposes.

* * *

Our analysis outlines the basic halakhic guidelines for women's tefillah groups. Women are obligated or strongly encouraged to pray privately. They therefore, may recite the entire tefillah at the women's service. But women are exempt from communal prayer, an exemption which excludes them from being counted into a minyan constituted for prayer. As a consequence, participants in women's tefillah groups omit any *davar she-bi-kedushah*, i.e., any part of the service which requires a minyan. While women's prayer groups may be public and communal from the perspective of the contemporary norm, they are private from a halakhic point of view.

Opponents of women's tefillah groups have claimed that they are a *ziyyuf ha-Torah*, a falsification of the Torah,[45] as the women

42. See *Mishnah Berurah* to *Shulḥan Arukh*, Oraḥ Ḥayyim 671:47, and *Bi'ur Halakhah*, ibid., s.v. *vayaish nohagin*.

43. *Responsa Rav Pe'alim*, pt. 2, Oraḥ Ḥayyim 62.

Once again, it would appear that if there is no problem of *periẓut*, women can be counted among the ten.

44. *Koret ha-Berit*, Yoreh De'ah 265:47. See Rabbi Frimer, "Women and *Minyan*," p. 75, n. 67.

45. Rabbi Schachter, "Ẓe'i Lakh be-Ikvei ha-Ẓon," p. 119.

See the statement of the five rabbis from Yeshiva University and Rabbi Abba Bronspigel's amplification of its content. Rabbi Bronspigel adds the issue of *ona'ah bein adam le-ḥavero* (deception).

The prohibition of *ziyyuf ha-Torah* even when Jewish lives are at stake, was introduced by *Rashal* in his *Yam shel Shlomo* to Bava Kamma 4:9 (see "*Ẓe'i Lakh be-Ikvei ha-Ẓon*," p. 119). It should be noted, however, that *Rashal*'s position is contradicted by Rabbenu Jonathan ha-Kohen of Lunel. He interprets the Mishnah (Bava Kamma 4:3) one way and then suggests that in a dispute with Christians (*minin*), an alternative explanation which distorts the halakhah can be given in order to protect the Jewish community (see *Shitah Mekubeẓet* to Bava Kamma 38a). For Rabbenu Jonathan, *ziyyuf ha-Torah* as defined by *Rashal* is not problematic. (Rabbenu Jonathan was a *rishon*. He lived in Provence in the twelfth century,

involved represent themselves as participating in a minyan. Such is not the case. Those who join in the *tefillah* are fully cognizant that their prayer service is halakhically limited to the private aspects of prayer. As women who are well versed in the process of *tefillah*, they know that without Kaddish, Kedushah, Barekhu, and the repetition of Shemoneh Esreh, their service is halakhically private, not public. For this reason, they refer to their prayer groups as women's tefillah groups, not as a women's minyan.

Unfortunately, critics of women's tefillah groups have almost always referred to them as a women's minyan.[46] The women's tefillah group is not a women's minyan and should not be mislabeled as such.

The reality is that women's tefillah groups are not an innovation, and not a new minhag (custom), because women's prayer services have been in existence for years. To this very day, for example, women's services take place in schools such as Beit Ya'akov, Lubavitch, and Yeshiva University High School for Girls.[47] There too, of course, the women are careful not to recite any *davar she-bi-kedushah*. Women's tefillah groups follow the same format as the women's yeshiva prayer groups—with one exception: the reading of the Torah from the Torah scroll.[48]

---

hundreds of years before *Rashal*. *Rashal* was apparently unaware of Rabbenu Jonathan's position.)

46. In the original statement of the five rabbis from Yeshiva University, the addendum of Rabbi Bronspigel, and the article by Rabbi Schachter, the question of the prayer groups is couched in the terminology of minyan. The real problem lies in mislabeling women's prayer groups as a minyan rather than a tefillah group.

47. In a December 29, 1989 letter to the New York Jewish Week, Sharon Hertzfeld describes a "tefillah for girls" which she, as a student at Rabbi Samson Raphael Hirsch ("Breuer's") experienced.

"After we shuffled into the school building each morning, the *chazonis*, a girl selected by our Hebrew teacher, stood in front of the classroom leading the morning prayers. In the fourth grade, our Hebrew teacher inculcated the importance of davening for girls by teaching us the meaning of the words we recited daily in addition to the tunes for the weekday, Shabbat and holiday prayers usually sung by the *shliach tzibbur* in shul."

"On Rosh Chodesh we assembled in the main sanctuary of the synagogue building, where we sat at the front of the shul . . . The *chazonis* for Rosh Chodesh stood in front of the ark, leading the prayers. I have vivid memories of my classmates from the Breuer's community giggling when they realized they were actually sitting in their father's, grandfather's or brother's seats. They would open the little wooden cabinet on the back of the seat in front of them to look at the tallis, tefillin, siddurim and sour candies."

48. Reading from the Torah scroll as part of the women's service would appear to constitute a new practice in synagogue custom. See chapter eight for a discussion of this issue.

Chapter Five

Women and Torah Study

THE EXEMPTION

At first blush, Torah reading for women seems bound to their right or obligation to study Torah. If women may or must study Torah, it would appear that they would be permitted to read from the Torah Scroll.

The Talmud concludes that since there is no obligation to teach women Torah, women are similarly not obligated to study Torah themselves. The Talmud states:

> And how do we know that she is not bound to teach herself? Because it is written, *ve-limaddetem* "and you shall teach" (Deuteronomy 11:19) *u-lemadetem* "and you shall learn" (Deuteronomy 5:1): the one whom others are commanded to teach is commanded to teach oneself; and the one whom others are not commanded to teach is not commanded to teach oneself. How then do we know that others are not commanded to teach her? Because it is written, "And you shall teach them [to] your sons" (Deuteronomy 11:19)—but not your daughters.[1]

The Mishnah in Sotah

The fundamental question is whether this exemption is extended to exclude women from *Talmud Torah* (Torah study). A statement by Rabbi Eliezer in the Mishnah seems to conclude that it does. "Rabbi

1. Kiddushin 29b.

Eliezer says: Whoever teaches his daughter Torah teaches her *tiflut* [sometimes translated as 'obscenity']."[2]

Although Rabbi Eliezer's dictum is often quoted as a primary source for excluding women from Torah study, an analysis of the passage in Tractate Sotah where Rabbi Eliezer's comment appears could yield a different conclusion.

A *sotah*, a woman suspected by her husband of infidelity, was forced to drink the bitter waters. If she was guilty, the waters had a devastating physical effect upon her. If she was innocent, the waters had no effect (Numbers 5:11–31).[3] Concerning the laws of *sotah*, the Mishnah states:

> If she has merit, it [causes the water] to suspend its effect upon her. Some merit suspends the effect for one year, another for two years, and another for three years. Hence, declared Ben Azzai, a man is under the obligation to teach his daughter Torah, so that if she has to drink [the waters of bitterness], she may know that the merit suspends its effect. Rabbi Eliezer says: Whoever teaches his daughter Torah teaches her *tiflut*.[4]

This is best understood within the larger context of Tractate Sotah. It is preferable that women not drink the *sotah* waters. The first three chapters of Tractate Sotah therefore describe how the rabbis use every legal means at their disposal to make it unnecessary for an accused woman to drink the bitter waters. Our mishnah

---

2. Sotah 20a or Mishnah Sotah 3:4.

Sotah 21b explains the position of R. Eliezer as follows: "Can it enter your mind [that by teaching her Torah he actually teaches her] *tiflut*? Read, rather: 'as though he had taught her *tiflut*?' R. Abbahu said: What is R. Eliezer's reason? Because it is written, 'I wisdom have made guile (*armah*) my dwelling' (Proverbs 8:12), i.e., when wisdom enters a person, guile enters with it."

Rashi to Sotah 21b, s.v. *ke'ilu*, understands *tiflut* as an ethical term. "Through [the learning of Torah] she learns guile (*armemut*) and can do things secretively." *Tiflut* for Rashi seems related to immorality. See Jeremiah 23:13, "And in the prophets of Samaria I saw *tiflah* (immorality)."

Tiferet Yisrael to Mishnah Sotah 3:4, n. 19, second interpretation, relates *tiflut* to vanity. Since she "will not have the mind to understand the reasons of the Torah, it will be laughable (*liẓeḥok*) in her eyes."

See Rambam, *Perush ha-Mishnayot* to Mishnah Sotah 3:4 and *Code*, Laws of Talmud Torah 1:13.

3. If the *sotah*'s husband had himself acted immorally, the bitter waters were inoperative. Soon after the destruction of the Second Temple, as immorality spread, Rabbi Yoḥanan ben Zakkai suspended the *sotah* ordeal. See Sotah 27b, Mishnah Sotah 5:1.

4. Mishnah Sotah 3:4, Sotah 20a.

states that even if a woman does have to drink them, they may be inoperative, for she may have merits that suspend their effects. Ben Azzai then declares that every father should teach his daughter Torah. With that merit, the waters will be rendered null and void. Rabbi Eliezer responds: If so, women may feel free to commit immoral acts, knowing the waters are ineffective.[5] From this perspective, Rabbi Eliezer's statement is not a sweeping restriction of woman's place in Torah study, but rather relates to the specific laws of *sotah.*

Rambam's View

Indeed, Rambam does not understand the passage to prohibit women from studying Torah.

> A woman who studies Torah receives a reward, but since she was not commanded to learn Torah it is not on the same level as [that of] men. For study was not imposed upon her as a duty, and one who performs a meritorious act which is not obligatory will not receive the same reward as one upon whom it is incumbent and who fulfills it as a duty, but only a lesser reward.[6] And even though she receives a reward, the sages have warned us that one should not teach his daughter Torah, as the majority of women do not have a mind suitable for its study, but, because of their limitations, will turn the words of Torah into trivialities. Our sages have said that whoever teaches his daughter Torah it is as if he taught her *tiflut.* This refers to the Oral Law; he ought not to teach her the Written Law in the first place, but if he did teach her [the Written Law], it is not as though he taught her *tiflut.*[7]

The contradiction in Rambam's reasoning is obvious. If a woman who studies Torah receives reward, why is teaching her Torah

5. This interpretation may be the view of *Tiferet Yisrael.* In his commentary to Mishnah Sotah 3:4, no. 16, he claims that the only *zekhut* that would suspend her sentence is her sending her children to learn or her waiting for her husband to come home from learning. Perhaps this idea can be extended to be the position of Ben Azzai, who says, let her study Torah so that the sentence is suspended. *Tiferet Yisrael,* loc. cit., no. 19 (his first interpretation) understands Rabbi Eliezer as formulated here. If she studies Torah, the waters will be rendered ineffective, giving her license to be immoral.

6. See Kiddushin 31a and Avodah Zarah 3a. Tosafot to Kiddushin 31a, s.v. *gadol ha-mezuveh ve-oseh,* and Tosafot to Avodah Zarah 3a, s.v. *gadol ha-mezuveh ve-oseh,* suggest that the person commanded to do a mitzvah feels pressure to fulfill his/her obligation, unlike one who is not mandated to perform a mitzvah, who does not feel that constant pressure.

7. Rambam, *Code,* Laws of Talmud Torah 1:13.

considered *tiflut?* Rambam may be suggesting that women who are self-motivated to study by themselves will obviously channel their Torah learning properly and as such will receive their reward. Women who do not learn on their own and must be taught may not be as sincere and may use Torah learning in vain. In the words of *Perishah.*

> [Rambam writes:] "The majority of women do not have a mind suitable for its study." But if she studied on her own, we see that she has left the "majority." Therefore, he [Rambam] wrote that she receives the Divine reward provided that she studied Torah with proper intentions and not to produce trivialities. But the father is not permitted to teach her, lest her learning lead to trivialities, since he does not know her inner intentions.[8]

By implication, if one's daughter is sincere and well motivated, teaching her is not considered *tiflut.* Indeed, Ḥida writes in his *Responsa Tuv Ayin:* "Beruriah [the wife of Rabbi Meir], who was recognized as having the intention to learn with all her heart and had a good mind [to learn], was taught [Torah]."[9] It follows that women possessing these characteristics may be taught Torah.[10]

Alternatively, there may be no halakhic difference between women studying Torah and women being taught Torah. Rambam may, however, view the statement of Rabbi Eliezer to be societal in nature, rather than a blanket prohibition against women studying. In mishnaic times, Rabbi Eliezer concluded that women might use learning for vain purposes, but if and when Torah study were used by women for positive reasons, it would be permissible for them to learn. This seems to be what Rambam means when he states that one should not teach his daughter Torah because she "will turn the words of Torah into trivialities." Presumably, if this were not the case, women could study Torah.

Rambam's position can be explicated as follows: In theory, women

8. *Perishah* to *Tur Shulḥan Arukh*, Yoreh De'ah 246:15. See also Rav Kook, *Iggerot ha-Re'ayah*, 467.

9. See *Responsa Tuv Ayin*, siman 4.

10. *Perishah*, loc. cit., seems to disagree, claiming that when a father teaches his daughter Torah he does not know what is in her heart. It is possible that *Perishah* is speaking of a situation where one's daughter has expressed neither interest nor disinterest in learning. If, however, she actively seeks to learn for sincere reasons, perhaps *Perishah* would agree that she can be taught.

may study Torah, and receive a reward for doing so. "A woman who studies Torah receives a reward." In reality, however, it was difficult to find a situation where women did not "turn the words of Torah into trivialities." Once this was no longer the case, i.e., once Torah study did not lead to "trivialities," women, according to Rambam, may study Torah.

Rambam appears to follow this approach by interpreting Rabbi Eliezer's statement to refer to the more complicated areas of Torah study which could be misunderstood. This is evident from his "cutting into" Rabbi Eliezer's dictum as relating in absolute terms to the study of the Oral Law, but a woman who post-facto learns the Written Law is not considered to have learned *tiflut*; even in the time of Rambam, this kind of Torah study did not lead to "trivialities."

In fact, *Tur* reverses the text of Rambam.

> Our sages have said that whoever teaches his daughter Torah, it is as if he taught her *tiflut*. This has reference to the Written Law; he ought not to teach her the Oral Law in the first place, but if he did teach her [the Oral Law], it is not as if he taught her *tiflut*.[11]

For *Tur* it is not *tiflut* if a woman studies the Oral Law.

Women and Talmud Torah

With time, many authorities increasingly encouraged women to study the Oral Law. *Torah Temimah*, quoting from *Responsa Mayan Ganim* (who was responding to a question asked by a woman concerning women and *Talmud Torah*), suggests that Rabbi Eliezer's statement relates only to the teaching of Torah to women who are young. He writes:

---

11. *Tur Shulḥan Arukh*, Yoreh De'ah 246 quotes Rambam, *Code*, Laws of Talmud Torah 1:13, but reverses part of the text.

Sefer Mitzvot Gadol, as quoted in *Haggahot Maimuniyyot* to Rambam, *Code*, Laws of Talmud Torah 1:13, s.v. *bameh devarim amurim*, cites the text of Rambam. *Beit Yosef* to *Tur Shulḥan Arukh*, Yoreh De'ah 246, s.v. *ve'af al pi sheyesh lah sakhar*, states that the text of our *Tur* is incorrect—*ta'ut sofer*. *Beit Yosef* concludes that the proper text of *Tur* is as found in Rambam, *Code*, Laws of Talmud Torah 1:13.

Perishah to *Tur Shulḥan Arukh*, Yoreh De'ah 246:16, prefers the text as written in the *Tur* "because in all of our texts it is so written." *Perishah* goes on to explain that it is more serious to misinterpret the Written Law than the Oral Law. In his words: "there is a greater loss when one uses the Written Law for vain purposes than when one uses the Oral Law [for vain purposes]."

Shulḥan Arukh, Yoreh De'ah 246:6, quotes the halakhah as it is found in Rambam, *Code*, Laws of Talmud Torah 1:13.

> The saying of our sages ["whoever teaches his daughter Torah it is as if he had taught her *tiflut*"] perhaps applies when a father teaches his daughter when she is young. . . . In that situation one can certainly suspect that most women [presumably younger girls] . . . are preoccupied with trivialities. . . . However, women who have decided on their own to come closer to the service of God [through learning Torah] . . . "dwell" in a higher spiritual place because they are role models. It is the obligation of the sages of their generation to exalt . . . strengthen . . . and encourage them. Do and succeed, and from Heaven you will be helped.[12]

Others play on the word *ke'ilu* (it is "as if" you taught your daughter *tiflut*); teaching one's daughter Torah *is as though tiflut* were taught, but if one's daughter was not taught Torah, *it is truly tiflut.* In the words of Rabbi Ben Tzion Firer, a contemporary rabbinic scholar:

> Today, the question is not whether or not to teach Torah to one's daughter. The question today is, should one's daughter study Torah or should she study something other than Torah? Indeed, this great pursuit of the Tree of Knowledge has taken hold of everyone—both men and women—and no one can possibly withstand such a powerful attraction. Rabbi Eliezer said: "Anyone who teaches Torah to his daughter teaches her *tiflut.*" The Gemara adds the words "it is as if" he teaches her *tiflut.* The young woman of our time who does not study Torah may instead study real *tiflut.* And clearly, if one had to choose between real *tiflut* and "as if teaching her *tiflut,*" we would choose the latter.[13]

Of great significance is the position of the Ḥafeẓ Ḥayyim:

> One who teaches his daughter Torah. . . . It seems that all this relates to eras in our past when our ancient traditions were so strong that every individual conducted himself just as his parents did, as the verse says, "Ask your father, he will inform you; your elders, they will tell you." We were then able to say that daughters should not study Torah, but should conduct themselves by emulating their righteous parents.

---

12. *Torah Temimah* to Deuteronomy 11: no. 48, quoting *Sefer Mayan Ganim* by Rabbi Samuel ben Elḥanan Jacob Rakvalti.

13. Rabbi Firer, "*Be-Inyan Limud Torah le-Banot,*" p. 134.

See also Rabbi Zalman Sorotzkin, *Moznayim la-Mishpat*, vol. 1, no. 42, who argues that today, when everyone is exposed to the challenges of contemporary society, one who does not teach his daughter Torah leaves her without direction, and as such, may be teaching her *tiflut*.

> But now, with our many sins, our ancient traditions have become much, much weaker. It is also prevalent that they do not live with their parents at all. For those young women, especially those who study the language and literature of the nations, it is a particularly great mitzvah to teach them Ḥumash, as well as Prophets and Writings and the ethical principles of our rabbis, such as *Pirkei Avot* and *Sefer Menorat ha-Ma'or* [aggadic writings and ethical teachings of Rabbi Isaac Aboab], so that our holy practices will be authenticated in the minds of these young women. If we do not do so, they are liable to depart entirely from the way of God and violate all the basic tenets of the faith (God forbid).[14]

In recent years, Rav Yosef Dov Soloveitchik approved the teaching of Talmud to women. Talmud is taught to females attending his elementary and high schools in Boston (Maimonides). Indeed, Rav Soloveitchik gave the inaugural Talmud *shiur* when the Beit Midrash program (where Talmud is taught) first opened at Stern College for Women, Yeshiva University.[15] And teachers like the revered Neḥama Leibowitz serve as extraordinary role models of Torah scholarship for women as well as men. Our yeshivot have yet to work through a consistent policy on this issue.[16] A good starting point would be the policy enunciated by Rabbi Aharon Lichtenstein.

> I have no objection to teaching girls Talmud. From a practical point of view it is somewhat difficult, as there is little motivation for this among girls . . . [and] I am not convinced that it is desirable to press girls to learn Talmud so intensively.
>
> . . . But if we speak of the ability to learn a page of Talmud, to understand it and enjoy it, then I see no reason not to educate girls to those goals. Indeed, there is a need to establish this as an integral part of the school curriculum, as an actual course. That is how I educate my daughter and that is how my wife was educated. And that seems to me to be the recommended road for our generation's girls.[17]

---

14. Ḥafetẓ Ḥayyim, *Likkutei Halakhot* to Sotah 20a.

15. A picture of the Rav giving the inaugural *shiur* appeared in Anglo-Jewish newspapers throughout the United States.

16. See the discussion of Dr. Joel B. Wolowelsky, "Modern Orthodoxy and Women's Changing Self-Perception," p. 79.

17. Rabbi Aharon Lichtenstein, "Ba'ayot ha-Yesod be-Ḥinnukhah shel ha-Ishah" [Fundamental problems in education for women], in Ben-Ẓion Rosenfeld, ed., *Ha-Ishah ve-Ḥinnukhah*, p. 159. See also R. Beni Brama, "Kavim le-Shitato shel ha-Rav ha-Gaon Yosef Dov Soloveitchik be-Hanhagat Yeshivat Rambam," regarding coed yeshiva education and Talmud study for girls. These sources are cited in Dr. Wolowelsky's article, n. 30.

THE OBLIGATION

"Whoever Does Not Learn Will Not Do"

There is yet another approach to women and Torah study. Basing itself on the biblical verse "And Moses called unto all Israel, and said unto them: Hear, O Israel, the statutes and the ordinances which I speak in your ears this day, that you may learn them and observe to do them" (Deuteronomy 5:1), the Talmud states: "Rabbi Yose said: Whoever says that he is only [interested in studying the] Torah, [but not in observing it] . . . [receives] no [reward] even [for the study of the] Torah. What is the reason?—R. Papa replied : Scripture said, 'that you may learn them and observe to do them'; whosoever is [engaged] in observance [of the laws of the Torah] is [also regarded as engaged] in study, but whosoever is not [engaged] in observance is not [regarded as engaged] in study."[18] In other words, if people do not implement that which they have learned, it is as if they had not studied.

The reverse may be equally true: If you do not learn, you will not do. In the words of *Torah Temimah:*

> And behold, just as we deduce that whoever does not observe receives no credit for learning, so is it possible to deduce the reverse, whoever does not learn will not do. . . . And it is possible to say that in accordance with this principle it states in Ethics of the Fathers, *lo am ha-areẓ ḥassid,* "the ignorant person cannot be pious."[19] And the matter is simple. Because of his lack of knowledge he will not know how to conduct himself in accordance with the Torah [he will not know how to fulfill the requirements of Jewish law].[20]

This principle may be the basis of the halakhah quoted by Rema: "Women are obligated to learn the laws which apply to them."[21]

In-Depth Knowledge

The meaning of learning "laws which apply to them" is the subject of considerable debate. Prior to Rema, *Sefer Ḥasidim* wrote:

---

18. Yevamot 109b.
19. Ethics of the Fathers 2:5.
20. See *Torah Temimah* to Deuteronomy 5:1.
21. Rema, *Shulḥan Arukh*, 246:6. See also *Shulḥan Arukh ha-Rav*, Talmud Torah 1:14.

> A person is required to teach his daughter the mitzvot, like the *piskei halakhot* [knowledge of the law, of what to do]. The statement "whoever teaches his daughter Torah teaches her *tiflut*" refers to a deep understanding of the reasons for the mitzvot and the secrets of the Torah. These are not taught to women and children. But he should teach her practical law. After all, if she doesn't know the laws of Shabbat, how can she observe the Shabbat, and so, too, with all of the mitzvot.[22]

For women, *Sefer Ḥasidim* contends, the mechanical knowledge of how to function as a Jew is enough. Others, however, suggest that it is necessary for women to delve into the intricacies of the law and to understand them in depth. Rabbi Firer writes:

> There is reason to question why *Sefer Mitzvot Gadol* (Moses ben Jacob of Coucy, who maintains that a woman's knowledge of the halakhah is enough)[23] has to say that a woman is obligated to study the laws pertinent to her. Is it not obvious that if she did not study, she would not know how to fulfill the commandments that are incumbent on her? If the Torah gave commandments to women, it is as though it obligated them to study those commandments [i.e., the Torah's giving commandments to women is tantamount to its requiring them to study those commandments]. It appears, however, that *Sefer Mitzvot Gadol* is speaking not only about women knowing in general terms those practical commandments that are incumbent on them, but also about their studying the matter by thorough analysis and a detailed understanding of the development of the law.[24]

From this perspective, women would be obligated to learn "virtually everything" in depth, as "most everything" applies to women: the prohibitive commandments, the positive commandments not fixed by time, the positive commandments fixed by time that women are required to perform, and even those that women are exempt

---

22. *Sefer Ḥasidim*, siman 313. See also Rabbi Samson Raphael Hirsch, *Horeb*, vol. 2, p. 371.
23. Ḥida (*Perush Azulai*), in his commentary to *Sefer Ḥasidim*, siman 313 (see previous note), quotes *Sefer Mitzvot Gadol*, positive commandment 12, as being in agreement with Rabbi Judah he-Ḥasid. (Moses ben Jacob of Coucy was a student of Rabbi Judah he-Ḥasid, author of *Sefer Ḥasidim*.)
24. Rabbi Firer, "*Be-Inyan Limud Torah le-Banot*," p. 132.

from performing, for in virtually every case the exemption does not imply exclusion.[25]

* * *

The upshot is clear. Within halakhic parameters women are encouraged and even obligated to learn Torah. Our sources are replete with examples of women who studied Torah. Deborah, who judged Israel (Judges 4–5), and Beruriah, Rabbi Meir's wife, who arbitrated many disputes, are but two examples.[26]

Indeed, a priority issue on the Jewish agenda ought to be the teaching of Torah to women on the same quantitative and qualitative level as men. Only then will we be able to replicate the era of Hezekiah, when a "search was made from Dan to Beersheba, and no ignoramus was found from Gabath to Antipatris, and no boy or girl, man or woman was found who was not thoroughly versed in the laws of *tumah* and *taharah*."[27]

25. See Rosh ha-Shanah 32b–33a; Rambam, *Code*, Laws of Ẓiẓit 3:9 (exemption does not imply exclusion, but blessings should not be said); Tosafot to Rosh ha-Shanah 33a, s.v. *ha* (exemption does not imply exclusion and blessings should be said). Note the claim of Targum Jonathan ben Uzziel to Deuteronomy 22:5 ("a woman shall not wear that which pertaineth unto a man") that donning *tefillin* or wearing *ẓiẓit* is included in the prohibition of wearing a garment specifically designed for a man (*beged ish*).

26. See Tosefta Bava Kamma 4:9.

27. Sanhedrin 94b. These laws are probably mentioned because of their difficulty.

For a review of the role of women with regard to *Talmud Torah* see Arthur M. Silver, "May Women Be Taught Bible, Mishnah and Talmud?"

See also Rabbi Elyakim Ellinson, *Ha-Ishah ve-ha-Mitzvot*, pp. 160–171, for a fine survey of sources dealing with the issue of women and Torah study.

Chapter Six

Women and Aliyot

KEVOD ẒIBBUR

If women are encouraged or even required to learn Torah, is there any obstacle that would prevent them from receiving an aliyah (being called to the Torah)? The Talmud quotes a baraita. "Our rabbis taught: All are qualified to be among the seven [to receive an aliyah], even a minor and a woman, only the sages said that a woman should not read in the Torah because of *kevod ẓibbur*."[1]

The precise meaning of *kevod ẓibbur* is unclear. Reviewing other places where the Talmud uses the phrase may give us a clearer understanding of its meaning.

> Ulla ben Rav inquired of Abbaye: Is a child in rags allowed to read from the Torah? He replied: You might as well ask about a naked one. Why is one without any clothes not allowed? Out of *kevod ẓibbur*. So here, [he is not allowed] because of *kevod ẓibbur*.[2]
>
> R. Huna ben R. Joshua said in the name of R. Sheshet: . . . It is not proper to roll up a scroll of the Law before the community because of *kevod ẓibbur*.[3]
>
> R. Tanḥum said in the name of R. Joshua ben Levi: The precentor (*sheli'aḥ ẓibbur*) is not permitted to strip the ark bare in the presence of the congregation because of *kevod ẓibbur*. [The ark was adorned

1. Megillah 23a.
2. Megillah 24b.
3. Yoma 70a. The service would be delayed as the scroll is rolled to another section. This would be burdensome for the congregation (*tirḥah de-ẓibbura*) and would constitute a violation of *kevod ẓibbur*.

> with hangings, and they could not be removed while the worshippers were present.][4]

> Rabbah and R. Joseph both concurred in ruling that separate *Ḥumashin* [one of the five books of the Pentateuch written on scrolls] should not be read from in synagogue because of *kevod ẓibbur.*[5]

In each case, *kevod ẓibbur* is associated with embarrassment. Reading the Torah in public gives honor to the community. However, reading the Torah naked or in rags, rolling it publicly as people await the commencement of another reading, removing the hangings adorning the ark in the presence of the congregation, and reading from a scroll that contains only one of the five books of the Pentateuch rather than the complete work "humiliates the Torah" and in the process violates the honor that Torah reading normally confers on the congregation.

The Shame of Ignorance

The obvious question is: Why should a woman's reading from the Torah scroll be an issue of *kevod ẓibbur?* Several explanations have been suggested. In talmudic times the *oleh la-Torah* (the person who was given an aliyah) was normally a male; after reciting his *berakhah* (blessing), he would read his portion from the scroll.[6] If women had been given *aliyot*, it might have been thought that the men were not being called because they were unable to read the Torah portion. This would have embarrassed the congregation by implying that it did not accord sufficient importance to Torah study.

Interpreting the baraita in this fashion, Yaveẓ writes:

> The latter part [of the baraita, "a woman should not read in the Torah because of *kevod ẓibbur*,"] has reference to a case where there are enough [men capable of reading the Torah]. The first [part of the baraita, "all are qualified to be among the seven, even . . . a woman"] refers to a case where seven males are not versed enough in reading

4. Sotah 39b. Rashi to Sotah 39b, s.v. *le-hafshit et ha-tevah be-ẓibbur*, states that the Torah scroll was brought from a well-protected place to the synagogue, where it would be placed in an Ark adorned by hangings. Since removing the hangings before returning the Torah to its permanent place would have been time-consuming and therefore a burden to the congregation, the Torah was removed first, to enable the congregation to leave the synagogue, and after this the Ark was "stripped bare."

5. Gittin 60a.

6. This custom is followed in many Yemenite and Syrian synagogues.

> the Torah and there is a woman who is versed. [In that situation a woman who is able may be called to the Torah] for it would be impossible to read without her.[7]

According to the latter part of the baraita, were women to read, it would leave the impression that men could not. According to the first part, there is no alternative but to have a woman participate among the seven.

Centuries before Yaveẓ, Ritva directly associated *kevod ẓibbur* with the shame of ignorance.

> Since we follow the view of R. Joshua ben Levi that women are obligated [to read the Megillah], they may therefore fulfill [their male counterparts' obligation]. However, [if they read the Megillah for men] it is not *kevod le-ẓibbur* and falls into the category of *me'erah* ("shame," literally "curse light"). [Since men normally perform the ritual reading, their failure to do so reveals their ignorance.][8]

---

7. Yaveẓ, *Haggahot ve-Ḥiddushim* to Megillah 23a.

See *Responsa Rivash* 326: "Since not all who were present were versed in Torah reading, they did not burden the congregation [with the requirement] to bring seven adults trained to read the Torah. And when they established that seven should read from the Torah, the enactment was that a minor who knew how to read could be counted towards the seven so as not to burden the congregation [with the requirement] that all seven should be adults when there may not be seven [adults] available trained to read [the Torah]. And even women were permitted [to read the Torah] for this reason were it not for *kevod ha-ẓibbur*."

Here, Rivash associates the right of a minor to read from the Torah with the situation where seven adult readers are not available. The same would be true for women were it not for *kevod ẓibbur*. If a woman read from the Torah, her male counterparts would be embarrassed by the implication that they were unable to perform the Torah reading ritual. The reason a minor may read "in a pinch," but not a woman, is that a minor's reading would be less embarrassing to the congregation. Calling a minor to the Torah would not necessarily imply that the congregation was ignorant; it could be viewed as a legitimate way of preparing the *katan* for his adult responsibilities.

8. Ritva to Megillah 4a. Thus, although women are as obligated to read the Megillah as men, they should not read it for their male counterparts, as this would imply that men who should know how to read the Megillah could not. Ritva's comment is especially significant in that he directly associates *kavod ẓibbur* with *me'erah*.

A similar case is that of Birkat ha-Mazon. Some maintain that even if a woman's obligation to recite the Birkat ha-Mazon is equivalent to a man's, women ought not to recite the prayer for men, as it would imply that the men were incapable of reciting Grace themselves. Berakhot 20b states: "A woman may say Grace on behalf of her husband [either because a woman's obligation to recite the Grace After Meals is also biblical, as is a man's, or her obligation is rabbinical, but we are dealing with a case where the man ate a quantity for which he is only rabbinically bound to say Grace]. But the sages said: A curse light (*me'eirah*) on the man whose wife or children must

Although the context relates to the reading of the Megillah on Purim, Ritva's comments may be extended to Torah reading. A woman should not read from the Torah scroll on behalf of men because of *kevod ẓibbur* or *me'erah.* Doing so would reveal that the men could not read the Torah.[9]

Modesty

Alternatively, *kevod ẓibbur* as it relates to *aliyot* for women might involve the issue of *ẓeniut* (modesty). A sense of frivolity or theatrics might prevail if men and women were forced to mingle while leading the service. This, in the end, would embarrass Torah and congregation alike.[10]

---

say Grace for him [because he cannot say it himself]."

See Sukkah 38a for a similar text. Rashi to Sukkah 38a, s.v. *she-ishto u-vanav mevarkhim lo,* explains *me'eirah* as relating to the man's ignorance. If the woman recites the Grace, it implies that the man has not studied. See also Tosafot to Sukkah 38a, s.v. *utehe lo me'erah.*

9. Rabbi Yehudah Herzl Henkin, "Mahu Kevod ha-Ẓibbur," p. 33, concurs. Quoting similar sources, he relates *kevod ẓibbur* to *me'eirah.*

10. *Sefer ha-Eshkol* (Hilkhot Ḥanukkah ve-Purim, chap. 9) writes that a woman may not read the Megillah for a man because of *kol be-ishah ervah* (a woman's voice as a source of sexual stimulation). Some extend this concern to Torah reading.

See, however, Rabbi Henkin, "Mahu Kevod ha-Ẓibbur," pp. 33–35, who disagrees. Rabbi Henkin deduces from *Sefer ha-Eshkol* that while *kol ishah* would prevent women from reading the Megillah for men, it would not prevent women from reading the Torah for men. For Rabbi Henkin, the issue of *kevod ẓibbur* as it relates to Torah reading is not based upon *kol ishah,* for in fact there is no problem of *kol ishah* in Torah reading.

Rabbi Henkin argues that *kol ishah* is more problematic in regard to the Megillah reading, for the Megillah is listened to with greater love and attentiveness, *shemeirov ḥavivuta yehavu daataihu lishmoah.* Moreover, the Megillah is read on Purim, a day of partying, and often in homes (especially when women read for men). Rabbi Henkin concludes that reading the Megillah even with trop (cantillation) "is not actually a violation of *kol be-ishah ervah,* but rather a situation where men could have frivolous thoughts during the reading. With this in mind, one could distinguish between Megillah reading and Torah reading."

(For an analysis of *kol ishah,* see Rabbi Saul J. Berman, "Kol Ishah.")

Even if one does not accept the contention that women reading the Megillah or Torah is an issue of *kol ishah,* it raises a larger question: the mingling of the sexes were women to read the Megillah or Torah for men.

Periẓut (immodesty) is a central issue in halakhah. For example, Berakhot 45b states that three or more women alone may recite the *zimmun,* the invitation to those present to recite Grace After Meals. Tosafot to Berakhot 45b, s.v. *shanei hatam de-ika de'ot,* concludes that three women *may* recite *zimmun,* while Rosh to Berakhot 45b, s.v. *tanu rabbanan nashim mezammnot le-aẓman,* concludes that three women *must* do so.

Berakhot 45b states that women may not be counted with men in the quorum of three because of *periẓut.* Ran to Megillah, chap. 2, end, s.v. *ha-kol,* distinguishes

THE KEY DEFINITION: EQUALITY OF OBLIGATION

Examination of a Tosefta parallel to our baraita ("All are qualified to be among the seven [to receive an aliyah], even a minor and a woman, only the sages said that a woman should not read in the Torah because of *kevod ẓibbur*") provides a clearer understanding of the *kevod ẓibbur* concept. The Tosefta reads: "All are included among the seven, even a woman and even a minor. But a woman is not brought forth to read in public [*ein mevi'in et ha'ishah likrot be-rabbim*]."[11]

The variant reading preserved in the Tosefta ("a woman is not brought forth to read in public," *ein mevi'in et ha-ishah likrot be-rabbim*"), replacing the baraita's term *kevod ẓibbur*, may hold the key to a correct understanding of *kevod ẓibbur*.[12] The change is significant and requires further analysis.

Private and Public Torah Study.

In outlining the Torah blessings that should be said every morning, the Talmud states:

> What benediction is said [before the study of the Torah]? Rav Judah said in the name of Samuel: "[Blessed are You, Lord our God, Ruler of

---

between the Megillah reading and Birkat ha-Mazon (Grace After Meals). In the former case, women may join men to make up the quorum of ten. The Megillah text is the same whether it is read individually or in a group, and thus the mixing of men and women does not constitute *periẓut*. However, the text of Grace After Meals changes when there is a quorum of three. Therefore, the combining of men and women to comprise three is considered *periẓut*. Women, however, may offer the appropriate responses when Grace is recited by three men forming such a quorum, since the women's presence does not cause any alteration in the text of the *zimmun*.

Ba'al ha-Ittur (*Tur Shulḥan Arukh*, Oraḥ Ḥayyim 689) maintains that women are not counted *ab initio* toward the quorum of ten for Megillah. Baḥ, ibid., s.v. *u-B"H katav*, understands the concern of *Ba'al ha-Ittur* to be *priẓutah*. (See chap. 4, n. 30.)

It is conceivable that the reason women are not counted with men as part of the quorum of three for *zimmun* is that women may only have a rabbinical obligation to say Grace After Meals, while men's obligation is biblical. See Berakhot 20b.

See *Haggahot Maimuniyyot* to Rambam, *Code*, Laws of Prayer 12: *resh*, where it is stated that in a city inhabited only by Kohanim (priests), the first and second aliyot are given to a Kohen (as a descendent of the tribe of Levi, a Kohen may come forth for the second aliyah), while the third may be given to a woman. In extenuating circumstances the issue of *kavod ẓibbur* (*me'eirah, ẓeniut*) is put aside so that the public reading of the Torah may take place.

11. Tosefta, Megillah 3:5. *Haggahot ha-Gra*, ibid., no. 19, indicates that his text of the Tosefta is the same as the baraita in Megillah 23a.

12. See Tosafot Rid to Megillah 23a: "This Tosefta is explained by the baraita."

> the universe] who has sanctified us by Your commandments, and commanded us to study the Torah (*la-asok*)." Rabbi Yoḥanan used to conclude as follows [in order both to open and close with a benediction]: "Make pleasant, therefore, we beseech You, O Lord our God, the words of Your Torah in our mouth and in the mouths of Your people the house of Israel, so that we with our offspring and the offspring of Your people the house of Israel may all know Your name and study Your Torah. Blessed are You, O Lord, who teaches Torah to Your people Israel (*ve-ha-arev*)." R. Hamnuna said: "[Blessed are You, Lord our God, Ruler of the universe] who has chosen us from all the nations and given us Your Torah. Blessed are You, O Lord, who gives the Torah (*asher baḥar*)." Rabbi Hamnuna said: This is the finest of the benedictions. . . . Therefore let us say all of them.[13]

Tosafot asks why a blessing over the *sukkah* (*leshev ba-sukkah*) is required each time one eats in a *sukkah* (perhaps several times a day), while Torah blessings recited in the morning cover the entire day of Torah learning even if there were intervals between the periods of study.

In response, Tosafot distinguishes between the mitzvah of eating in the *sukkah* and learning Torah.

---

13. Berakhot 11b. Rif and Rosh attribute these last words to R. Papa.

Whether these paragraphs constitute two or three Torah blessings is disputed by Tosafot and Rambam. Tosafot to Berakhot 46a, s.v. *kol ha-berakhot kulan*, suggests that *ve-ha-arev* is connected to *la-asok* and hence there are two blessings (*asher baḥar* being the second). For Tosafot the two blessings are both *arukot*, as they both begin and end with *Barukh atah Hashem*. The first (*la-asok* and *ve-ha-arev*) deals with the Oral Law, while *asher baḥar* concentrates on the Written Law, upon which the oral tradition is based. According to Tosafot, one would add the conjunctive *vav* before *ha-arev* to indicate its link to *la-asok*. See *Haggahot Maimuniyyot* to Rambam, *Code*, Laws of Prayer 7:30, and *Shulḥan Arukh*, Oraḥ Ḥayyim 47:6, where the use of the conjunctive *vav* is mentioned. Appropriately, sections from the Written and Oral Law are then recited.

Rambam, *Code*, Laws of Prayer 7:10–11, maintains that *ha-arev* is an independent blessing, and hence there are three Torah blessings (*la-asok* [Rambam's text is *al divrei Torah*] and *ha-arev* would both be *berakhot keẓarot*, beginning *or* ending with *Barukh atah Hashem* but not both). For Rambam, the Torah blessings correspond to the three major forms of blessings: *la-asok* to *birkhot ha-mitzvot* (blessings recited before performing a mitzvah), *ha-arev* to *birkhot ha-nehenin* (blessings recited on pleasurable activities, e.g., eating), and *asher baḥar* to *birkhot hoda'ah* (blessings of thanksgiving). See Rambam, *Code*, Laws of Blessings 1:4, who lists these three types of blessings.

Abudarham in *Sefer Abudarham ha-Shalem* (Jerusalem: Hoẓa'at Usha, 5723), p. 44, quotes Rabbi Zeraḥiah ha-Levi, who maintains that the three blessings correspond to the portions from the Pentateuch (*Parashat Ẓav*), Mishnah (*Eizehu Mekoman*), and Talmud (*Rabbi Yishmael Omer*) that follow the blessings in the prayerbook. It may also refer to the portions from the Written Law, Mishnah, and Gemara found immediately after the blessings.

> Torah [study] is different as it never leaves one's mind. One is obligated to study every moment, as it is said, "and you shall meditate on it day and night" (Joshua 1:8), and it is as if he were sitting [and learning Torah] all day without interruption. But eating in the *sukkah* has fixed times.[14]

Tosafot's interpretation is this: the mitzvah of *sukkah* relates to actually being in the *sukkah;* it begins upon one's entry into the *sukkah* and concludes when one leaves it. A second meal, even if eaten on the same day, would therefore require another blessing. On the other hand, the process of learning Torah never ceases during the day.[15] All human actions, even those that do not involve Torah study per se, relate to Torah learning in some way, since every aspect of human existence involves the implementation of Torah principles. From this perspective, one never finishes learning Torah as long as one is awake. Reciting the morning Torah blessings is therefore sufficient for the whole day.

An obvious question arises: If the Torah blessings recited each morning cover the entire day, why may one repeat the blessing *asher baḥar* when receiving an aliyah? Does this not constitute a *berakhah le-vattalah*, a blessing said in vain?[16]

Rabbenu Tam suggests that public Torah reading is not part of the halakhah of learning Torah (*Talmud Torah*). In his words:

> The blessings before and after the Torah reading are not linked to *Talmud Torah*. This is obvious, since even one who has said *ve-ha-arev* [the morning blessings] repeats the blessings [at the public reading of the Torah]. [Similarly] this is obvious because if there is no Levi, the Kohen reads [the Torah] in his place and recites the blessings again even though he recited these blessings in his first reading [first aliyah].[17]

---

14. Tosafot to Berakhot 11b., s.v. *shekvar niftar be-Ahavah Rabbah*.

15. *Shulḥan Arukh*, Oraḥ Ḥayyim 47:11, quotes two views concerning the repetition of the Torah blessings if one has slept during the day. See *Arukh ha-Shulḥan*, Oraḥ Ḥayyim 47:23, and *Mishnah Berurah* to Oraḥ Ḥayyim 47:25.

16. Berakhot 33a: "Rava, or as some say Resh Lakish, or again, as some say, both Resh Lakish and R. Yoḥanan, have said: Whoever recites a blessing which is not necessary transgresses the command of 'Thou shalt not take [the name of the Lord thy God in vain]' (Exodus 20:7)!"

See Rambam, *Code*, Laws of Blessings 1:15, and *Shulḥan Arukh*, Oraḥ Ḥayyim 215:4.

17. Rabbenu Tam on Rosh ha-Shanah 33a, Tosafot, s.v. *ha*. An understanding of the larger context within which Rabbenu Tam comments is in order.

Rosh ha-Shanah 32b–33a discusses whether the exemption of women from partic-

Here Rabbenu Tam distinguishes between the private responsibility to study Torah, which falls within the halakhic category of *Talmud Torah*, and the obligation to read Torah publicly. *Shulḥan Arukh* echoes this very point in distinguishing between private *Talmud Torah* and public Torah reading. He writes:

> Even if one recited the private Torah blessings and immediately afterwards was called to read the Torah [in public], he must again repeat the blessing *asher baḥar* when he reads from the Torah [in public] as that blessing was enacted to give honor to the Torah when read before the congregation.[18]

Arukh ha-Shulḥan makes a similar point:

> All who are called to the Torah recite blessings before and after the reading. And these blessings are not connected to the Torah blessings [recited in the morning], as these blessings were recited to give honor to the Torah.[19]

This distinction yields a solution to our question. The recitation of Torah blessings each morning permits one to study Torah as an individual; it is the *matir* (permit) for the private mitzvah of *Talmud Torah*. On the other hand, the blessings (including *asher baḥar*) recited when the Torah is read in synagogue refer to the fulfillment of the mitzvah of public Torah reading. The blessing *asher baḥar* may be identical to the morning Torah blessings, but its purpose is entirely different.

---

ular mitzvot implies exclusion. Two tannaitic views are recorded.

Rambam concurs with the view that exemption does not imply that women are barred from performing certain mitzvot. However, he contends that women should not recite blessings over these mitzvot (probably because it is inaccurate for women to say *ve-ẓivanu*, "you have commanded *us*"). See Rambam, *Code*, Laws of Ẓiẓit 3:9, where he rules that women may put on *ẓiẓit* without a *berakhah*.

In contrast, Rabbenu Tam (in Tosafot, s.v. *ha*) states that women may recite blessings on commandments they are exempt from performing (probably because *ve-ẓivanu* is not in the singular form, but is a plural term relating to the community as a whole, of which women are, of course, an equal part). See below, chap. 7, n. 29.

Ri bereb Yehudah in Tosafot, s.v. *ha*, attempts to support Rabbenu Tam's position by quoting in part the baraita in Megillah 23a that states (in its first part) that women may be counted towards the seven receiving aliyot, despite the fact that they are not obligated to fulfill the mitzvah of *Talmud Torah*.

Rabbenu Tam rejects this proof, since being called to the Torah is not a halakhah of *Talmud Torah*. In his words: "This is not a proof. The blessings before and after the Torah reading are not linked to *Talmud Torah*." It is here that Rabbenu Tam distinguishes between private *Talmud Torah* and public Torah reading.

18. *Shulḥan Arukh* to Oraḥ Ḥayyim 139:8.
19. *Arukh ha-Shulḥan* to Oraḥ Ḥayyim 139:9.

Kevod Ẓibbur Defined

The distinction between private *Talmud Torah* and the obligation to read Torah publicly is the key to our understanding of *kevod ẓibbur.* Women, like men, possess the innate capacity to reach the highest spiritual levels. For this very reason, halakhah encourages and, according to some, mandates that women study Torah. This is reflected in the first parts of the Tosefta and baraita which state that women can in theory come forward to receive aliyot. However, by reading the Torah publicly, women cannot fulfill the male congregants' duty of *keri'at ha-Torah be-ẓibbur* (public Torah reading), since women, unlike men, are not required to participate in the public Torah reading.

In short, public Torah reading, unlike private *Talmud Torah,* requires a minyan; women, however, are excluded from minyan. This is precisely what the Tosefta means when it concludes that a "woman should not be brought forth to read in public." Not having the same obligation, women cannot fulfill their male counterparts' responsibility in regard to public Torah reading.

The baraita that concludes, "The Sages have said that a woman should not read from the Torah because of *kevod ẓibbur,*" makes the same point. *Kevod ẓibbur* in this context means that the reader has the same obligation as the assembled. If women (for whom the public Torah reading is not obligatory) read for men (for whom it is), the *kevod ẓibbur,* the honor which the act of reading the Torah normally confers on the congregation, is diminished.

This analysis of *kevod ẓibbur* becomes more evident when we analyze the very meaning of the term. The word *kavod* "contains within it the root of the word *kaved.*" Indeed *kavod* is linked etymologically to *kaved.*[20] *Kaved* means "heavy." In concrete terms, heaviness is determined by the pull of gravity upon an object; in conceptual terms, weight is determined by the degree of responsibility one has. The greater the responsibility (*kaved*), the greater the potential honor (*kavod*) once those obligations are fulfilled.

The meaning of the talmudic dictum now becomes clear: In principle all women may come to the Torah. But, the baraita con-

20. Although offering different understandings of the relationship between *kavod* and *kaved,* Rabbi Samson Raphael Hirsch and, *yibadel le-ḥayyim,* Rav Aharon Soloveichik both note that these terms are intrinsically bound to each other. See Rabbi Hirsch's commentary on the Bible, Exodus 20:12, and Rav Soloveichik, "A Deeper Insight into the Miracle of Chanukah," p. 4. The quotation "contains within it the root of the word *kaved*" is found in Rav Soloveichik's article.

cludes, women do not read from the Torah because they do not have the same responsibility in regard to public Torah reading as their male counterparts. The exclusion of women from aliyot is not a socio-psychological phenomenon through which a woman's reading would detract from the honor of the congregation per se, but rather a legal concern. Women do not read Torah publicly because of *kevod* (*kaved*) *ẓibbur.* Lacking the same obligation (*kaved*) as her male counterparts (*ẓibbur*), a woman is not permitted to recite the Torah blessings required for the public Torah reading. The Tosefta reinforces this idea when it declares that "women should not be brought forth to read in public."

There is an alternative explanation. Originally, only the first and last readers recited the Torah blessings—the first prior to his reading, and the last following his reading. In time, it was decreed that all who read should recite blessings.[21] The Tosefta and baraita that first permitted women to come to the Torah were referring to the middle aliyot, those which originally did not require blessings. Since they required no blessings, nothing prevented women from coming to the Torah and reading from the scroll. Once it was established, however, that each aliyah required blessings, even the middle aliyot could only be recited by individuals for whom the public Torah reading was obligatory—i.e., individuals who could be counted into a minyan—thus excluding women. In the words of Meiri:

> The words ["All are qualified to be among the seven, even . . . a woman"] apply to the time when the middle aliyot were read without blessings, and a woman could read in the middle [aliyot]. But now that everyone [who comes to the Torah] recites a blessing, a woman may not read at all. This is logical. How can she recite a blessing [and fulfill the obligation of the listeners with respect to *keri'at ha-Torah be-ẓibbur*] if she is exempt [from public Torah reading]?[22]

---

21. Megillah 21b: "A tanna stated: The one who reads first recites a blessing before the reading, and the one who reads last recites a blessing after it. Nowadays all make a blessing both before and after the reading. The reason the rabbis ordained this: to avoid error on the part of people entering and leaving synagogue. [People who come in after the reading has commenced, on seeing a subsequent person start to read without saying a blessing, might think that no blessing is necessary before the reading. Similarly, those who leave before the reading is concluded might think that no blessing is necessary after the reading.]"

22. Meiri to Megillah 23a. See also Rabbenu Tam on Rosh ha-Shanah 33a, s.v. *ha* (end), and *Arukh ha-Shulḥan*, Oraḥ Ḥayyim 282:11.

See Ran to Megillah 23a (in Ran's commentary on Rif, 13a), s.v. *ha-kol olin*, who

The Tosefta therefore concludes: "Women should not be brought forth to read in public." Lacking the duty men have concerning public Torah reading, women cannot recite the public blessings for their male counterparts. If they did so, they would detract from *kevod* (or *kaved*) *ẓibbur*. Hence, the final decision of the baraita: "The sages said that a woman should not read in the Torah because of *kevod ẓibbur.*"

WOMEN AND PUBLIC TORAH READING

Our analysis of *kevod ẓibbur* rests on the premise that women are not legally bound to hear a public Torah reading. Some critics of women's tefillah groups have disagreed,[23] citing *Magen Avraham* to support their position. At first blush they seem correct. Commenting on the statement in *Shulḥan Arukh*, "all are qualified to be among the seven [to receive an aliyah], even a woman . . . only the sages said that a woman should not read before the congregation because of *kevod ha-ẓibbur*,"[24] *Magen Avraham* states:

> From here we can deduce that a woman is required to listen to the reading of the Torah. And even though it was enacted because of

argues that once the blessings were introduced for each aliyah, a woman could have come forward for any of the aliyot were it not for *kavod ẓibbur*. See *Beit Yosef* to *Tur Shulḥan Arukh*, Oraḥ Ḥayyim 282, s.v. *ha-kol olin*, where he quotes Ran.

Although it may seem forced to interpret *ha-kol olin le-minyan shivah*, "all are qualified to be among the seven," as referring only to the middle aliyot, many authorities suggest that the phrase means that women can come forward for *some* but not *all* aliyot.

See Ran and *Beit Yosef*, ibid., who understand *ha-kol olin* as *olin le-hashlim*, "come forward to complete the count," but not for every aliyah.

Magen Avraham to *Shulḥan Arukh*, Oraḥ Ḥayyim 282:5 states: "[they can come forward] to the count of seven but not to the count of three." Rabbi Akiva Eger (*Haggahot Rabbi Akiva Eger*, Oraḥ Ḥayyim 282, s.v. *Magen Avraham*, no. *hay*) suggests that *Magen Avraham* permits a woman to receive one of the seven aliyot. However, when less than seven are called to the Torah (as on Yom Kippur, when six are called, or a holiday, when five are called, or Rosh Ḥodesh, when four are called, or on Shabbat afternoon and Monday and Thursday mornings, when three are called), women may not come forth. Rabbenu Tam (Tosafot to Rosh ha-Shanah 33a, s.v. *ha*) suggests that it refers to receiving the seventh aliyah.

However, Rema, *Shulḥan Arukh*, Oraḥ Ḥayyim 282:3, suggests that women may be included in *some* but not *all* the aliyot whenever the Torah is read. See Rabbi Akiva Eger, ibid.

All these views interpret *ha-kol olin le-minyan shivah* as a reference to one or some but not all of the seven aliyot. They would agree that women today may not receive aliyot because of *kevod ẓibbur*.

23. See, for example, the brief statement of the five rabbis from Yeshiva University, Rabbi Bronspigel's elaboration on the statement, and Rabbi Schachter, "Ẓe'i Lakh be-Ikvei ha-Ẓon," p. 118.

24. *Shulhan Arukh*, Oraḥ Ḥayyim 282:3.

> *Talmud Torah*, which is not obligatory for women, nonetheless it is a mitzvah for them to listen, like the mitzvah of *Hakhel*, which is also incumbent on women and children.[25]

But a reading of the entire passage in *Magen Avraham* leads to a very different conclusion. After making the above comment, *Magen Avraham* immediately states: *umihu yesh lomar, af al pi she'einun ḥayyavot olot le-minyan*, "however, one can say that even though [women] are not obligated [in regard to *keri'at ha-Torah be-ẓibbur*], they are qualified to be among the count [of seven, for an aliyah]."[26] In simple terms, *Magen Avraham* maintains that although women may be called forward, they may, nonetheless, be exempt from *keri'at ha-Torah be-ẓibbur.*

Magen Avraham's final comment is especially revealing. Although he quotes the statement in Tractate Soferim that women, like men, are required to listen to the reading of the *Sefer Torah*, and it is a mitzvah to translate the Torah portion for them to ensure that they understand it,[27] he rejects this view and concludes: "and here our custom is that women leave the synagogue [when the Torah is read]."[28]

Indeed, two of the most important halakhists of the twentieth century, *Arukh ha-Shulḥan* and *Mishnah Berurah*, conclude that women are not obligated to hear the public Torah reading. *Arukh ha-Shulḥan* states in precise terms that the intent of Tractate Soferim

> was not to establish a complete obligation [for women in *keri'at ha-Torah*]. . . . After all, women are exempt from *Talmud Torah* and there is no greater positive commandment fixed by time. . . . And one should not compare this to *Hakhel*, concerning which the Torah commands that men, women, and children should assemble [to hear the Torah read], because *Hakhel* is a unique mitzvah which occurs once in seven years when the king himself reads Deuteronomy. . . . But to conclude from this that women are obligated every Shabbat to hear the Torah

---

25. *Magen Avraham* to *Shulḥan Arukh*, Oraḥ Ḥayyim 282:6.
26. Ibid.
27. Massekhet Soferim 18:4.
28. *Magen Avraham*, loc. cit.

Rabbi Henkin, "Mahu Kavod ha-Ẓibbur," p. 39, understands the first part of *Magen Avraham* to mean that if women are already in synagogue they are obligated to listen to the Torah reading. *Magen Avraham*, however, concludes that this is not our custom. Here "women leave the synagogue [before the Torah is read]" even if they are already in synagogue.

reading is astounding. And current custom proves this point [most women did not attend *keri'at ha-Torah be-ẓibbur*]. . . . But the intent of Massekhet Soferim was to teach correct conduct. That when the Torah was translated [for those assembled], it was appropriate to translate for women . . . in order to deeply instill in their hearts fear and love of God.[29]

Paraphrasing *Magen Avraham*'s conclusion, *Mishnah Berurah* writes: "However, women are not careful about this [listening to the reading of the Torah]. On the contrary, there are communities where it is customary for women to leave [the synagogue] during the reading [of the Torah]."[30]

Commenting on *Mishnah Berurah*, Rabbi David Auerbach concludes: ". . . and from the language of *Mishnah Berurah*, it appears that women were careful to leave. In other words, not only did they not come to listen, but those who came to synagogue were accustomed to leave [when the Torah was read]."[31]

While nowadays it is more common for women to hear *keri'at ha-Torah*, there is virtually no authority who supports the position that women are required to attend the public Torah reading.[32] In fact, one prominent critic of women's tefillah groups wrote: "Since a woman has no obligation to participate in communal prayer, she need not seek a minyan or pray with it if one is present. . . . Women are not required to participate in public prayer and hence cannot lead public prayer."[33]

The reason for this exemption is consistent with our analysis. Were women mandated to hear *keri'at ha-Torah* it would make it difficult, and at times impossible, for them to fulfill their preferred home role if they so wished.[34]

Our conclusion remains intact: While women are encouraged and perhaps required to engage in private *Talmud Torah*, they are not

29. *Arukh ha-Shulḥan*, Oraḥ Ḥayyim 282:11.

30. *Mishnah Berurah to Shulḥan Arukh*, Oraḥ Ḥayyim 282:12.

31. Rabbi Auerbach, *Halikhot Beitah*, p. 62, n. 4.

32. If women are required to hear the public Torah reading, rabbis should insist that they attend services on Mondays, Thursdays, Rosh Ḥodesh, holidays, and Shabbat mornings, as well as Shabbat afternoons. And if the obligation of women to hear Torah reading refers only to Shabbat (see *Magen Avraham*, loc. cit., and *Mishnah Berurah* to *Shulḥan Arukh*, Oraḥ Ḥayyim 282:11), there should be a concerted effort to have women arrive at synagogue on Shabbat prior to the Torah reading.

33. Rabbi Moshe Meiselman, *Jewish Woman in Jewish Law*, p. 136.

34. See above, chaps. 1 and 4.

legally bound to hear a public Torah reading. In consequence, they may not recite blessings at the Torah for those who are obligated, because of *kevod ẓibbur.*

TORAH BLESSINGS AT WOMEN'S TEFILLAH GROUPS

It follows that the Torah reading at a women's tefillah group is a function of private Torah learning. Although *societally* public in that it involves a group gathering, the reading remains halakhically private. For this reason, women's Torah readings (and tefillah groups) may take place with fewer than ten women present, with minors reading from the Torah and leading the service, and without the Torah blessings recited at a traditional minyan.

In practical terms this means that Barekhu, which falls into the category of *devarim she-bi-kedushah* and requires a minyan, is omitted.[35] Recitation of the first *berakhah* (*asher baḥar*) would depend upon whether the Birkhot ha-Torah had been recited within the Birkhot ha-Shaḥar If they had been, the recitation of *asher baḥar* would be prohibited, since it would constitute a *berakhah le-vatalah* (a blessing said in vain).[36] If the morning blessings had not been recited, the blessing *asher baḥar* could be recited during the Torah reading as a partial fulfillment of one's obligation to say Birkhot ha-Torah. *Shulḥan Arukh* states:

> If he was called to read from the Torah before reciting his individual Torah blessings, he is relieved from reciting the [morning] blessing of

35. *Shulḥan Arukh*, Oraḥ Ḥayyim 55:1 and *Mishnah Berurah* to ibid., 55:2.

36. Note that the recitation of Ahavat Olam or Ahavah Rabbah (*Shulḥan Arukh*, Oraḥ Ḥayyim 47:7 and 60:1) fulfills one's obligation to recite the Torah blessings if one studies Torah immediately afterwards. These prayers include aspects which deal with learning Torah, and constitute a blessing (*Mishnah Berurah* to Oraḥ Ḥayyim 47:14). Levush (quoted by *Mishnah Berurah* to ibid., 47:15) indicates that Shemoneh Esreh is not considered an interruption. Therefore, if one recited Ahavat Olam or Ahavah Rabbah and studied Torah after Shemoneh Esreh, one has fulfilled the Torah blessing obligation.

Be'ur ha-Gra and *Eliyahu Rabba* (quoted in *Mishnah Berurah* to *Shulḥan Arukh*, Oraḥ Ḥayyim 47:17) state that the recitation of Keri'at Shema is a function of prayer and not of learning Torah. *Mishnah Berurah* (ibid. 47:15) points out that Ahavah Rabbah is meant to introduce the Keri'at Shema as a prayer and not as Torah learning.

It is best for women who wish to recite the blessing *asher baḥar* at the Torah to omit the morning Torah blessings and recite Ahavah Rabbah with the intention of *not* fulfilling the obligation of reciting the Birkot ha-Torah. See *Peri Megadim* (quoted in *Biur Halakhah* to *Shulḥan Arukh*, Oraḥ Ḥayyim 47, s.v. *poteret*), who states that someone who recites Ahavah Rabbah without the intention of fulfilling his Torah blessing obligation is still obligated to recite the Torah blessings.

asher baḥar. [His recitation of *asher baḥar* at the Torah relieves him of his personal obligation to say this very same blessing privately.][37]

Whether participants in women's tefillah groups may recite the final blessing of *asher natan lanu Torat emet* is unclear. Some argue that since the *berakhah* is linked to public Torah reading (it is not found in the private Torah blessings of Birkot ha-Shaḥar), it should be omitted. Others suggest that *asher natan lanu* is a separate *berakhah* which may be recited by individuals after studying from a *Sefer Torah.*

The basic source supporting this position is a halakhah found in Tractate Soferim. There it states:

> And what does one say [when reciting the Torah blessings]?
>
> Before ten they say: "Bless the Lord who is to be blessed" (*Barekhu et Hashem ha-mevorakh*).
>
> When alone, when rising to read (*ke-shehu mashkim likro*) [presumably from the Torah scroll] he says: "Blessed are You, Lord our God, Ruler of the universe, who has given us the Torah from the heavens above (*asher natan lanu Torah min ha-shamayim*) for eternity. Blessed are You, O Lord, Giver of the Torah." He then rolls [presumably, the Torah scroll] together and says (*ve-golel ve-omer*): "Blessed are You, Lord our God, Ruler of the universe, who has given us the Torah of truth (*asher natan lanu Torat emet*) and has planted everlasting life in our midst. Blessed are You, O Lord, Giver of the Torah."[38]

Independent of the obligation to read from the *Sefer Torah* during the public prayer service, it was common to study Torah from the Torah scroll.[39] Separate honor was given to this learning process by

37. *Shulḥan Arukh*, Oraḥ Ḥayyim 139:9.

Magen Avraham to *Shulḥan Arukh*, Oraḥ Ḥayyim 139:12, states that even though reciting *asher baḥar* at the Torah relieves one of the private responsibility to recite *asher baḥar, ve-ha-arev* and *la-asok* must still be said.

38. Massekhet Soferim 13:8.

39. The issue of *Torah metammei et ha-yadayim* ("hands which touch a Torah scroll become *tameh*") suggests that it was common for the *Sefer Torah* to be used for learning purposes. See below, chap. 7, n. 30, for a discussion of this issue.

In *Eleh Ezkerah* ("These shall I recall"), recited during the Yom Kippur service, the story of the Ten Martyrs is told. Rabbi Ḥananya ben Teradyon was one of the victims. "[The ruler] ordered that Rabbi Ḥananya ben Teradyon be brought from his study hall, and they burned his body with bundles of branches. They placed saturated wool sponges on his chest to delay his death—as soon as they were removed, he was burned together with a Torah scroll."

Rabbi Ḥananya was executed for violating the Roman decree against teaching Torah publicly. The Romans took the *Sefer Torah* from which Rabbi Ḥananya

reciting blessings before and after the study period. A literal reading of the Massekhet Soferim text indicates that when a *ẓibbur* of ten studied from a Torah scroll, Barekhu was recited. When someone studied or read alone, Barekhu was not recited, but *asher natan lanu Torah min ha-shamayim* was said prior to the reading, and *asher natan lanu Torat emet* after. *Asher natan lanu Torat emet* may therefore be recited by individuals after learning from a Torah scroll.[40] Since the reading from the Torah at a women's tefillah group is a function of *Talmud Torah*, it follows that the final *berakhah—asher natan lanu Torat emet*—may be said.

It could also be argued that Massekhet Soferim would have individuals recite *asher natan lanu Torat emet* as part of their obligation to recite Birkhot ha-Torah every morning. Indeed, *ke-shehu mashkim likro*, "when rising to read," may relate to what an individual does when privately reciting Birkhot ha-Torah. The halakhah in Massekhet Soferim reveals that every morning one would recite *asher natan lanu Torah min ha-shamayim*, learn from a Torah text (which was in scroll form), and then close the text (roll it together) and say *asher natan lanu Torat emet*.[41] It follows that *asher natan*

---

apparently used to learn and teach Torah, and wrapped him in it before setting him ablaze. To intensify his pain, they "saturated wool sponges on his chest to delay his death." The Midrash relates that Rabbi Ḥananya then said: "The parchment is consumed, but the letters fly up in the air."

This tragic episode may suggest that Rabbi Ḥananya studied and taught Torah from a Torah scroll.

For a similar reading of this atrocity, see *Kinnot* (Lamentations) of Tishah be-Av, *Arzei ha-Levanon* ("The cedars of Lebanon").

40. I heard this analysis of Massekhet Soferim from Rabbi Saul Berman.

41. The wording in Massekhet Soferim may support this contention. The halakhah states: *ke-she-hu mashkim likro*, "when rising to read," which implies that one has just awakened and is ready to recite the Birkhot ha-Torah.

The term *ve-golel* ("to roll together") used in the latter part of the baraita, could refer to a *Sefer Torah*, as individuals often studied from the Torah scroll. It is also possible that *ve-golel* does not refer to a *Sefer Torah*. It was common for people to learn Torah from a text which was in scroll rather than book form. See Rashi to Gittin 60a, s.v. *be-ḥumashin*. Indeed, it does not explicitly state in Massekhet Soferim that the case of the individual ("when alone") deals with one who reads from a Torah scroll.

See, however, *Naḥalat Ya'akov* to *Massekhet Soferim* 13:8, s.v. *ve-golel ve-omer*, where the following argument is made: "it [the blessing *asher natan lanu Torat emet*] refers to the above ["before ten they say"]. Concerning the Torah blessings said in public [before ten] after [the reading], he first rolls the Torah and then recites the blessing [*asher natan lanu Torat emet*]."

For *Naḥalat Ya'akov*, the term *ve-golel ve-omer* refers to the situation where ten are present. The halakhah then indicates that the blessing *asher natan lanu Torat emet* is said in public after the Torah is rolled together. In that setting (i.e., before ten) the blessing *asher natan lanu Torat emet* is recited. According to *Naḥalat*

lanu Torat emet was recited in the daily Birkhot ha-Torah.[42]

Of course, women could recite the blessings before and after the Torah reading without including God's name (*Shem u-Malkhut*). They could also substitute verses from *Tanakh* or the liturgy which do not require a minyan, or omit the blessings in their entirety.[43] The Torah reading would retain its private characteristics if any of these options were followed.[44]

Ya'akov's understanding of Massekhet Soferim, *asher natan lanu Torah emet* is said with a minyan.

42. For an analysis of the position of Rav Yosef Dov Soloveitchik, Rav Moshe Feinstein, and Rabbi Shlomo Goren concerning the recitation of these *berakhot* at the women's prayer service, see below, chap. 8.

43. Rav Yosef Dov Soloveitchik has been quoted as suggesting substitute texts for the *berakhot* women would omit when coming to the Torah during the service at a women's tefillah group. See below, chap. 8, for a discussion of Rav Soloveitchik's view on the issue.

44. While acknowledging that "it is permissible for any person to read or to study from a Torah Scroll at any time," Rabbi J. David Bleich ("Religious Experience? *tefillah betzibbur?*" p. 148) writes that since the Written Law may now be studied from a printed text rather than a properly written scroll, "there is absolutely no cogent reason for utilizing a Torah Scroll rather than a printed *Chumash* for purposes of Torah study. On the contrary, use of an unvocalized text can only lead to error yielding misinformation. . . . Since use of a *Sefer Torah* is halakhically meaningful only when it is used for purposes of fulfillment of the rabbinic commandment [to read the Torah in public], the use of a Torah Scroll by women who candidly acknowledge that they do not thereby fulfill the rabbinic requirement borders on the farcical."

In my conversations with participants in women's tefillah groups, I have not found this to be the case. For many, the challenge of mastering their Torah portion has added immeasurably to their learning experience. Preparing and then reading from the unvocalized Torah scroll has been for them a joyous expression of *Talmud Torah*, motivating them to intensify their study of Torah. Rather than lead to error, it has contributed significantly to their understanding of every nuance and meaning of the Torah text.

Were Rabbi Bleich's position followed with consistency, a moratorium should be called on the *ba'al peh* program, a program which enhances talmudic study in yeshivot by encouraging students to memorize pages of Gemara. With the Oral Law now committed to writing, what is the value of learning Talmud by heart? Couldn't this "lead to error yielding misinformation"? Clearly, however, the *ba'al peh* method contributes to the learning process and facilitates greater mastery of Talmud. The same is true for women who prepare and then read from the Torah scroll.

It is, as Rabbi Bleich states, "permissible for any person to read or study from a Torah Scroll at any time." For those attending women's tefillah groups, this practice has enhanced their Torah study.

Chapter Seven

Women and *Sifrei Torah*

In recent years, sincere Jewish women have asked for the right to dance with the Torah scroll during their own independent *hakafot* on the holiday of Simḥat Torah, to kiss the scroll as it passes the *ezrat nashim* (women's section of the synagogue), to themselves carry the scroll through the *ezrat nashim* in order to feel a greater connection with the Torah, and most strikingly, to have direct contact with the Torah as part of their reading from the Torah scroll during the services held by women's tefillah groups.

All of these practices would involve women in physically touching or holding a Torah scroll. Somehow, a tradition has arisen in our communities which deprives women of the right to touch a *Sefer Torah*. Many individuals have expressed to me the belief that women are enjoined from physically having contact with the *Sefer Torah* when they are *niddot* (i.e., during their menstrual cycle). The subject of this chapter is to evaluate whether this belief is, in fact, correct. Our investigation is divided into two sections: first, the tracing of the origin and development of the laws of *tumat niddah* as they are found in the Talmud; second, an analysis of the laws pertaining to women and *Sifrei Torah* as they appear in halakhic literature. It is hoped that through this study we will be better able to judge the merits of the issue.

THE TALMUDIC SOURCES

"Words of the Torah Are Not Susceptible to Tumah"

Our starting point is a baraita in Berakhot 22a which states:

> It has been taught, Rabbi Judah ben Bathyra used to say: The words of the Torah are not susceptible to *tumah* [commonly translated "im-

> purity"].[1] It happened that a disciple standing before Rabbi Judah ben Bathyra spoke hesitatingly [evidently because he was *tameh*—being a *ba'al keri*, one who has had a seminal emission—and thought that he was debarred from uttering words of Torah]. He said to him: My son, open your mouth and let your words be clear, for the words of the Torah are not susceptible to *tumah*. For it is said: "Is not My word like fire, says the Lord" (Jeremiah 23:29)? As fire is not susceptible to *tumah*, so are words of Torah not susceptible to *tumah*.

Based on the verse from Jeremiah, this tannaitic source concludes that an "invisible wall" surrounds the words of Torah which cannot be penetrated by *tumah*. The Gemara concludes that the halakhah is in accordance with Rabbi Judah ben Bathyra.[2] Accordingly, Rambam states:

> All who are *tameh* are obligated to recite Shema, and they recite the blessing before and after Shema while they are *tameh*. . . . And all of Israel are already accustomed to read in the Torah and to recite the Shema while they are *ba'al keri*, because the words of Torah are not susceptible to *tumah*.[3]
>
> All who are *tameh* need only wash their hands (without immersion) . . . and may pray.[4]
>
> A person who is *tameh* is permitted to recite all of the blessings.[5]

In the Laws of Sefer Torah, Rambam extends Rabbi Judah ben Bathyra's principle to include the touching of a *Sefer Torah*.[6] There he states:

---

1. There is no precise term that adequately defines *tumah* and its antonym, *taharah*. In the course of this chapter, an attempt will be made to offer a general analysis of these concepts. The two major categories of *tumah* that will be dealt with are *niddah* (Leviticus 15:19–24) and *ba'al keri* (Leviticus 15:16–18). Since *tumah* and *taharah* have no appropriate English translation, all forms of the terms *tumah* and *taharah* will be used in their original Hebrew throughout this chapter.

2. See Berakhot 22a: "Rav Naḥman bar Isaac said: It is the general custom to follow these three elders: Rabbi Il'ai, as to first fleece; Rabbi Josiah, as to mixed kinds; and Rabbi Judah ben Bathyra, as to words of Torah." See Hullin 136b for a similar Gemara.

3. Rambam, *Code*, Laws of Keri'at Shema 4:8.

4. Ibid., Laws of Prayer 4:4.

5. Ibid., Laws of Blessings 1:9.

6. The precise source of this extension is not at all clear. See *Or Same'aḥ* on Rambam, *Code*, Laws of Sefer Torah 10:8. There he quotes as a source of the halakhah Bava Batra 19a–20b, from which *Or Same'aḥ* deduces that "a *Sefer Torah* is not susceptible to *tumah* and serves as a barrier preventing the spread of *tumah*," and Sukkah 26b, from where *Or Same'aḥ* deduces that "one who has had a seminal issue may don tefillin." Interestingly, when the issue of women touching *Sifrei Torah* is mentioned in *Shulḥan Arukh*, Oraḥ Ḥayyim 88:1 and Yoreh De'ah 282:9, it is not associated with Rabbi Judah ben Bathyra's halakhah.

All who are *tameh* and even *niddot* and even a *Kuti*, may hold the scroll of Torah and read from it,[7] because the words of Torah are not susceptible to *tumah*. All this is permissible with the proviso that one's hands should not be unclean or soiled with clay, in which case they should wash their hands and afterwards touch it.[8]

Ba'al Keri and Niddah

Rambam's general classification of *tumah* ("all who are *tameh*," "a person who is *tameh*") indicates that he understands Rabbi Judah ben Bathyra's halakhah to apply to all forms of *tumah*.[9] Although the specific case which precipitated Rabbi Judah ben Bathyra's halakhah deals with *ba'al keri*, it would be equally applicable to *niddah*. Indeed, a further analysis of talmudic sources dealing with *ba'al keri* clearly shows that for the purpose of Torah study and prayer (Rambam would extend the similarity to touching a *Sefer Torah*), *niddah* is treated the same as *ba'al keri*.[10]

Biblically, although a *ba'al keri* is *tameh* (Leviticus 15:16), he may pray or learn Torah. After the return from the Babylonian exile, Ezra the Scribe attempted to introduce legislation mandating that a process of ritual immersion was also necessary before a *ba'al keri* could study Torah or pray.[11] Ezra's additional prohibition was not associated with the laws of *tumah* and *taharah*. The requirement of ritual immersion for a *ba'al keri* before praying or studying, it was assumed, would induce people to limit their sexual activity and

---

7. The change of language in Rambam from "all who are *tameh*" to "all who are *tameh*, even *niddot*, and even a *Kuti*," is somewhat strange. It can be suggested in the case of Shema, tefillah, and *berakhot*, prayers which women are either obliged or strongly encouraged to recite, that women who are *niddot* are obviously included in the phrase "all those who are *tameh*." However, women and for that matter *Kutim* are certainly not obligated to touch a *Sefer Torah*. In order to make certain that the reader understands that this halakhah pertains to them, Rambam adds "even *niddot* and even a *Kuti*."

8. Rambam, *Code*, Laws of Sefer Torah 10:8.

9. That Rabbi Judah ben Bathyra's halakhah applies to all forms of *tumah* may be an obvious inference. Otherwise, no one would be able to touch a *Sefer Torah* today as we are all *temeai meit*. See *Sefer ha-Pardes*, chap. 271, Laws of Niddah 3b, Ehrenreich ed., p. 3, where the school of Rashi alludes to the same argument. However, see *Responsa Yeḥaveh Da'at*, siman 8, who mentions a zoharic passage on Exodus which states that *niddah* is the most stringent *tumah*, but circumscribes its application to one who has had relations with a *niddah*, and not a *niddah* proper.

10. The similarity would indicate that if *niddot* cannot learn, pray, or touch a *Sefer Torah*, neither can *ba'alei keri*.

11. See Berakhot 22b, Bava Kamma 82a for Ezra's *takkanah*. How far Ezra extended this *takkanah* is a subject of controversy.

thereby devote their full attention to lofty, spiritual undertakings.[12] During and immediately after the return from the Babylonian exile, a time when the spiritual purity of Israel was seriously challenged, it was especially important to institute *takkanot* designed to counterbalance the spiritual erosion that had deeply affected Israel during the Babylonian experience.[13]

Several tannaitic sources, with variant interpretations, outline the halakhic consequences of Ezra's ruling. For example: "A *ba'al keri* recites [the Shema] mentally but does not say the benedictions before it and after it. And for food, he says the Grace after it but not benedictions before it. Rabbi Judah says: He says the benedictions before them and after them."[14]

Even if Ezra's legislation had been accepted permanently, it would have had rabbinical status; hence it would only have had the power to obviate a rabbinical ordinance. The recitation of the Shema is of biblical origin, and *Tanna Kamma* (an anonymous opinion treated as authoritative) maintains that Ezra would have had the *ba'al keri* recite the Shema, but only "in his heart," not articulating it "with his lips." The blessings preceding and following the Shema, which were introduced by the rabbis, would, however, have been cancelled by Ezra's *takkahah*. Similarly, Ezra would have had the *ba'al keri* forgo the blessings preceding a meal, as they are rabbinical, but recite the Grace After the Meal, which is biblical. Rabbi Judah's divergent opinion indicates that he disagreed with *Tanna Kamma* as to how far Ezra extended his *takkanah*.[15]

Relative to our subject, the key tannaitic source is a passage in Tractate Berakhot.[16] There it states that a *niddah* who expelled seed (presumably from a sexual encounter which preceded the onset of her menstrual cycle), although maintaining her *niddut* status,

---

12. There are different reasons which explain why Ezra introduced this *takkanah*. For example, Berakhot 22a suggests that it was an attempt to prevent people from overindulging in sexual activity. In the words of the Talmud, "so that scholars should not be frequently with their wives." Yerushalmi Berakhot 3:4 suggests that Ezra's *takkanah* was introduced to limit sexual activity and thereby allow more time for Torah study.

13. There are numerous examples of Ezra's *takkanot* and special provisions. See Bava Kamma 82a, which lists the other *takkanot* introduced by Ezra; or the fourth chapter of Kiddushin, beginning 69a, which discusses Ezra's attempts to maintain the family purity of Israel after the Babylonian exile.

14. Berakhot 20b and Rashi loc. cit.

15. Berakhot 22a. Rabbi Judah disagrees with *Tanna Kamma*, maintaining that Ezra's *takkanah* applied only to Torah and not to blessings.

16. Berakhot 26a.

must, according to Ezra, immerse before praying or studying Torah (since, in effect, she had become a *ba'alat keri*). This indicates that a *niddah*, who is biblically *tameh* (Leviticus 15:19), could even in the time of Ezra occupy herself with Torah and prayer, as the words of Torah are not susceptible to *tumah*. Here, too, Rabbi Judah disagrees with *Tanna Kamma*, maintaining that Ezra did not extend his *takkanah* to this situation where a more inclusive form of *tumah* remains.[17] With the passage of time, Ezra's enactment became virtually obsolete.[18] Precisely how Ezra's *takkanah* was cancelled is a subject of dispute.[19]

---

17. Ibid. According to Rabbi Judah, Ezra only prohibited learning for the *ba'al keri* if, through immersion, one could become *tahor*. Ezra's *takkanah* would not apply to a *niddah* who expelled seed, because her status of being *niddah* would still remain after immersion. For a precise synopsis of Rabbi Judah's view here and in Berakhot 20b, see *Tiferet Yisrael*, Berakhot 3:6, comment 38.

18. *Magen Avraham* to *Shulḥan Arukh*. Oraḥ Ḥayyim. 88, comment 1, states that the enactment became nullified because it seriously limited the learning of Torah (rather than immerse, people chose not to learn) or the fulfillment of the mitzvah "be fruitful and multiply" (to avoid immersion, individuals opted to refrain from cohabitation).

19. An analysis of Rambam on this issue as it relates to Torah study and the Shema may be indicative of the importance of Rabbi Judah ben Bathyra's halakhah in the nullification process. Rambam, *Code*, Laws of Keri'at Shema 4:8, states: "and this *takkanah* did not spread in all of Israel, and the majority of the community did not have the strength to sustain it, and therefore it became nullified. And it is already the custom of all Israel to read in the Torah and to read the Shema while they are *ba'al keri*, because the words of Torah are not susceptible to *tumah* but they eternally retain their *taharah*."

Rambam's formulation of the halakhah is difficult. Having stated that the ordinance was nullified because the majority of the people rejected it, why did he find it necessary to include as the reason that "the words of Torah are not susceptible to *tumah*"? Apparently, without Rabbi Judah ben Bathyra's halakhah it would have been necessary for a subsequent court of greater stature to nullify Ezra's enactment. Such a court never existed. Therefore, Rambam adds that the halakhah of "the words of Torah are not susceptible to *tumah*" was operative during the time of Ezra, which may explain why Ezra's attempt to extend the restriction of a *ba'al keri* to include study and the Shema never took hold. Rambam, therefore, uses the expression *batla*, "it became nullified," rather than *bitteluha* "it was nullified by another court."

Rambam's distinction between *batla* and *bitteluha* in this passage is noted by the *Kesef Mishneh* on this passage in Rambam's *Code*. Note also that *Kesef Mishneh* understands the first two phrases as being interdependent: "and this *takkanah* did not spread in all of Israel, because the majority of the community did not have the strength to sustain it, and therefore it became nullified."

However, Tosafot to Bava Kamma 82b, s.v. "he came and enacted it even for words of Torah" suggests that Ezra may never have introduced this enactment; or that the enactment stipulated that anyone who wished to nullify the law might do so; or that the prohibition did not spread to the majority of Israel.

Magen Avraham to *Shulḥan Arukh*, Oraḥ Ḥayyim 88:1, states that no subsequent court was required to nullify the *takkanah* because it was not widely accepted by the

THE HALAKHAH

The Difficult Rema

The position of Rabbi Judah ben Bathyra would appear to permit anyone to pray, study, or touch the Torah. However, a reading of the halakhah as found in the *Shulḥan Arukh* points to some interesting and important observations. In Oraḥ Ḥayyim, *Shulḥan Arukh* offers an historical overview of Ezra's *takkanah* and its nullification.

> All who are *tameh* read in the Torah and read the Shema and pray. Except for one who has had a seminal emission, whom Ezra removed from the general category of *temeim* and forbade him to learn Torah, to read the Shema, to pray the Shemoneh Esreh, until he immerses himself, in order that the sages should not frequent their wives too often. And afterwards they nullified this enactment and established the matter in accordance with the law, that even one who has had a seminal emission is permitted to study Torah, to read the Shema, and to pray the Shemoneh Esreh without a ritual immersion, and without washing himself in nine *kabim*. And this is the way the custom spread.[20]

However, Rema, in his addendum, formulates what appears to be a rather inconsistent position.

> There are those who have written that a woman who is in the midst of her menstrual flow may not enter a house of prayer, or pray, or mention God's name or touch a *Sefer*. And there are those who maintain that all of this is permissible and this is the essential [law]. But the custom in our lands is as presented in the first position. And during her clean days [the seven-day period between the cessation of the menstrual flow and immersion in the mikvah], the custom is to permit. And even in a place where the custom is to be stringent, on the High Holy Days and [days] like that, when many gather to go to the synagogue, women [who are *niddot*] may go to the synagogue like other women, because it is greatly saddening to them, if all would gather in the synagogue while they stand outside.[21]

---

majority of Jews. For this reason alone, "it never took hold."

See *Tur Shulḥan Arukh*. Oraḥ Ḥayyim 88, quoting Rabbenu Hai amongst others, who states that Ezra's *takkanah* should still be followed on some level. *Tur* concludes, however, that in "all of our places" the *takkanah* of Ezra is not followed.

20. *Shulḥan Arukh*, Oraḥ Ḥayyim 88:1.

21. Ibid., Rema. Rema is reflecting a distinction which was already present in the gaonic period.

See *Oẓar ha-Ge'onim*, (edited by Dr. B. Lewin), vol. 1, Tractate Berakhot, sec. 119, which states that a "*niddah* is permitted to enter a synagogue to pray . . . as long as her clothes have no *dam* (blood)."

The inconsistency in Rema's position, as followed in "our lands," is obvious. The status of *tumat niddah* remains even after the cessation of the actual menstrual flow until immersion in the mikvah. Why should a woman during her seven "clean days" be permitted to do all that is forbidden during her flow, if her *tumah* remains in full force throughout the seven-day period?

Similarly, why does Rema suspend the prohibitions during the High Holy Days? Can restrictions resulting from *tumat niddah* be obviated by the pain that some women would feel if forced to remain outside during the Rosh ha-Shanah—Yom Kippur services?

There is yet a second place in *Shulḥan Arukh* where the issue is discussed. Once again, Rema's position (or lack of position) raises a serious difficulty. In Yoreh De'ah, Rabbi Joseph Karo states: "All who are *tameh*, even *niddot*, may hold the scroll of Torah and read from it. All this is permitted with the proviso that their hands not be unclean or dirty."[22]

What is striking is that Rema offers no comment on this halakhah. His lack of reaction seemingly indicates that he is in agreement with *Shulḥan Arukh*. Yet we know from Rema's statement on the passage in Oraḥ Ḥayyim that he in fact disagrees. Why doesn't Rema in Yoreh De'ah offer a brief synopsis of his position, which appears to be very different from the view posited by *Shulḥan Arukh*?

Tumah and Uncleanliness: A Conceptual Analysis

Through a brief analysis of the *tumah* concept, we may understand Rema's comments in Oraḥ Ḥayyim and his omission of any statement in Yoreh De'ah. It is hoped that this analysis will also explain Rema's position vis-à-vis women and *Sifrei Torah*.

Tumah has often been defined as physical uncleanliness. If this were true, *taharah*, the antonym of *tumah*, would by implication be synonymous with cleanliness. However, Phinehas ben Jair, in a famous comment which was to contribute the outline of Rabbi Moses Ḥayyim Luzzatto's *The Path of the Just* (*Mesillat Yesharim*), said that Torah, precision, zeal, cleanliness, restraint, *taharah*, saintliness, meekness, and fear of sin in that order lead to holiness.[23] We learn from this statement that cleanliness and *taharah*

22. *Shulḥan Arukh*, Yoreh De'ah 282:9.

23. Avodah Zarah 20b. See Mishnah Sotah 9:15 and Yerushalmi Shekalim 3:3, where the version varies. The text quoted here follows the order of the statement as understood by Rabbi Luzzatto.

are two distinct categories. So, too, is physical uncleanliness not synonymous with *tumah.*[24]

There have been many attempts to conceptualize *tumah.*[25] Rav Aharon Soloveichik, in one of his classic *hashkafah* classes years ago,[26] suggested that the meaning of *tumah* may be derived from the verse in Psalms which says: "The fear of the Lord is *tehorah*, enduring forever" (Psalms 19:10). *Taharah* therefore means that which is everlasting and never deteriorates. *Tumah*, the antithesis of *taharah*, stands for mortality or finitude, that which withers away. A dead body is considered a primary source of *tumah*, for it represents decay in the highest sense not only because the corpse itself is in the process of decaying, but also because the living individual who comes in contact with the corpse usually suffers emotionally and endures a form of spiritual fragmentation, a counterpart of the corpse's physical falling away. The *meẓora* (leper), whose body is encompassed with skin lesions, is also considered in a state of *tumah*. The leper is *tameh* because he is slowly "disintegrating," while those who associate with him decline emotionally as they observe the wasting away of another human being. The *ba'al keri* and the *niddah* may fall into the same framework, for they represent in the strictest sense the loss of potential life.

Rav Aharon's thought may explain conceptually why "words of Torah are not susceptible to *tumah*." Torah represents infiniteness; that which is eternal. *Tumah*, reflective of breakage or dissolution, does not have the power to penetrate Torah, which endures forever.

---

24. I first heard this thought from Rav Aharon Soloveichik in a *shiur* given at Yeshiva University in the spring of 1962. Rabbi Lamm, in *A Hedge of Roses*, pp. 43–47, describes the popular association of *niddot* with uncleanliness as a "semantic tragedy." As much as we have tried to teach the real meaning of *tumat niddah*, there are still so many who believe that halakhah links *niddot* with that which is dirty. This myth must be shattered, a myth that has made it emotionally difficult for many women, especially those on the religious fringes, to accept the laws of family purity. Commenting on the mistranslation of *tumah* as uncleanliness, Rabbi Lamm writes: "No wonder that so many young people reject the whole institution (of family purity) offhand: certainly in this scientific age, with our technological progress in hygiene and sanitation, we do not need to abide by ancient ritual regulations in order to keep clean!" Rabbi Lamm then proceeds to beautifully articulate a deeper understanding of *tumat niddah* and *mikvah*.

25. For example, Rabbi Samson Raphael Hirsch, *Horeb*, vols. I and II, pars. 222, 420, 442, 447, 464, 717; and Rabbi Lamm, *A Hedge of Roses*, pp. 79–93.

26. The same *shiur* mentioned in note 24. Although the major idea of relating *taharah* to that which is everlasting is Rav Aharon's, the precise application of the concept to a *meit*, *meẓora*, *ba'al keri*, and *niddah* as it appears here, is not.

The Rema: A Possible Explanation

But whatever *tumah* means, one thing remains very clear—it has nothing to do with the physical state of uncleanliness. *Tumah* and *likhlukh* (or *tinnuf*) are independent conditions and should not be confused. With this in mind, Rema's position on women and *Sifrei Torah* may become clear. Both Rema and *Shulḥan Arukh* agree that the words of the Torah are not susceptible to *tumah*. For this reason, Rema, after stating that women should not enter a synagogue, pray, mention God's name, or touch a *Sefer*, adds that the correct position is that all of this is permissible. Having taken this position, Rema expresses a different concern relative to his own community; not a concern which relates to *tumah* but one which is associated with physical uncleanliness. Rema, therefore, concludes that in his city all was prohibited, as women struggled to maintain their cleanliness during their menstrual flow. But these restrictions were only operative during the actual period of menstruation when the problem of physical uncleanliness existed. During the seven clean days the only remaining consideration was *tumah*. However, since the "words of Torah are not susceptible to *tumah*," all was permitted.[27] Likewise, on Rosh ha-Shanah and Yom Kippur, when so many come to synagogue, women would have experienced great sadness if pre-

---

27. A similar argument is expressed in *Kaf ḥa-Ḥayyim* to *Shulḥan Arukh*, Oraḥ Ḥayyim 88:11. There he states: "It is important to warn women during the time that *dam* is flowing to cease reading and also to change the cloth, so they be as clean as possible during the time of prayer. . . . Similarly, it is important to warn women not to enter the synagogue when they know that *dam* is flowing, because of the *kavod*."

The concern of *Kaf ha-Ḥayyim* is clearly physical cleanliness. Even women who are *tameh*, if they are physically clean, may, according to *Kaf ha-Ḥayyim*, pray and enter the synagogue.

Responsa Kerem Ẓevi, chap. 41, formulates a similar position vis-à-vis women touching a *Sefer Torah*.

See *Kesef Mishneh* to Rambam, *Code*, Laws of Keri'at Shema 4:8, s.v. "All who are *tameh*," who distinguishes between physical uncleanliness and *tumah*. There he states: In the case of a place which is unclean "we can clearly see the despicable item, or feel its smell, and it appears as if the one who is saying Torah there [in this unclean place] is embarrassing the Torah. However, *tumah* of the *temeim* is not physically felt but is rather a mental state, and therefore 'words of the Torah are not susceptible to *tumah*.' "

See Sukkah 26b. Our rabbis taught: "If he forgot and had sexual intercourse while wearing his tefillin, he should not take hold either of a strap [of the tefillin] or of a capsule [of the tefillin] to remove them until he washes his hands, since hands touch things automatically [and may therefore have touched an unclean spot]." Although we are dealing with a different holy object (the *Sefer Torah*) and a different form of *tumah* (*tumat niddah*), permission to touch tefillin is mentioned in the Talmud as being contingent upon one's being in a state of physical cleanliness.

vented from attending services. Since *tinnuf* is the crucial consideration, Rema may be suggesting that the sadness felt could overcome the problem of physical uncleanliness.[28]

In Yoreh De'ah, Rema offers no comment because there *Shulḥan Arukh* added a phrase not found in Oraḥ Ḥayyim: "All who are *tameh*, even *niddot*, may hold the scroll of Torah and read from it. All this is permitted with the proviso that their hands are not unclean or dirty."[22] The particular concern of Rema in Oraḥ Ḥayyim was physical uncleanliness. Once *Shulḥan Arukh* in Yoreh De'ah adds the proviso that a *niddah*'s hands must be clean, Rema finds no reason to offer an alternative view, for this in fact is his position.[29]

A Synopsis of Halakhic Sources

It seems, therefore, that for a variety of reasons, women may touch and carry a *Sefer Torah*. First, we follow the view of Rabbi Judah ben Bathyra that words of the Torah are not susceptible to *tumah*.[30]

---

28. Note that *Magen Avraham to Shulḥan Arukh*, Oraḥ Ḥayyim 88, comment 3, already extends the High Holy Days to begin with the first day of Seliḥot.

29. Interestingly, Rema in *Shulḥan Arukh*, Oraḥ Ḥayyim 38:3, also states that even those women who wish to don tefillin should be prevented from doing so. Commenting on Rema, *Magen Avraham* in comment 3 says: "Because they require a clean body [in order to wear tefillin] and women are not zealous to be careful [on this matter]. But if they were obligated, they would not be exempt for this reason."

It seems that Rema's view that women should be prevented from wearing tefillin is, according to *Magen Avraham*, not related to *tumah* but rather to physical cleanliness. Perhaps Rema would have arrived at a different conclusion if cleanliness had not been a problem.

Whether women may or may not wear tefillin is the subject of great controversy. Targum Jonathan ben Uzziel (Deuteronomy 22:5) views tefillin as a distinctly male garment and hence concludes that women may not "put on" tefillin. Maimonides, although silent on the tefillin issue, seems to conclude that women may don tefillin, but without blessings. See Rambam, *Code*, Laws of *Ẓiẓit* 3:9, where he says that women may put on *ẓiẓit* without a *berakhah* (probably because they cannot say *ve-ẓivanu*, "You have commanded us to wear *ẓiẓit*"). From Rabbenu Tam in Rosh ha-Shanah 33a, Tosafot, s.v. *ha*, it appears that women may even wear tefillin and recite the blessings (perhaps because *ve-ẓivanu* is not a "singular" expression, but rather a term which relates to the community as a whole, of which women are, of course, an equal part).

For a good collection of sources related to this issue, see Rabbi Meiselman, *Jewish Woman in Jewish Law*, pp. 147–151.

30. The issue of *Torah metammei et ha-yadayim*, "hands which touch a Torah scroll become *tameh*," is not problematic. Mishnah Zavim 5:12 states that a scroll renders *terumah* unfit. This is because of what happened when the priests stored *terumah* near the Holy Scriptures. Mice gnawed the *terumah* and also nibbled the scroll. To prevent this desecration, it was declared that Holy Scriptures were in the second degree of *tumah*, rendering *terumah* unfit. In order to ensure that the sacred

Second, Rema in Oraḥ Ḥayyim states that the view that *niddot* may enter a synagogue, pray, mention God's name, and touch a *Sefer* is the correct position.[31] Third, Rema's statement that in his cities women in the midst of their menstrual flow did not enter a synagogue, pray, mention God's name, or touch a *Sefer* is linked to the issue of cleanliness. In a world where *niddot* can take far greater

---

scrolls would not be touched by bare hands, it was further enacted (Mishnah Yadayim 3:2) that hands which touched a scroll became *tameh* in the second degree and therefore rendered *terumah* unfit. Shabbat 14a, Megillah 32a, and Rashi, loc. cit., relate the prohibition of touching a *Sefer Torah* to touching it barehanded. See Shabbat 14a, Tosafot, s.v. *ha-oḥez*, who suggests that the prohibition could be extended to all Holy Writings, citing Yadayim 3:5 as proof.

Shulḥan Arukh, Oraḥ Ḥayyim, 147:1, states that it is forbidden to touch a *Sefer Torah* barehanded, without a *mitpaḥat*. Rema extends the prohibition to all holy writings and then indicates that the custom is to apply the prohibition only to *Sifrei Torah*. Rema concludes that while it is best to wash one's hands before touching any of the holy writings, it would nonetheless be forbidden to touch the *Sefer Torah* barehanded even after washing one's hands.

Ḥayyei Adam 40:20 states that if one had touched a *Sefer Torah* or tefillin or one of the Megillot written on parchment in the middle of a meal, he would require *netilat yadayim* (washing of the hands) without a *berakhah* before continuing to eat. *Be'ur Halakhah* on *Shulḥan Arukh*, Oraḥ Ḥayyim 164, s.v. *laḥzore velitol yadav*, concludes that if one touches a *Sefer Torah* during a meal, *netilat yadayim* without a *berakhah* would only be required if one wishes to consume *terumah*, but for regular food an additional *netilat yadayim* would not be required.

As the *Sefer Torah* is touched or carried through the medium of a cloth (the binder [*gartle*] or Torah covering), *Torah metammei et ha-yadayim* is not a problem. While *Magen Avraham* in his introductory comments to *Shulḥan Arukh*, Oraḥ Ḥayyim 147, and *Baḥ* in his commentary to *Tur Shulḥan Arukh*, Oraḥ Ḥayyim 147, s.v. "it is forbidden to hold a *Sefer Torah* without a *mitpaḥat*," suggest that it is forbidden to hold the handles of the *Sefer Torah* barehanded, most *poskim* maintain it is permissible. See *Mishnah Berurah* on *Shulḥan Arukh*, Oraḥ Ḥayyim 147:2 and *Sha'ar ha-Ẓion*, ibid. comment 4. The whole issue of women touching a *Sefer Torah* becomes academic if one bears in mind that a person carrying a Torah scroll only handles the covering and *eẓ ḥayyim* and not the scroll itself.

31. Even the first view mentioned by Rema in Oraḥ Ḥayyim (that women should not enter a synagogue, or pray, or utter God's name or touch a *Sefer*) is understood by the Vilna Gaon as a "mere stringency." See *Be'ur ha-Gra* to *Shulḥan Arukh*, Oraḥ Ḥayyim 88, s.v. "and there are those who say that they are permitted in everything." The noted commentary *Dammesek Eliezer*, ad loc., states: "and even those who are stringent are only stringent relative to entering a synagogue." According to *Dammesek Eliezer*, even those who followed the stringent ruling (*ḥumrah*) of the Rema never applied it to touching a *Sefer Torah*. The *Gra*, ibid., also refers his readers to *Shulḥan Arukh*, Yoreh De'ah 282:9, where it says that *niddot* may touch the Torah as long as their hands are clean.

Both the *Gra*, ibid., and *Magen Avraham* to *Shulḥan Arukh*, Oraḥ Ḥayyim 88:3 make reference to the last mishnah of the third chapter of Berakhot (Berakhot 26a). *Maḥzit ha-Shekel* comments on *Magen Avraham*'s reference to this mishnah by stating: "In other words, that there it is explained that certainly the law of *niddah* [Rema's injunction against *niddot*] is a precautionary measure without any real halakhic foundation. For there we learned, if a *zav* became a *ba'al keri*, or a *niddah*

hygienic precautions, we may presume that women, even during their menstrual flow, can remain clean and therefore would be permitted to learn, pray, or touch a Torah.[32] Fourth, *Shulḥan Arukh* explicitly states that *niddot* may touch a Torah as long as their hands are clean, and Rema (through his silence) agrees.

The essential right of women to touch a *Sefer Torah* is mentioned by many other authorities. Those *posekim* (rabbinic decisors) who record that some women do not touch a *Sefer Torah* invariably speak of this practice as being a "mere stringency" or as having "no [real] basis." For example, the school of Rashi states: "There are women who refrain from entering a synagogue when they are *niddot* and from touching the *Sefer:* this is a mere stringency, and they do not have to do this."[33]

---

expelled seed, there is a difference of opinion between the first tanna and Rabbi Judah about whether she needs immersion. Because even if they immerse, they would retain their status of *tumah*, as one would still be a *zav*, while the other would still be a *niddah*. From here we can conclude that if the *niddah* did not expel seed, even in the time of Ezra's enactment, she would be permitted to do everything. Certainly this would be the case today after the enactment has been nullified."

Note *Magen Avraham* to *Shulḥan Arukh*, Oraḥ Ḥayyim 88:2. Commenting on the first view of Rema he states: "This requires much consideration. For there are those who say that women are biblically obligated to recite Grace After Meals. If so, how can women be exempt from the performance of a biblical law, by a custom which has no foundation?"

32. In addition, if today we follow the view of Rema (in his cities), that women may not touch *Sifrei Torah* during their flow, why should it not be similarly prohibited for these women to enter a synagogue or pray or mention God's name? Moreover, Rema, as already indicated, suspends his *ḥumrah* on Rosh ha-Shanah and Yom Kippur, days when women attended synagogue. Preventing *niddot* from coming to shul on the High Holy Days would have caused these women great sadness. This emotional sadness had the power to override the issue of physical uncleanliness. Today when many women attend public tefillah every Shabbat and holiday, would Rema's suspension be operative on a weekly basis? Would it not be painful for today's *niddot* to remain at home on Shabbat or the holidays? Note that when Rema states that his *ḥumrah* was cancelled on the High Holy Days because of the sadness involved, he used the expression "on the High Holy Days and [days] like that."

33. *Sefer ha-Pardes*, chap. 271, Laws of Niddah 3b, Ehrenreich ed., p. 3; note that in *Sefer ha-Orah*, vol. 2, chap. 1, in the Buber ed., p. 167; and in *Maḥzor Vitry*, end of chap. 498, in the Horowitz ed., p. 606, the words "and from touching the *Sefer*" do not appear. See also *Issur ve-Heter*, chap. 306.

It seems clear from the context of *Sifrei Rashi* that Rashi's closing words, *aval makom tahara lahem ve-yafeh hen osot* (in *Sefer ha-Orah* the text is *aval makom tahara hu ve-yafeh hen osot*), apply only to entry into a synagogue and not to touching a *Sefer Torah*. This can be fortified by the following Ashkenazic authorities who clearly relate *ve-yafeh* to entering a synagogue and make no mention whatsoever of the *Sefer Torah* issue. *Haggahot Maimuniyyot*, chap. 4, *Hilkhot Tefillah*, letter *gimmel; Mordechai*, Berakhot 3:86 end; *Sefer ha-Agur* 1388; *Ravyah*, Berakhot, chap. 68. Moreover, the term *makom* (rather than *derekh* or *minhag*) relates more easily to a synagogue than to a *Sefer Torah*.

The only *rishon* (early authority) that I am aware of who *clearly* suggests that it is improper for women to touch a holy book during their days of *tumah* is *Or Zaru'a*, who explicitly states, however, that this minhag is a "mere stringency."[34] The later authorities seem to reject the opinion of *Or Zaru'a* as evidenced by *Shulḥan Arukh ha-Rav*, who states: "And the custom of some women not to mention the name of God while they are *niddot*, or not to touch the *Sefer* . . . this custom has no real basis."[35]

In our contemporary period this opinion was followed by Rabbi Eliyahu Shmuel Wind (a *posek* of the *edah ḥaredit* community in Jerusalem) in his work *Sugah ba-Shoshanim*, who writes: "The custom of women who are *niddot* not to touch a *Sefer*—this custom has no real basis."[36] The preponderance of opinion supports the position that it is in fact permissible for women to touch *Sifrei Torah*.[37]

* * *

Our analysis of the laws of *niddut* and *ba'al keri* indicates that there are no fundamental halakhic barriers that would prevent women from touching a *Sefer Torah*. While one should be sensitive

34. *Or Zaru'a* 1:360 states: "There are women who follow the custom of not entering a synagogue or touching a holy book during their days of *tumah*, and this is mere stringency, and what they are doing is proper." While the *Or Zaru'a* does say *ve-yafeh hen osot*, "what they are doing is proper," he indicates that it is a mere stringency. Whether the term *Sefer* used by *Or Zaru'a* applies only to a *Sefer Torah* or to all *sefarim* is unclear. Note Rabbi Eliyahu Shmuel Wind in *Sugah ba-Shoshanim*, Laws of Taharah 27:17. If *Sefer* means all holy books, then one who follows *ve-yafeh* with regard to a *Sefer Torah* should also not touch any holy book.

35. *Shulḥan Arukh ha-Rav*, Oraḥ Ḥayyim. 88:2.

36. Rabbi Wind in *Sugah ba-Shoshanim*, Laws of Taharah 27:17. The opinion of authorities like *Binyamin Ze'ev*, chap. 153, quoted in *Magen Avraham* to *Shulḥan Arukh*, Oraḥ Ḥayyim 88:2, and Rashal quoted by Taz in *Shulḥan Arukh*, Oraḥ Ḥayyim 88:2, that *niddot* should not look at the *Sefer Torah* when it is shown to the people is understood by Rabbi Wind to be a unique halakhah of *hagbah*, from which no conclusion can be deduced with regard to *niddot* touching a *Sefer Torah*. See *Sugah ba-Shoshanim*, Laws of Taharah 27:18. After stating that *niddot* should not enter a synagogue, look at the *Sefer Torah*, or pray near their friends, *Binyamin Ze'ev*, chap. 153, concludes that this is done "out of *kavod* rather than because of a prohibition." Note *Sugah ba-Shoshanim*, Laws of Taharah 27:18, who states that the custom of women not to look at the Torah during *hagbah* is done "out of *kavod* rather than because of a prohibition."

37. *Responsa Yeḥaveh Da'at*, vol. 3, siman 8, states that *niddot* are permitted to follow the stringencies of not entering into a synagogue, not touching a *Sefer Torah*, and not looking at the *Sefer Torah* when it is shown to the people. Here again, Rav Ovadiah is saying that *niddot* may be stringent, clearly indicating that they need not follow this *ḥumrah*. Rav Ovadiah, however, states that *niddot* may not refrain from praying or reciting blessings.

to those women who wish to follow the *ḥumrah* of Rema, equal sensitivity is required for the many women who sincerely feel that holding the *Sefer Torah* would allow them to feel much more a part of communal tefillah. We must ask ourselves whether the common practice of banning women from carrying the Torah justifies the numerous benefits that would accrue from adopting this practice.

Prayer is a moment of deep relationship between the human being and God. For many that moment is more deeply expressed when carrying, holding, touching, kissing the deepest reflection of God's love—the Torah. The right of women to experience this moment—indeed, their right to have contact with the *Sefer Torah*—has a clear basis in the halakhah.[38]

---

38. The *meḥiẓah* of our new shul in Riverdale is built in such a way that when the Torah is carried through the men's section, it is virtually impossible for the women to kiss it. (The *meḥiẓah* bisects the sanctuary, merging into the walls which surround an elevated *bimah* in the center of the shul and an elevated *aron kodesh* against the eastern wall. Both the *bimah* and the *aron* are therefore equally placed within the men's and women's sections.) A group of women asked that the Torah be carried through the *ezrat nashim*. They were sincere, sensitive people whose request was deep and real. Since it was felt that it would be immodest for the ḥazzan to walk through the women's "domain," it was decided that after the Torah was taken through the men's area, it would be transferred to a woman who would then carry the Torah through the women's section.

As expected, the decision promoted much discussion. The intensity of the debate was indicative of the seriousness of the issue and the earnestness of those deliberating the matter. A few women, not accustomed to this procedure, were upset. Other women, excited by their involvement, found it difficult to understand the feelings of those who were hesitant or even loath to come near the Torah. The penning of the original version of this chapter, for publication in *Tradition*, was in part prompted by the need for all involved to clearly understand the halakhic concerns related to this matter.

Chapter Eight

Additional Issues

During the course of our study, we have in passing attempted to respond to arguments presented by those opposing women's tefillah groups.[1] Some criticisms deserve further analysis.

AN INCOMPLETE FULFILLMENT OF PRAYER

Some opponents of women's tefillah groups claim that since *devarim she-bi-kedushah* must be omitted from these services, the mitzvah of prayer is incomplete (*ha-mitzvot hen she-lo bishlemuton*). It would be preferable, these critics claim, for women to be present at public prayer, where they can fulfill the mitzvah of prayer in its complete form by hearing Kaddish, Kedushah, and Barekhu,[2] and by praying in synagogue, where "attendance carries a guaranteed return. . . . 'The Holy One, blessed be He, does not disdain the prayer of the multitude' refers only to *tefillah be-ẓibbur*, not the prayer of groups of individuals, of any sex, which do not constitute a *minyan*."[3]

Yet *gedolei Torah* (Torah scholars) and yeshiva educators have never applied this reasoning to women's groups. No one has ever suggested, for example, that a minyan of older men be brought in so that female students at "Breuer's" (Beth Jacob High School of Yeshiva Rabbi Samson Raphael Hirsch) or Lubavitch or Yeshiva University High School for Girls could pray each morning in the context of *tefillah be-ẓibbur*. All-female prayer groups are the norm

1. The criticisms already dealt with are: (a) *ziyyuf ha-Torah*, falsification of Torah (see chap. 4, end); (b) the contention that women are obligated to hear the public Torah reading (see chap. 6, end); (c) reading from a Torah scroll for reasons other than fulfilling the commandment of public Torah reading (see chap. 6, n. 44).
2. Rabbi Schachter, "Ze'i Lakh be-Ikvei ha-Ẓon," pp. 118–119.
3. Rabbi Bleich, "Religious Experience? *tefillah be-ẓibbur*?" pp. 146–149.

in these high schools and seminaries, even though the young women have reached the age of mitzvot.

In any event, women are not obligated to participate in public prayer, i.e., in *devarim she-bi-kedushah* or *tefillah be-ẓibbur.*[4] Their participation in halakhic women's tefillah groups is therefore a fulfillment of their complete responsibility in prayer.[5]

A more correct formulation of the issue is whether women should be permitted to fulfill their requirements of tefillah in a way which brings them to a higher religious level, even though this would in the process eliminate their presence at public worship services, where they could "receive credit" for *devarim she-bi-kedushah* and *tefillah be-ẓibbur.* In broader terms, may one fulfill an obligatory mitzvah in a subjectively preferred manner and in the process choose to forgo other, separate, nonobligatory acts?[6]

For some women, it may in fact be halakhically *preferable* to attend women's prayer groups. Many participants have said they lack kavvanah (intention or devotion) in the synagogue setting. The halakhic question for them is whether women's tefillah groups with greater kavvanah should supersede public prayer with less kavvanah. An understanding of the principle of kavvanah within the prayer experience is necessary to resolve this issue.

---

4. See above, chap. 4, for a discussion of the exemption of women from public prayer, and chap. 6, for a discussion of the exemption of women from public Torah reading.

5. Rabbi Schachter, in "Ẓe'i Lakh be-Ikvei ha-Ẓon," p. 119, notes that according to some *posekim* (rabbinic decisors) women are required to hear *Parashat Zakhor*, the special Torah portion for the Sabbath before Purim, with a minyan. It would appear that according to those authorities, if a women's tefillah group read *Parashat Zakhor* without saying Barekhu, this would constitute an incomplete mitzvah. Yet it is common practice to read *Zakhor* from a Torah, for women who missed the regular reading, even though the *berakhot* are not said.

Note also *Sefer ha-Ḥinnukh*, commandment 603. The author maintains that women are exempt from *Parashat Zakhor.* See also *Kaf ha-Ḥayyim* to *Shulḥan Arukh*, Oraḥ Ḥayyim 685:30, who states that while women are obliged to remember the incident of Amalek, they are exempt from hearing *Parashat Zakhor.* And even those who maintain that women are required to hear it may not demand that they specifically hear it on *Shabbat Zakhor*, when *Parashat Zakhor* is read, but that they hear the portion of Amalek sometime during the year (for example, when *Parashat Ki Teẓe* is read).

For a fine survey of a woman's obligation in respect to *Parashat Zakhor*, see Rabbi Auerbach, *Halikhot Beitah*, pp. 63–66.

6. This formulation of the question was presented by Rabbi Saul Berman in a lecture on women's prayer groups given at Lincoln Square Synagogue, December 10, 1986. The tape of the lecture is available through Lincoln Square Synagogue in New York City.

Kavvanah in Prayer

• Of the various types of kavvanah in prayer, the first has to do with understanding the literal meaning of the words recited.

The Mishnah states: "The pious people of old used to wait an hour before praying in order that they might concentrate their thoughts upon their Father in heaven."[7]

The implication is that in earlier times pious people meditated an hour before prayer; by the time the Mishnah was written, however, this was no longer commonly practiced. Nonetheless, it was essential that every word of the prayer service be understood.

A baraita quoted in the Talmud states that while it is optimal to have kavvanah throughout the Shemoneh Esreh, b'-de-avad (post-facto), it would be sufficient if one had kavvanah only while reciting the first paragraph (the paragraph of *Avot*).

> When one recites the tefillah [i.e., the Shemoneh Esreh], he must say all the blessings attentively, and if he cannot say all attentively, he should say one attentively. Rav Ḥiyya said in the name of Rav Safra, who had it from a member of the school of rabbis: This one should be the blessing of the Patriarchs (*Avot*).[8]

Rambam accordingly concludes: "One who has prayed but did not sustain kavvanah should repeat the prayer with kavvanah. But if one had kavvanah for the first blessing, he need not [pray] again."[9]

Concurring with Rambam, *Shulḥan Arukh* states: "One who is praying [the Shemoneh Esreh] should sustain kavvanah for all the blessings. And if he can't have proper kavvanah for all the blessings, he should minimally have kavvanah in *Avot.*"[10]

Rema adds: "And today we do not repeat [the Shemoneh Esreh] for lack of kavvanah. Because even if one repeats the prayer, it is

---

7. Mishnah Berakhot 5:1, Berakhot 30b. Some suggest that *ḥassidim ha-rishonim*, "the pious people of earlier times," refers to the *vatikim*, people of exceptional piety. See Berakhot 9b and 26a.

See Tosafot Yom Tov to Mishnah Berakhot 5:1, s.v. *sha'ah aḥat*, and *Tiferet Yisrael, Yakhin*, n. 2, where *sha'ah* is defined as *sha'ah davkah* and not a short interval. *Magen Avraham* to *Shulḥan Arukh*, Oraḥ Ḥayyim 93:1, understands *sha'ah* as being one-twelfth of the day period. This period of meditation refers to the pious; others would wait just a few moments to gather their thoughts prior to prayer. See also *Shulḥan Arukh*, Oraḥ Ḥayyim 90:20.

8. Berakhot 34b.

9. Rambam, *Code*, Laws of Prayer 10:1.

10. *Shulḥan Arukh*, Oraḥ Ḥayyim 101:1.

virtually certain that he will still not have *kavvanah.* Under these circumstances, why repeat the prayer?"[11]

It is clear that over a period of time the level of *kavvanah* declined.[12] Although Rema concludes that one should not repeat the Shemoneh Esreh if *kavvanah* is lacking, understanding the words is surely central to prayer. Optimally, kavvanah is necessary throughout Shemoneh Esreh, minimally, during *Avot.*

• The second component of kavvanah in prayer is the kavvanah of recognizing that one is praying to fulfill the mitzvah of prayer. *Shulḥan Arukh* states: "There are opinions that mitzvot do not require kavvanah [referring to the kavvanah that one is fulfilling the mitzvah], and there are those who say that they do require kavvanah, and this is the law."[13]

While *Magen Avraham* suggests that this halakhah only applies to biblical and not rabbinical commandments,[14] the Vilna Gaon applies it to both.[15] *Ḥayyei Adam* maintains that kavvanah is considered lacking when it is clear that the mitzvah is not being performed. For example, if one is studying Torah, and learns the Shema while doing so (Deuteronomy 6:4–9), the fact that this occurred during a study session is a clear indication that there was no intent to fulfill the mitzvah of praying the Shema. However, if one recites the Shema in the context of a prayer service, even if there is no active intent to fulfill the mitzvah of Shema, its recitation within

---

11. Rema, ibid.

12. The decline in kavvanah is discernible in respect to the Shema as well. Mishnah Berakhot 2:5, Berakhot 16a states: "A bridegroom is exempt from reciting the Shema on the first night [of his marriage]." This is because the bridegroom, intent on performing his marital duty, lacks the proper concentration (kavvanah) to recite the Shema.

A thousand years later, Tosafot to Berakhot 17b, s.v. *Rav Shisha*, states that people no longer pray with such concentration even in normal circumstances, hence the bridegroom should read the Shema on his wedding night. In fact, says Tosafot, were he not to recite the Shema, he would appear arrogant, as if trying to create the impression that he normally prays with proper kavvanah. Here again, kavvanah is crucial in the recitation of Shema, but the decline in kavvanah over the course of history is readily observed.

The Mishnah does not speak of the bride because women are exempt from reciting Keri'at Shema (see Berakhot 20a). As indicated in chap. 2, with the passage of time women were obligated to accept the Yoke of the Kingdom of Heaven and recite Shema.

13. *Shulḥan Arukh*, Oraḥ Ḥayyim 60:4. See Eruvin 95b, Pesaḥim 114b, Rosh ha-Shanah 28b, where this issue is debated.

14. *Magen Avraham* to *Shulḥan Arukh*, Oraḥ Ḥayyim 60:3 in the name of Radbaz.

15. Gra to *Shulḥan Arukh*, Oraḥ Ḥayyim 489, quoted in *Mishnah Berurah* to *Shulḥan Arukh*, Oraḥ Ḥayyim 60:10.

the service is sufficient for this type of kavvanah. It is viewed as a kind of passive *kavvanah* which is deemed sufficient.[16]

Mishnah Berurah, however, declares: "All this is post-facto. Optimally it is certain that one should be careful to have the intention before every mitzvah to fulfill the obligation of performing the mitzvah."[17]

Indeed, authorities distinguish between commandments of action and commandments of speech. R. Jonah Gerondi states:

> Even those who rule that mitzvot do not require intention only rule so where the mitzvah is the performance of some act, since here the act takes the place of the intention. . . . Mitzvot which, however, depend on speech alone (like prayer) certainly require intent, since the recital is to be performed with the heart. If, in these cases, the worshipper has no intent, and he performs no overt act, he has not performed any mitzvah whatever.[18]

• A third element of kavvanah is the kavvanah of recognizing that one is praying in the presence of God. *Ḥiddushei Rav Ḥayyim ha-Levi*, Rav Soloveitchik's grandfather, analyzes this form of kavvanah by noting a contradiction in Rambam.

Rambam first states:

> What is meant by kavvanah of the heart? Any tefillah [referring to the Shemoneh Esreh] which lacks kavvanah is not considered tefillah. If one prays without kavvanah he must repeat the tefillah with kavvanah. If his thoughts are confused and his heart burdened, he is forbidden to pray until his mind is calmed [i.e., he regains his composure]. Therefore, if one returns from a journey and is tired or distressed, he should not pray until his mind is calm. Our sages have said, one should wait three days until his mind rests and is cleared, and [only] afterwards should he pray.[19]

---

16. See *Ḥayyei Adam*, Laws of Zehirut Mitzvah 68:9, and *Ḥayyei Adam* quoted in *Mishnah Berurah*, ibid. This principle seems to apply to biblical law. In rabbinical law, the mitzvah is considered fulfilled without "active" or "passive" kavvanah.

17. *Mishnah Berurah* to *Shulḥan Arukh*, Oraḥ Ḥayyim 60:10.

18. Rabbi Jonah Gerondi at the end of the first chapter of Berakhot, s.v. *omnam*. See *Beit Yosef* to *Tur Shulḥan Arukh*, Oraḥ Ḥayyim 589, s.v. *veẓarikh she'yekavein*. See also *Ḥayyei Adam*, Laws of Zehirut Mitzvah 68:9.

19. Rambam, *Code*, Laws of Prayer 4:15. See Berakhot 30b. See also Eruvin 65a: "The father of Samuel after having returned from a journey did not pray for three days." Apparently, he was tired, confused, and distracted and lacked the proper kavvanah. The same talmudic passage adds: "Said Rav Ḥiyya ben Ashi in the name of Rav, anyone whose mind is not calm should not pray."

See *Kesef Mishneh* to Rambam, *Laws of Prayer* 4:15, s.v. *lefikhakh* and *maẓa dato*.

Rambam then states:

> One who prayed [the Shemoneh Esreh] but did not have kavvanah should repeat the prayer with proper kavvanah. But if one had kavvanah in the first blessing [*Avot*], he need not repeat [the prayer].[20]

The contradiction is obvious. Rambam first declares that kavvanah is necessary throughout the Shemoneh Esreh. Without kavvanah one should not pray even if it means waiting three days for the proper devotion required for tefillah. Rambam then proclaims that kavvanah during the blessing of *Avot* is sufficient.

In resolving the contradiction, *Ḥiddushei Rav Ḥayyim ha-Levi* maintains that Rambam distinguishes between two types of kavvanah: the kavvanah of *perush ha-millim*, understanding the words being said, and the kavvanah of *da lifnei mi atah omed*, recognizing that one is praying in the presence of God.

> It would seem that there are two kinds of kavvanah in prayer. The first is the kavvanah of the meaning of the words. This is the foundation of kavvanah. The second is the kavvanah that one realizes that he stands before God. . . . It would seem that this [second] aspect of kavvanah is integral to the act of prayer. If his heart does not turn from other things, and he does not see himself as standing before God and praying, then this is not an act of prayer. He is like one who is busy with other matters and not involved in the mitzvah act (*mitasek*). Therefore, lack of this kind of kavvanah prevents proper prayer in all of the Shemoneh Esreh. For when he is involved in other things, he is judged as not having prayed at all, as if he skipped those words. Certainly, since this affects the very essence of prayer, it prevents proper prayer in any of the Shemoneh Esreh. When he has kavvanah and realizes what he is doing and knows that he stands in prayer, yet he does not know the meaning of the words, then this is a matter only concerning prayer—an added law of kavvanah. It is this aspect which is the subject of the Gemara in Tractate Berakhot: "He who prays must have the proper kavvanah in all the *berakhot*. If he cannot have kavvanah in all of them, then he should have kavvanah in one of them. Rav Ḥiyya in the name of Rav Safra in the name of one of the students said: He should have kavvanah in the *Avot*."[21]

---

20. Rambam, Laws of Prayer 10:1, based on Berakhot 34b.

21. *Ḥiddushei Rav Ḥayyim ha-Levi*, second comment in the volume. The translation here is based on Rabbi David Derovan's translation, published by the National Commission on Torah Education, Stone-Saperstein Center for Jewish Education, Yeshiva University, in the *Halakha Yomit* prepared for Yeshiva University High School Seminar, February 12–16, 1976.

The kavvanah of understanding the words is necessary throughout the Shemoneh Esreh, but post-facto, knowing the meaning of *Avot* is enough. However, awareness of being in the presence of God is, for Rav Ḥayyim, even more fundamental than kavvanah of understanding the words. It falls into the category of *mitasek*. Without this knowledge it is as if the words were not recited, "he is judged as not having prayed at all." This awareness is necessary throughout the tefillah.

Kavvanah is therefore crucial to the prayer experience, intrinsic to the very essence of tefillah. To borrow from the terminology of Rav Yosef Dov Soloveitchik, there exists the *pe'ulah*, the action of prayer, and the *kiyyum*, the fulfillment of prayer. In tefillah, *pe'ulah* relates to the enunciation of the external words; *kiyyum*, to the kavvanah, the inner intent while praying. In the case of prayer, *pe'ulah* merges with *kiyyum*. They are inextricably bound. Without kavvanah, prayer is devoid of substance; it lacks meaning; it is body without soul. Explicating the position of Rambam, Rav Soloveitchik says:

> Thus, for Rambam, "service of the heart" (*avodah she-ba-lev*) encompasses man's whole being, and vocalizing the words of prayer is not enough. The heart must do its share. Of course, "service" involves external acts and performance. . . . But the act of prayer (*ma'aseh*) cannot in itself exhaust all that is implied in the concept of "service of the heart," which encompasses all of man's being, wherever he is and whatever opportunities are available to him, both his joys and sorrows, his grief as well as his rejoicing. . . . The act of prayer is merely the performance (*pe'ulah*) of the precept while its fulfillment (*kiyyum*) remains within the realm of the heart.
>
> The best proof of this is the fact that even those sages who argued that "intention" was not a necessary component in the observance of the commandments, admitted that conscious intent is a prerequisite for prayer, for its very fulfillment must come from the heart.[22]

* * *

The relevance of kavvanah to women's tefillah groups is clear. Women are mandated to pray and should do so in ways which allow them to maximize their kavvanah. If they choose women's prayer groups as most conducive for a heightened prayer experience, and in the process forfeit an unrelated, nonobligatory opportunity in

---

22. Pinchas H. Peli, *On Repentance in the Thought and Oral Discourses of Rabbi Joseph B. Soloveitchik*, pp. 82–83. Rav Soloveitchik made his observation based on Rambam, *Code*, Laws of Repentance 10:3.

connection with *devarim she-bi-kedushah* or *tefillah be-ẓibbur*, they have that halakhic right.[23]

How, then, can it be said that the option of *tefillah be-ẓibbur* is superior to increased kavvanah in a more private realm? The answer, says Rav Moshe Feinstein, in response to a man who asked whether to pray *be-ẓibbur* even though private prayer might yield additional kavvanah, is that the *possibility* of increased kavvanah cannot outweigh the *definite fulfillment* of the obligation to pray with a *ẓibbur*.[24]

But women have no such obligation! Just as the halakhah creates separate rules and obligations for men and women, it grants them different options for religious fulfillment. In this case, women have been granted the option of non-*ẓibbur* tefillah if they prefer it.

THE APPEAL TO CONTEMPORARY TORAH SCHOLARS

A most troubling component of the contemporary debate on women's prayer groups has been the misleading use of the appeal to the authority of our generation's Torah scholars.

> And behold, it is well known that the two great sages of our generation, to whom all of us turn for their opinion, our teacher, the Gaon Rav Yosef Dov Soloveitchik, and our teacher, the Gaon Rav Moshe Feinstein, both oppose the practices mentioned above, i.e., *hakafot* specifically designated for women, "minyanim" [for women] for prayer, the reading of the Torah Scroll, and the reading of the Megillah.[25]

But these two Torah scholars had ample opportunity to publicly condemn such groups, and they very carefully held back from any *issur* (prohibition) and always held open the real possibility of these groups functioning within the halakhic community.

---

23. Nor is it appropriate to demand that women have kavvanah in the normative public prayer setting. Not everyone is spiritually motivated in the same way. For some women, the mainstream service is optimal. For others it is difficult and at times impossible to pray with deep devotion at regular public services. Their feelings ought to be respected.

24. Rav Moshe Feinstein, *Iggerot Mosheh*, Oraḥ Ḥayyim 3:7.

25. Rabbi Schachter, "Ze'i Lakh be-Ikvei ha-Ẓon," p. 126.

See also the statement of the five *Roshei Yeshiva* from Yeshiva University, and Rabbi Abba Bronspigel's amplification of its content.

Rav Yosef Dov Soloveitchik

In the early 1970s, Rav Soloveitchik indicated to some rabbis that under certain guidelines, women's tefillah groups are permitted.[26] On one occasion, the Rav carefully detailed the format of women's tefillah groups, and suggested substitute texts for the *devarim she-bi-kedushah* that women would omit in their prayer groups.[27] Some have claimed that in recent years, Rav Soloveitchik, concerned about fragmentation within the Jewish community, has been less forthcoming. Nevertheless, the Rav has never objected to women's prayer groups on halakhic grounds.

This is not to say that the Rav has never been quoted as objecting to a specific practice of these groups. But opponents have unfortunately been willing to generalize these objections and cast them as total opposition to women's prayer groups. For example, Rabbi Moshe Meiselman outlined the procedure whereby some women's prayer groups allow the personal Birkhot ha-Torah to be said out loud before the reading from the *Sefer Torah*.[28] He then notes that "My revered teacher, Rabbi Joseph B. Soloveitchik, has told me that he is *opposed to such aliyot* and has never told any rabbi that they are permitted."[29]

Yet Rabbi Kenneth Auman remarked: "Long before the current controversy, Rabbi Moshe Meiselman quotes his 'revered teacher Rabbi Joseph B. Soloveitchik' as being *opposed to women's prayer groups*."[30]

Rabbi Meiselman, himself no fan of these groups, was careful to indicate that the opposition was only to a specific form—the recitation of blessings before and after the Torah reading.[31] But he is

---

26. Rabbi Shlomo Riskin on numerous occasions indicated that Rav Soloveitchik had told him that women's tefillah groups are halakhically permissible.

27. Rabbi Saul Berman, in a lecture given at Lincoln Square Synagogue on December 10, 1986, told of a colleague who asked Rav Soloveitchik about women's tefillah groups. The Rav responded very positively and suggested substitute texts for the *devarim she-bi-kedushah* women would omit. The tape of Rabbi Berman's lecture is available through Lincoln Square Synagogue in New York City.

28. Rabbi Meiselman, *Jewish Woman in Jewish Law*, pp. 144–145.

29. Ibid., p. 197, n. 64 (emphasis added).

30. Rabbi Kenneth Auman, "Orthodoxy Requires Sage Discussion," pp. 145–146 (emphasis added).

See also the statement by the five rabbis from Yeshiva University, Rabbi Bronspigel's amplification, and Rabbi Schachter's "Ẓe'i Lakh be-Ikvei ha-Ẓon," p. 126.

31. As indicated above, other rabbis have quoted the Rav as suggesting substitute texts for the *devarim she-bi-kedushah* women would omit when coming to the synagogue. See above, chap. 6, end, for a further discussion of the recitation by women of blessings before and after the Torah reading.

quoted by others as the authority presenting the Rav's opposition to the groups per se.

Rav Moshe Feinstein

Rav Moshe Feinstein states in an opinion issued on his stationery through his grandson and assistant, Rabbi Mordechai Tendler:

> In reality, it is hard to find a situation where this problem [of women whose motivation is insincere][32] does not exist. Therefore, it is hard for us to say that any "women's *minyan*" does not have this problem.
>
> And only in the theoretical realm itself can one say that if there is a group of righteous women whose intention is purely for the sake of Heaven without intending to undermine God's Torah or Jewish practice, then, of course, why prevent them from praying together?
>
> And they may also read from the Torah Scroll, provided that they take care not to do it in such a way that one might erroneously believe it to be actually a public reading, i.e., they should not say the Torah blessings in public [out loud]. They should either rely on the blessings which they said earlier, or in the event that they have not yet said the blessings, they may say them to themselves.[33]
>
> There are, of course, additional details included in our *Iggerot Mosheh* which one should take careful note of in this matter. Each *ba'al hora'ah* [arbiter of halakhah] should conduct himself in this matter in a way which is in line with this outlook.[34]

Those who are aware of the careful formulation of the written and oral responsa of Rav Soloveitchik and Rav Feinstein know that they do not hesitate to speak in definitive terms, declaring a matter to be halakhically permitted or prohibited, when they deem it necessary. At other times, these great Torah authorities adopt a more neutral stance, neither condemning nor condoning. They often reveal per-

---

32. See Rav Feinstein's *Iggerot Mosheh*, Oraḥ Ḥayyim 4:49.

33. Rav Feinstein is concerned about *ziyyuf ha-Torah*. By reciting blessings "one might erroneously believe it [the reading from the Torah scroll] to be actually a public reading." It can be argued that participants in women's tefillah groups are fully aware that without Barekhu their Torah reading is halakhically private and not public in nature. Moreover, the Torah reading is part of the larger women's tefillah service, where Kaddish, Kedushah, and Barekhu are not recited. The likelihood of women believing that their Torah reading is public and representing themselves as participating in a minyan is virtually nil.

See chap. 4, end (*ziyyuf ha-Torah*), and chap. 6, end (blessings at the Torah), for a further discussion of these issues.

34. The teshuvah (dated 4 Sivan 5743) has been widely circulated. Rav Feinstein's opinion was translated by Rabbi Louis Sherby.

sonal reservations on a particular issue, without declaring a halakhic *issur*. In these situations, it is crucial not to confuse concerns about public policy with halakhic *pesak* (binding opinion). Their equivocal position on certain matters is usually a purposeful attempt on their part to allow rabbis to evaluate the situation or conditions prevalent in their own community and then decide (*pasken*) accordingly.

This is the gist of Rav Feinstein's position vis-à-vis women's tefillah groups. He neither supports their initiation nor insists they be discontinued, but leaves it to each individual rabbi to decide. His concluding sentence underscores this point: "Each *ba'al hora'ah* should conduct himself in this matter in a way which is in line with this outlook."

For Rav Feinstein, women's tefillah groups are halakhically permissible if conducted by women who fulfill the criteria of sincerity outlined in *Iggerot Mosheh*. Whether the women involved fall into this category is a decision to be made by each *ba'al hora'ah*.

In a subsequent explanation of Rav Feinstein's position Rabbi Mordechai Tendler wrote:

> Upon consultation with my grandfather the following clarification [concerning women's *tefillah* groups] is being offered. As stated in my letter the detailed discussion was purely in a theoretical sense. My grandfather pragmatically feels that the possibility of a group of women or for that matter men existing in any one community which will fulfill the lengthy philosophical criteria mentioned in his printed *teshuvah* is extremely remote. Therefore, realistically speaking he doesn't commend or actually condone the establishment of women's prayer groups.[35]

Here Rav Feinstein reemphasizes that participants in women's tefillah groups should be the most sincere women who fulfill "lengthy philosophical criteria," criteria which are so extensive that the possibility of finding such women "is extremely remote." Nonetheless, while not commending or condoning the establishment of women's prayer groups, Rav Feinstein does not denounce them either. He never claims that women's tefillah groups are halakhically prohibited. In fact, he maintains that they are in principle halakhically permissible. And while Rav Feinstein states "that the possibility of a group of women or for that matter men existing in any one

35. This letter, written in English, has been widely circulated.

community which will fulfill the lengthy philosophical criteria . . . is extremely remote," he leaves open the possibility that if enough women who fulfill his criteria might be found they could conduct and participate in women's prayer groups.[36]

Rav Feinstein dismisses the *entire theoretical basis* of those who object to women's tefillah groups. The most sincere women need not be advised that *tefillah be-ẓibbur* is preferable to private prayer; the existence of women's prayer groups is not in and of itself in any way antithetical to the spirit or letter of the halakhah; and participating in such groups, including the reading from a *Sefer Torah*, is in no way a *ziyyuf ha-Torah*. This is not to say that Rav Feinstein, on a practical level, had no serious reservations about these groups. But to quote him as an authority in a discussion of the theoretical arguments against these groups is misleading at best. Rav Feinstein's position is exactly analogous to his published *teshuvah* on women wearing a tallit during tefillah.[37] While on a practical level he might question the motives of women who want this option, he will in no way allow himself to say that it is prohibited when, in fact, it is a valid halakhic option.

* * *

It should also be noted that Rabbi Shlomo Goren, the former Ashkenazi Chief Rabbi of Israel, in a responsum that was intended as a private, confidential *pesak*, but which has since been widely circulated, concluded that women's tefillah groups are halakhically permissible and that women may recite *devarim she-bi-kedushah*. Only one group follows this opinion.[38]

---

36. Rav Feinstein's position in his teshuvah may follow the same reasoning developed by Rambam in his analysis of whether women may study Torah (see above, chap. 5). In theory, both *Talmud Torah* and prayer groups for women are permissible. In reality, however, there was concern that the study of Torah by women would lead to trivialities (Rambam), and that the women involved in prayer groups are insincere (Rav Feinstein).

As indicated (chap. 5), Rambam did not prohibit women from studying Torah if it would not be used for vain purposes. And today, women study Torah on all levels, as it does not lead to trivialities.

Similarly, Rav Feinstein does not prohibit women's tefillah groups if the participants' "intention is purely for the sake of Heaven," and indeed would see them as permissible if conducted by sincere women.

37. Rav Feinstein, *Iggerot Mosheh*, Oraḥ Ḥayyim 4:49.

38. The responsum of Rabbi Goren is dated 11 Kislev, 5735 (November 25, 1974) when he was the Ashkenazi Chief Rabbi of Israel. It was written by Rabbi Goren as an individual rabbi, but was issued on the stationery of the Chief (Ashkenazi) Rabbi of Israel.

Rabbi Goren asserts that the right of women to say *devarim she-bi-kedushah* at

Also in a *shiur* (Torah session) given at Stern College, Yeshiva University (Spring 1986), Rabbi Avraham Shapiro, the Ashkenazi Chief Rabbi of Israel, was asked about women's prayer groups. He responded that he personally did not condone the services, as he saw little value in them. When I asked him afterwards whether his statement constituted a halakhic *pesak*, i.e., whether in fact, women's tefillah groups were halakhically *assur* (prohibited), he responded in clear terms: "I did not say that these prayer groups are *assur.*"

Rabbi Shapiro affirmed this position in a letter he recently wrote. He concludes that a "woman's minyan where *devarim she-bi-kedushah* (are recited) is contrary to halakhah and minhag." The implication is clear. A woman's tefillah group where *devarim she-bi-kedushah* are not said is not halakhically prohibited.[39]

---

women's tefillah groups depends on whether they may recite blessings on commandments they are exempt from performing (see chapter 5, note 25, chapter 6, note 17 and chapter 7, note 29).

Rambam states that women may not recite such blessings (see Rambam, *Code* Laws of Ẓiẓit 3:9). It follows, writes Rabbi Goren, that from this perspective, *devarim she-bi-kedushah* must be omitted at women's prayer groups.

Rabbenu Tam is of the opposite opinion. Women may recite blessings on commandments they are exempt from performing (see Rosh ha-Shanah 33a, Tosafot, s.v. *ha*). Similarly, Rabbi Goren maintains that from this point of view, the exemption of women from *devarim she-bi-kedushah* does not deny them the right to recite these prayers at a women's service.

Rabbi Goren concludes: "We [referring to the Ashkenazi community] follow the view of Rabbenu Tam. . . . [Indeed] on all holidays, women recite blessings on positive commandments fixed by time. It is logical, therefore, to conclude that women may arrange a minyan for public prayer and recite Kaddish, Kedushah, and Barekhu. This is not considered a blessing said in vain. Just as it is permissible for women to recite blessings with the name of God on positive time-bound commandments they are exempt from performing and include the word *ve-ẓivanu* ('and you have commanded us'), [so too] may they pray in a minyan for themselves."

Rabbi Goren strictly limits this *heter* (permission) to women's tefillah groups, which are, of course, attended exclusively by women. In a conversation with this writer (Spring 1989), Rabbi Goren affirmed his support for his responsum.

Virtually all women's prayer groups have decided not to rely on this teshuvah and have chosen instead to omit these liturgical items in consonance with the arguments presented in chapters 4, 6, and 8.

Just prior to the publication of this study, Rabbi Goren in a letter to Rabbi Mordechai Eliyahu, the Sephardi Chief Rabbi of Israel, dated 1, Tevet, 5750 (December 29, 1989) withdrew from his previous position and concluded that women may not recite *devarim she-bi-kedushah*. Rabbi Goren insists that his prior *heter* was not meant as a practical *pesak*, but rather as an interesting theoretical analysis (*le-iyun be-almah ve-lo ki-fesak halakhah*) which in any case should never have been made public.

39. The letter written to Mr. Y. Yudson, is dated 30, Kislev, 5750 (December 28, 1989). For Rabbi Shapiro, like the other Torah scholars, women's tefillah groups are

IMITATIONS OF NON-JEWISH PRACTICES

Offshoots of the Feminist Movement

Critics have claimed that women's tefillah groups are prohibited because they are "an imitation of non-Jewish practices"; specifically, the contemporary women's liberation movement. In the words of one opponent:

> And behold, it is known that these practices [women's tefillah groups] were not introduced in a vacuum, but as a direct offshoot of the women's liberation movement, whose essence and purpose in this area is for licentiousness, to make women identical to men in every possible way.[40]

The implication that women's tefillah groups, as offshoots of the feminist movement, may include elements of licentiousness is particularly unfortunate.

Throughout Jewish history, rabbinic authorities have been able to articulate the halakhic response to different phenomena as they arose in every generation. Using the precise methodology of the halakhic process, Jews have always been able to maintain a sense of modernity, while retaining a meticulous allegiance to the halakhic system.

As new movements emerged, halakhists scrutinized their multifaceted elements. Those aspects that ran contrary to halakhah were rejected. But those that inspired Jews to draw closer to God and Torah were ennobled by the halakhah and then carefully incorporated into the mainstream of Jewish observance. For example, some

---

not halakhically prohibited. Their concern relates to the realm of public policy—will women's tefillah groups fragment the community? are they conducted by sincere women? do they have any value?—leaving it to each rabbi to decide whether these services permissible on purely halakhic grounds, are appropriate for his community.

For this writer, the distinction between public policy and a binding halakhic opinion became clear in a related discussion I had with Rav Soloveitchik concerning the carrying of the *Sefer Torah* by women through the *ezrat nashim* (women's section). In conversation with the Rav I asked whether he felt this was prohibited. I remember the Rav's response with great clarity: "Don't do it." I then asked: "But Rebbe, are you saying it is *assur?*" The Rav answered: "I didn't say it's *assur.* It's *mutar* (permissible), but I want to protect you."

Here again, the Rav's "don't do it" was not a halakhic *pesak*, but an expression of concern—a concern which in this case, the Rav felt, would protect me—but a suggestion which was certainly not halakhically binding, and one which I have respectfully chosen not to follow.

40. Rabbi Schachter, "Ze'i Lakh be-Ikvei ha-Zon," p. 131. See also the statement of the five *Roshei Yeshiva* and Rabbi Bronspigel's amplification.

aspects of nineteenth-century nationalism contributed to the emergence of the modern Zionist movement and the establishment of the modern State of Israel, *reshit ẓemiḥat ge'ulatenu.* And those elements of feminism which in the early part of the twentieth century motivated many Jewish women to seek greater Torah education deserve support.[41] *Rimon matzanu. Tokho akhalnu ukelipato zaraknu.*

Thus, if some principles of feminism have in any way stimulated today's women to seek a more powerful prayer experience through their own tefillah groups, they should be warmly embraced. These prayer groups are a good example of the balance struck between women who wish to intensify their tefillah and the halakhic system, which sets rigid guidelines on such services.[42]

The reality is that participants in women's tefillah groups are primarily motivated by increased Torah learning and not by the feminist movement. Generally, the leaders of women's tefillah groups are women from observant homes and yeshiva backgrounds. Their involvement is the result of Torah study, which has given them greater knowledge and, in turn, greater incentive to experience more. It is based on a meticulous commitment to the letter and spirit of halakhah. Indeed, these women have rejected the practical option of participating in non-halakhic prayer services.

Interestingly, one of the critics of the organizers of these groups has changed his views somewhat. Originally, he wrote:

> It would seem that the main motivating factor in establishing these groups is . . . simply to innovate and gain publicity in the newspapers, to gain honor and be recognized as a leader. . . . Among the founders are women who tend to learn in Schechter's Seminary [Jewish Theological Seminary], women whom we ourselves have heard to say . . . that these activities are only the "beginning," as they really intend to "uproot it all."[43]

Later, he wrote:

> Among the women who participate [in these prayer groups] are educated women, fully committed and some even covering their hair; and

41. See above, chap. 5, for a discussion of this issue.
42. For a similar understanding of the possible positive impact of some aspects of the feminist movement, see Arlene Pianko, "Women and the Shofar," p. 53.
43. Rabbi Schachter, "Ẓe'i Lakh be-Ikvei ha-Ẓon," pp. 126–127.

> most likely among them are those who are acting for the sake of Heaven—to come closer to God by more personal involvement in the fulfillment of mitzvot.[44]

In any event, as Rabbi Yehuda Herzl Henkin pointed out, there is no justification for objecting to these groups on the basis of any alleged similarity to the feminist movement, for "the Torah prohibits specific acts, not movements,"[45] and as we have argued, there is no specific act to which serious objection can be raised.

While Performing a Mitzvah of the Torah

Citing the discussion of Deuteronomy 12:30 in the Torah commentary of Ramban, critics have also asserted that women's tefillah groups especially violate the prohibition of "imitating non-Jewish practices" since they involve the performance of a mitzvah. In the words of one opponent: "There is a special prohibition against performing a mitzvah of the Torah in accordance with their [non-Jewish] practices."[46] An analysis of what Ramban actually says in the cited passage, however, reveals that this argument, as it relates to women's tefillah groups, is flawed.

In Deuteronomy 12:29–31, the Torah states:

> When the Lord your God shall cut off the nations from before you . . . and [you] dwell in their land. Take heed to yourself that you not be ensnared to follow them after they are destroyed from before you; and that you inquire not after their gods, saying: "How were these nations accustomed to serve their gods? even so will I do likewise." You shall not do so unto the Lord your God; for every abomination to the Lord, which He hates, have they done unto their gods; for even their sons and their daughters do they burn in the fire to their gods.

Commenting on this passage, Rashi states: "After you see that I destroy them from before you, you should pay attention as to why these [nations] were destroyed—because of their corrupt practices. So you, too, should not do the same, so that others not come and destroy you."[47]

---

44. Rabbi Schachter, "Be-Inyanei Beit Knesset," pp. 66–67.
45. Rabbi Henkin, "Mahu Kevod ha-Ẓibbur," p. 40.
46. Rabbi Schachter, "Ze'i Lakh be-Ikvei ha-Ẓon," p. 131. See also the statement of the five *Roshei Yeshiva* and Rabbi Bronspigel's amplification.
47. Rashi to Deuteronomy 12:30, s.v. *aḥarei hishamdam mi-panekha.*

Ramban summarizes Rashi's position in these words: "This is Rashi's language. And if so, this verse becomes an admonition and warning against idol worship." He then offers an alternative explanation.

> Up to here he has commanded many times that when we come into the land we are to uproot the idols . . . and destroy their names, and . . . that we do this immediately upon dispossessing the nations. Now he stated that when the Eternal has cut off these nations from before us, and the names of the idols are forgotten in the land, and we dwell in their land securely, we should not [worship the true God in the manner that] . . . the nations did to their gods . . . (thinking) it will be pleasing to Him. . . . "For even their sons and their daughters do they burn in fire to their gods." [Hence any form of service instituted by people capable of such cruelty is considered an abomination by God, and no ceremony of theirs is to be adopted by us].[48]

For Rashi, the verses in Deuteronomy prohibit the worship of idols. For Ramban, the verses enjoin the adoption of any part of an idolatrous ceremony used by those who sacrificed children to their gods—even in the worship of the true God. The prohibition against performing a mitzvah of the Torah in accordance with non-Jewish practices means, according to Ramban, the specific replication of any element of idolatry in the service of God.

The claim that women's tefillah groups violate this prohibition as spelled out by Ramban—since they incorporate elements of contemporary feminism in prayer to God—borders on the absurd. Whatever one may think of feminism, it does not involve human sacrifice and the worship of idols. And the women who participate in such groups are not guilty of praying to God in abominable, idolatrous, and licentious ways.

MINHAG: A NEW PRACTICE IN SYNAGOGUE CUSTOM

Claims have been made against women's tefillah groups based on the principle that such services constitute a new practice in synagogue custom. In the words of a critic: "Since women have never fulfilled the mitzvah of prayer and reading from the Torah in this

---

48. Ramban to ibid., s.v. *hishamer lekha*.
The translation of Ramban and the final comment in the brackets are from Dr. Charles B. Chavel's translation of *Ramban: Commentary on the Torah, Deuteronomy* (New York: Shilo Publishing House, 1976), pp. 155–158.

manner, we should not change the tradition of our fathers . . . and introduce new customs, *hanhagot meḥudashot.*"[49] A full treatment of the principles of minhag (custom) which underlies this contention go beyond this study.[50] However, a response needs to be offered to some of these fundamental claims to demonstrate the acceptability of women's prayer groups.

Prohibition Based on Novelty

The prohibition of a minhag based purely on its novelty is incorrect. Were this principle followed, many customs that are now carefully observed would never have been introduced. The following, for example, would be prohibited: the wearing of skullcaps;[51] the mourners recitation of Kaddish;[52] the recitation of Yizkor;[53] the suggestion of the Lubavitcher Rebbe that single women (even young females) should light Shabbat candles; and the minhag of reciting *Tefillah li-Shelom ha-Medinah* (the Prayer for the Welfare of the State of Israel) or *Mi-she-berakh le-Ẓahal* (the Prayer for Israel's Defense Forces). Minhagim should not be proscribed on the basis of their being new.

Improper and Insincere

It has also been argued that the women's tefillah group is a minhag that should be forbidden because it is improper, and was introduced by insincere, even rebellious, women.[54] Even if these propositions are true,[55] as presented throughout this study, women's tefillah groups are halakhically valid and the participants are sincere.[56]

Approbation of Noted Scholars

Detractors have additionally stated that minhagim must have the approbation of noted scholars, approval which they contend is

49. Rabbi Schachter, "Ẓe'i Lakh be-Ikvei ha-Ẓon," p. 128.

50. For a thorough analysis of minhag, see Dr. Menachem Elon, *Ha-Mishpat ha-Ivri*, pp. 713–767.

51. *Shulḥan Arukh*, Orah Hayyim 2:6 and *Mishnah Berurah*, ibid., nos. 10–12. See also Samuel Krauss, "The Jewish Rite of Covering the Head."

52. Rema in *Shulḥan Arukh*, Yoreh De'ah 376:4; Orah Ḥayyim 132:2; *Ba'er Heitev*, ibid., no. 5. See also Rabbi David De Sola Pool, *The Kaddish*.

53. See Ismar Elbogen, *Ha-Tefillah be-Ẓibbur*, pp. 151–152.

54. Rabbi Schachter, "Ze'i Lakh be-Ikvei ha-Ẓon," pp. 126–127.

55. See Dr. Menachem Elon's extensive treatment of the rabbinic principle *minhag mevatel halakhah* (custom overrides the halakhah) in his *Ha-Mishpat ha-Ivri*, pp. 734–737. See also Rabbi Dr. Daniel Sperber's analysis of minhagim which derive from non-committed circles in his *Minhagei Yisrael*, pp. 9–19, 222–234.

56. See above, Imitations of Non-Jewish Practices.

lacking in the case of women's tefillah groups.[57] As indicated in this chapter, it is not at all clear that women's tefillah groups lack this approval.[58] There is, furthermore, room to believe that rabbinic approbation is necessary only for the assigning of binding character to a minhag, but not for its continuation as an individual voluntary activity.[59]

"We Never Saw"

Commenting on the argument that women's tefillah groups constitute a new minhag, Rabbi Eliezer Berkovits cites two responsa from Rabbi Jehiel Jacob Weinberg's *Seridei Eish.*[60] In the first, Rabbi Weinberg discusses whether it is permissible to administer an anesthetic to one being circumcised.[61] In the second, he deals with the right of young women to celebrate their 'bat mitzvah'.[62] Both situations involve introducing a minhag.

Rabbi Weinberg concludes that the cases are different. Pain killing drugs existed in Talmudic times; nonetheless, they were never used during circumcision. The situation then was no different from today. As it was forbidden then, it is forbidden now. "*Minhag avoteinu Torah hi*, the custom of our fathers is Torah;"[63] we must not offend it.

Bat mitzvah is different. It was never forbidden. Facing different circumstances, young women were brought up differently; they never expressed a desire to celebrate their bat mitzvah. "There was," in Rabbi Berkovits' words, "no minhag, but an unplanned and unintended absence, a complete vacuum." Things are different today. Blessed with intensive Torah education, young women seek to celebrate their bat mitzvah. Such celebrations are permissible as they do not contravene any prior minhag. They fall within the ambit of legitimate Torah observance.

Women's tefillah groups, Rabbi Berkovits argues, are analogous to bat mitzvah. There was never any minhag which forbade them. In his words: "Their [women's prayer groups] nonexistence was not

57. Rabbi Schachter, "Ẓe'i Lakh be-Ikvei ha-Ẓon," p. 126.
58. See above, The Appeal to Contemporary Torah Scholars.
59. See Tosafot to Pesaḥim, 51a, s.v. *ee atah* and Rambam's *Introduction to Mishneh Torah, Hakdamat ha-Rambam le-Mishneh Torah.*
60. Rabbi Eliezer Berkovits, *Women in Time and Torah*, pp. 79–81.
61. *Responsa Seridei Eish* 3:93.
62. *Responsa Seridel Eish* 3:96.
63. See Tosafot to Menaḥot 20b, s.v. *nifsal.*

due to any rejection of an existing demand for such services. The situation was entirely different from what it is today. We never saw such services before because women did not have the kind of education and participation in the life of the community that they have today. No one called for such services because no one felt the need for them. The nonpractice of women's services was not a minhag, and to introduce them in our times is not violating an established custom."

Paraphrasing Rabbi Berkovits: Women's tefillah groups do not abolish anything; they do not conflict with any minhag. They have a meaningful function in the context of Torah observance.

LOCATION: IN THE HOME OR THE SYNAGOGUE?

Even in communities where women's prayer groups have been approved by the rabbinic leadership, the synagogue has, with few exceptions, been declared off limits to them. In virtually all cases, they are held in homes or rented hotel facilities. They are "hidden" rather than "open"; unofficial rather than formally approved.

One major factor has contributed to this phenomenon. As long as women's prayer groups are kept out of the synagogue, they can be viewed as a passing fad, a kind of religious experience that is tolerated more than permitted, satisfying the whims of those attending, but lacking real legitimacy. Once in the synagogue, women's tefillah groups would by definition be affirmed as a viable halakhic option.

But if women's tefillah groups are halakhically permissible—and they are—those involved should not be treated as pariahs, but formally accepted as part of the larger community. And since it is halakhically preferable to pray—even privately—in the synagogue rather than at home, the most appropriate place for women's tefillah groups is in the synagogue as well.

The Rationale

Various rationales have been offered to explain this preference. The Divine spirit is considered ever-present in the synagogue. Indeed, the Talmud Yerushalmi states: "R. Abbahu in the name of R. Abbahu: 'Seek the Lord where He may be found' (Isaiah 55:6). Where is He found? In synagogues and houses of learning."[64]

---

64. Yerushalmi Berakhot 5:1.

In the synagogue setting, one is potentially able to reach a higher state of kavvanah. In the words of Meiri: "Whenever one is able to pray in a synagogue he should do so, because the intent of the heart (*kavvanat ha-lev*) is found there."[65]

The Legal Preference

The legal preference for praying in the synagogue together with the congregation is found in the Talmud.

> R. Yoḥanan said in the name of R. Simeon b. Yoḥai: What is the meaning of the verse: "But as for me, let my prayer be made unto You, O Lord, in an acceptable time" (Psalms 69:14)? When is the time acceptable? When the congregation (*ẓibbur*) prays.[66]

Basing himself on this text, *Tur Shulḥan Arukh* states: "An individual must only pray in synagogue with the *ẓibbur*."[67]

Baḥ understands *Tur* to mean that there is only an advantage to praying in synagogue when ten have gathered there to pray. "But when there is no *ẓibbur*, there is no difference between praying in synagogue and in another [private] home."[68]

Another talmudic text indicates that it is proper to pray in a synagogue even when the community has not gathered there to pray. "It has been taught: Abba Binyamin says: The prayer of an individual is only heard in a synagogue, as it says: 'to listen to the joy (*ha-rinnah*) and to the prayer (*ha-tefillah*)' (1 Kings 8:28). In the place where there is joy there is prayer."[69]

Rambam in his *Code* accordingly states: "A person should always

65. Meiri to Berakhot 6a.

66. Berakhot 7b–8a.

67. *Tur Shulḥan Arukh*, Orah Ḥayyim 90. *Tur* bases himself on variant readings of the text as recorded in Rif and Rosh to Berakhot 8a (in Rif 4a).

68. *Baḥ* to ibid., s.v. *lo yitpallel adam*.

Baḥ also suggests that R. Yoḥanan could be understood to mean that an individual who is praying alone should still pray in a synagogue.

Note also Rabbenu Jonah to Berakhot 8a (in Rabbenu Jonah's commentary to Rif, 4a s.v. *eimatai*) who states in the name of the geonim, "even when the congregation is not praying one should pray in the synagogue, since it is specifically designated for prayer." See also *Beit Yosef* to ibid., s.v. *lo yitpallel adam*.

69. Berakhot 6a.

attend synagogue morning and evening, because prayer is only heard at all times (*be-khol et*) in the synagogue."[70]

Leḥem Mishneh comments: "Our rabbi [Rambam] maintains that even if one engages in private prayer, he must enter into the synagogue [to pray]."[71]

Shulḥan Arukh follows this line, stating that it is better to pray in synagogue than at home. In his words: "And if one is in extenuating circumstances . . . and must pray individually [i.e., without a minyan], nonetheless he should pray in a synagogue."[72]

Mishkenot Ya'akov concurs, concluding that it is best to pray alone in a synagogue, rather than with a minyan in one's home. He understands the sentence "to listen to the joy and prayer" to mean, "in the place of *rinnah*, where the *ẓibbur* always prays, there should be tefillah, even of an individual."[73]

While recognizing that the arguments presented for this legal preference have heretofore been understood and applied only in relation to men who are obligated in *tefillat ha-ẓibbur* (communal prayer), the logic of the position would apply equally to women who are not obligated in *tefillat ha-ẓibbur* but for whom there is always additional potential for *kavvanah* through tefillah *be-makom ẓib-*

---

70. Rambam, *Code*, Laws of Prayer 8:1.

71. *Leḥem Mishneh* to ibid, s.v. *she'ain tefillato.*

Similarly, *Kesef Mishneh*, ibid., s.v. *u-le-olam*, concludes that in Rambam's view, an individual should pray in synagogue even when the *ẓibbur* is not davening, "because it [the synagogue] is designated for public prayer." It is, therefore, more conducive for the prayer of an individual. He adds that it is possible at times for prayer uttered outside of the synagogue to be heard (presumably if one prays with proper kavvanah), but in a synagogue, one's prayer is always heard.

72. *Shulḥan Arukh*, Oraḥ Ḥayyim 90:9.

73. *Mishkenot Ya'akov* to Oraḥ Ḥayyim 87 as formulated by Rabbi Fuchs in *Ha-Tefillah be-Ẓibbur.*

Ẓlaḥ explains Abba Binyamin's position (see n. 69) as referring to when the *ẓibbur* is completing its prayer service in synagogue. In that case, it is best for an individual, even one who has arrived late, to begin his prayers in synagogue. He interprets the sentence "to listen to the joy and to the prayer" to mean, in the place where God listens to *rinnah*—the joy of communal prayer—at that very time God listens to the tefillah, the prayer of the individual.

Ẓlaḥ apparently has a variant text of Abba Binyamin's statement. It reads: "The prayer of an individual is only heard in synagogue during the time when the *ẓibbur* [community] is praying." *Mishkenot Ya'akov*'s reading of the Gemara is as it appears in our text: "The prayer of an individual is only heard in a synagogue."

For a discussion of these variant texts, see *Baḥ* to *Tur Shulḥan Arukh*, Oraḥ Ḥayyim 90, s.v. *lo yitpallel adam* and Rabbi Fuchs in *Ha-Tefillah be-Ẓibbur*, p. 19.

bur (tefillah in the place where the community normally prays, i.e., the synagogue). Indeed, women ought also take advantage of tefillah *be-makom ẓibbur* as much as possible as the locus for private prayer. While in the past it may not have been possible for women to stop at a shul and *daven* (pray), women who today can, ought consciously attempt to utilize tefillah *be-makom ẓibbur* as a vehicle for the intensification of their own *kavvanah*. By the same token, when women gather in tefillah groups, the additional intensification which is available to them through their taking place *be-makom ẓibbur* should be recognized.[74]

Rabbi Aharon Lichtenstein writes:

"There is a *kiyum* (fulfillment) of *davening* in the *beis haknesses* (synagogue) even when you are not davening in *ẓibbur* (with the community). . . .

The purpose of davening in a *beis haknesses* is twofold. First is the psychological factor . . . The person in a *shul* feels more completely that the time that he is there is devoted to *avodah shebalev* (service of the heart). This is the primary consideration because being able to *daven* under circumstances which on the whole are more conducive to *kavvanah* is crucial. . . .

The other factor is that *beis haknesses* is a *mikdash me'at* (miniature Temple) and there is a particular *kiyum* of tefillah in relation to *mikdash*. There is a certain presence of *shechinah* (the indwelling) in there. In some sense, we do feel that *shechinah* is more of an indwelling presence in certain times and in certain places than in others, and *mikdash* has this element. Moreover, *mikdash* is a place symbolic of *knesses* of *klal yisroel*. *Mikdash* is a communal place and the same idea applies to *beis haknesses* as well, so that when a person is *davening* in a *beis haknesses* even when there is no *ẓibbur* present at the time, there is a sense of *davening* through a certain identification of *ẓibbur*. Thus, *beis haknesses* has the *kedushah* of the *mikdash* itself, especially by the presence of the Torah, and then it has a certain *kedushah* through its affiliations with the *ẓibbur*."[75]

---

74. We have not posited in this study that it is meaningless for women to pray *be-ẓibbur*. There is great value for women to *daven be-ẓibbur*. What we have suggested (see beginning chapter 8) is that the women's tefillah group is an alternative, and for some women a superior model for prayer, one which allows these women to achieve a higher level of *kavvanah*. Since women are not obligated in *tefillah be-ẓibbur*, they are entitled to utilize this alternate vehicle to achieve what ultimately is the same purpose, to pray with the best and fullest experience of one's soul.

I am indebted to Rabbi Saul Berman for helping formulate this issue.

75. Rabbi Aharon Lichtenstein, "Imperatives and Advantages of Communal Prayer Studied in Depth," *Hamevaser* 6, no. 5 (28 Adar 5728, March 28, 1968): p. 5.

* * *

Women are not required to participate in public prayer and are not mandated to fulfill their obligation of private prayer in the synagogue. Nonetheless, if they choose to participate in prayer groups, it is preferable that they do so in a synagogue rather than in a non-synagogue setting.[76]

---

76. Even if it is impossible (for logistical reasons) for a women's prayer group to take place in a room that has *kedushat beit ha-kenesset* (the sanctity of the synagogue), it is still preferable that the service be held within the synagogue complex. This guarantees that the women involved will remain within the social framework of the shul, preventing any "separation from the community."

For a fine survey of the preference for the synagogue as a place of prayer, see Rabbi Fuchs in *Ha-Tefillah be-Ẓibbur*, pp. 17–21.

Conclusion

The conclusion is clear. Within halakhic guidelines, women may participate in women's prayer groups, as long as these groups fall into the halakhic category of tefillah and not minyan. Rabbinic and lay leaders, in synagogues and yeshivot, have a responsibility to organize and sustain women's tefillah groups, providing logistical support (e.g., making available synagogue facilities and *Sifrei Torah*). Classes teaching women to read the Torah and Haftarah, and to lead the services, should be arranged for those who seek this type of learning and religious experience.[1]

One should not infer from this conclusion, however, that women's prayer groups are suited for everyone. Within halakhic guidelines, there are many stylistic possibilities in public prayer. Some men, for example, enjoy Bnei Akiva or Young Israel type davening, while others are more comfortable in an Agudah, shteibel, or Ḥasidic setting. Some opt to pray in a homogeneous atmosphere; others in a more open and heterogeneous community. These preferences are valid halakhic options. The Ba'al Shem Tov noted that in the Amidah, we acknowledge "the God of Abraham, the God of Isaac, and the God of Jacob" (not "the God of Abraham, Isaac, and Jacob"), because, although praying to the same Deity, each Patriarch approached God differently; their pathways to God were not identical. Similarly, the "atmosphere" of public prayer need not be the same at all services.

This principle would obviously apply to women as well. Women who wish to pray at home or in the regular public prayer service should be blessed, and those who feel more religiously inspired in the women's tefillah group have every halakhic right to pray there.

Prayer is a dialogue, a rendezvous with God. It is a song, a tear, a meditative thought, a joyful smile which helps bridge the tremen-

1. In some synagogues, trop, the method of cantillation for chanting from the Torah scroll and the Haftarah, is taught to women. For example, trop classes are offered at the Hebrew Institute of Riverdale and the Lincoln Square Synagogue.

dous chasm between the mortal human and the infinite God. That distance is not easily spanned. Every fiber of intellectual concentration and emotional strength is needed to achieve that instant when we feel the spark of God and breathe that spirituality into our being. For many women, the moment becomes more possible, the experience more intense, through women's tefillah groups.

Participants in such groups are not rebelling against Torah Judaism. Quite the contrary. They are seeking to instill greater religious meaning in their lives. Their purpose is not to diminish the Torah, but to enhance their Jewish commitment and halakhic observance.[2] It would be a great disservice to our communities if we were to deny these women the right to participate in women's tefillah groups, a right which has a clear basis in the halakhah, and a right which, for many, heightens the prayer experience. Their quest to reach nobly to attain this lofty objective should be applauded.[3]

---

2. It is not unusual for the leaders of those seeking greater involvement in synagogue ritual to be observant (often with yeshiva background), meticulously concerned with every detail of halakhah.

3. Rabbi J. David Bleich, a critic of women's prayer groups, made a comment in a different context which seems to lend support to women's tefillah groups. He wrote: "I frankly confess that when the *Lubavitch* movement began erecting *menorahs* on public property my reaction was, *vos darf man dos?* (Why do we need this?) Such *menorahs* serve no halakhic function, either obligatory or discretionary. . . . Now I applaud those efforts. . . . I discovered that the sight of the *menorah* prominently displayed in a public place has stirred feelings of pride and has kindled a spark of Jewish consciousness in countless numbers of otherwise disaffected Jews. I need not explain, or even understand, that phenomenon. It is sufficient to say that it is real and it is salutary." (Rabbi J. David Bleich, "The Constitution and the Jewish Problem," p. 125.)

From my perspective, women's tefillah groups serve a very real halakhic function. But even from the perspective of those who disagree, Rabbi Bleich's comment on the menorah could apply equally to women's tefillah groups.

Indeed, the growth in Torah and prayer that flows from women's prayer groups is real and salutary. As more people realize this, they too will come to applaud these efforts.

Women and the Reading of the Megillah*

May women read the Megillah for other women, and for that matter, may women read the Megillah for men?

I. TANA'ITIC TEXTS

Two primary Tana'itic texts deal with this issue, texts which on the surface seem contradictory. The Mishnah states (*Megillah* 19b), "*Ha-kol kesherim likrot ha-Megillah,*" "all are qualified to read the Megillah." Commenting on this Mishnah, the Talmud (*'Arakhin* 2b-3a) states: "*La-atuyei mai? La-atuyei nashim, u-khe-de-Rebbi Yehoshua ben Levi, de-amar Rebbi Yehoshua ben Levi, nashim ḥayyavot be-mikra Megillah she-af hen hayu be-oto ha-nes.*" "What is the word '*ha-kol*' meant to include? It is meant to include women, in accordance with the view of Rabbi Yehoshua ben Levi, for Rabbi Yehoshua ben Levi said: Women are obliged to read the Megillah because they, too, were included in that miracle."

From this text it would appear that women are mandated to read the Megillah. Based on the principle that one can fulfill the responsibility for another if they are on the same level of *ḥiyyuv*, it would seem that women can also fulfill the obligation for men.[1] Since women are duty bound to read the Megillah, they can fulfill the obligation for males who are similarly obliged to read the Megillah.

There is an alternative Tana'itic source which seems to maintain the reverse. The Tosefta states (*Megillah* 2:4): "*Ha-kol ḥayyavin bi-keriyat Megillah, Kohanim, Levi'im, Yisraelim . . . kulan ḥayyavin u-*

*I am deeply indebted to my son, Rabbi Dov Weiss, with whom I had the great joy and *zekhut* to learn this issue. Many of the insights and creative elements are his. While acknowledging Dov's contribution, I assume complete responsibility for all aspects of this article.

moẓi'in et ha-rabbim yedei ḥovatan. Androginus moẓi mino ve-lo et she-eno mino; tumtum eno moẓi lo et mino ve-lo et she-eno mino. . . . Nashim ve-'avadim u-ketanim peturin, ve-en moẓi'in et ha-rabbim yedei ḥovatan." "All are obligated in the reading of the Megillah, Priests, Levites, Israelites . . . all are obligated and fulfill the obligation of others. [An] *androginus* (a person with both male and female characteristics) fulfills the obligation for another *androginus*, but not of a non-*androginus*; a *tumtum* (a person either male or female, but it is not clear which) does not fulfill the obligation for another *tumtum* or a non-*tumtum*. . . . Women, '*avadim*,[2] and minors are exempt and cannot fulfill the obligation for others."

The simple reading of the last sentence of the Tosefta is that women, unlike all of those previously mentioned, are exempt from reading the Megillah, and, therefore, cannot fulfill the obligation for their male counterparts who are mandated to read.

The contradiction is obvious. The Mishnah seems to proclaim that women are obliged to read the Megillah and can therefore do so for men, while the Tosefta says that women are exempt from reading and therefore can not fulfill the obligation for men.

II. RISHONIM

1. *Pre-eminence of the Mishnah*

Rishonim deal with this question in different ways. Some insist that while the contradiction remains, the Mishnah has pre-eminence. In the words of *Or Zarua'* (R. Isaac of Vienna, 13c., Vienna) : "It seems to me since the Tosefta is not mentioned in our Talmud, we do not rely on it."[3] Meiri (R. Menaḥem ben Shlomoh, late 13c., Provence) concurs: "And the essential position is not to push aside our well-thought-out talmudic [discussion] because of a Beraita [ịe, the Tosefta]."[4]

From this perspective, *Or Zarua'* and Meiri definitively maintain that women can read the Megillah for men. *Or Zarua'* writes "concerning Megillah, it appears to me that the practical halakhah (*halakhah le-ma'aseh*) is that women are obligated to read the Megillah and can fulfill the obligation for males." Meiri consents: " Let us rely on the well known principle, all who are obligated in the matter may fulfill the obligation for others."

Both *Or Zarua'* and Meiri agree with Rashi's position in his commentary on the *'Arakhin* passage that: "[Women] are obligated to read the Megillah, and they may read it and fulfill the obligation for men."[5] In fact, *Or Zarua'* says explicitly, "It seems to me that the essential view is that of Rashi. [*'Ha-kol'*] is meant to include women who are obligated in reading Megillah and are qualified to fulfill the obligation for men."[6]

Other Rishonim, while not dealing with the Tosefta, explicitly state that women can fulfill the Megillah obligation for men. *Sefer ha-Mikhtam* (R. David ben Levi, 13c., Provence) writes: "And if a woman knows how to read, she fulfills the obligation for men."[7] Rid (R. Yishayahu of Trani ha-Zaken, early 13c., Italy) and Riaz (R. Yishayahu Aharon ben Eliyahu of Trani, 13c., Italy) state: "Women . . . are obligated in its [Megillah] reading. And it seems to me that they fulfill the obligation of the many."[8] *Nimukei Yosef* (R. Yosef H.aviva, 15c., Spain) adds: "Women recite a blessing on reading Megillah, and they fulfill the obligation of men."[9]

There are other Rishonim who, while not explicitly stating that women can fulfill the obligation for men, seem to agree. Rambam writes: "Everyone is obligated in its reading [of the Megillah], men, women . . . ," not making any differentiation between the two. He then adds, "Both the reader and listener fulfill their obligation as long as it is heard from one who is obligated."[10] Here, *Maggid Mishneh* (R. Vidal of Tolosa, 14c., Spain) states: "From our rabbi [Rambam] it can be deduced that she fulfills the obligation of others, and this is the essential view."[11]

Similarly, *Sefer Yere'im* (R. Eliezer ben Shmuel of Metz, 12c., France) states, "All are qualified to read the Megillah. . . ." Here, again, no distinction is made between men and women. *Sefer Yere'im* then concludes: "This is the principle. Whoever is not obligated in the matter cannot fulfill the obligation of others."[12]

Sefer ha-Manhig (R. Avraham ben Nathan ha-Yarḥi, 12c., Provence) follows a similar approach when stating that "women are obligated in the reading of the Megillah . . . and so are they obligated in Hanukkah candles."[13] It follows that as women can light Hanukkah candles for men[14] so can they read Megillah for their male counterparts.[15]

2. *Reconciling the Mishnah and Tosefta*

A. "External Reasons"

There are other Rishonim who fundamentally believe that women can read the Megillah for men, but for external reasons are enjoined from doing so. These external reasons include *kol ishah, zila milta* and *kevod ha-ẓibbur.*

Sefer ha-Me'orot was the first to attribute to *'Aseret ha-Dibbrot* (Ba'al ha-'Ittur—R.Yiẓḥak ben Abba Mari, 12c., Provence) the idea that women cannot fulfill the obligation for men through their reading because of *kol ishah 'ervah*, the voice of a woman is licentious.[16] *Orḥot Ḥayyim* (R. Aharon ben Ya'akov ha-Kohen mi-Lunel, 14c., Provence) and *Kol Bo* (authorship unknown) follow in his footsteps by similarly attributing to Ba'al ha-'Ittur the position that women may not read for men because of *kol ishah.*[17] This position, however, does not appear in our editions of the *'Ittur.*[18]

Tosafot explains the position of Bahag (Ba'al Halakhot Gedolot) that women cannot read the Megillah for men, because it is considered "*zila milta*," a process which results in a diminution of dignity.[19]

Semag (*Sefer Miẓvot Gadol* of R. Moshe of Coucy, 13c., France) associates the external inability of women to read the Megillah for men with *keriyat ha-Torah.*[20] This seems to relate to the Talmudic passage which states that women cannot read the Torah for men because of *kevod ẓibbur* (*Megillah* 23a). In fact, Ritva (R. Yom Tov ben Avraham Ibn Asevilli, 14c., Spain) explicitly states that since women are "obligated [in reading the Megillah] they also can fulfill the obligation [of men] but this is not *kavod* to the *ẓibbur.*"[21]

However, assuming this approach, ịe., that were it not for other considerations, women *could* fundamentally read the Megillah for men, how is one to understand the Tosefta which explicitly concludes "women are exempt from Megillah?"

Alternative versions of the Tosefta resolve the problem. *Semag* insists that the Tosefta's last sentence, "women are exempt," does not appear in the original text. However, he adds that from the inability of a *tumtum* to read the Megillah for another *tumtum*, we can deduce that women cannot read the Megillah for men because of external considerations. His reasoning is as follows: In principle, even if the *tumtum* is a female, she should be able to read the Megillah for a *tumtum* who is male, because both of them are on the same level of reading obligation. This, however, is not done for external reasons. In the words of *Semag*, "The reading of the Megillah is to be compared to *keriyat ha-Torah*" where women do not read for men because of *kevod ha-ẓibbur.*[22]

Alternatively, the Meiri,[23] Rashba,[24] Ran[25] (R. Nissim ben Reuven, 14c., Spain) and others quote a different ending of the Tosefta. For them, the concluding statement reads, "Women are obligated but still cannot fulfill the obligation of men." One can understand this alternative version to mean that women, like men, are indeed obligated to read the Megillah but still cannot fulfill the obligation for men for external reasons.

Given these alternate readings, one can reconcile the Tosefta with the Bavli by insisting that the Bavli reflects a post facto (*be-de'avad*) rule. Optimally (*le-khathila*), it is best that women not read for men for any of the external reasons cited above. The Bavli, however, says, if they do read for men, post facto, the men have thereby fulfilled their obligation. Alternatively, the Gemara of "*le-atuyei nashim*" means that women can read the Megillah for other women. For other women—but, for "external" reasons, they cannot read the Megillah for men.

B. Reading vs. Hearing

There are other Rishonim who believe that women cannot fulfill the obligation for men not for external reasons but because they are on different levels of obligation. This inability of women is fundamental, rather than external, in nature. While men are obligated to *read* the Megillah, women are only obligated to *hear* the Megillah. This is the position of Ba'al Halakhot Gedolot (Bahag) as quoted by Tosafot.[26]

There are other Rishonim who agree with the view of Tosafot. Rabbenu Ḥannanel (ben Ḥushiel, 11c., Tunisia) maintains that "women are obligated to listen to the reading of the Megillah."[27] Roke'aḥ (R. Elazar of Worms, 12c., Germany) concurs: "Women . . . are obligated to listen [to the Megillah]."[28] Similarly, Ba'al ha-'Ittur states: "Women . . . are obligated to listen to the reading of the Megillah . . . but they are not obligated to read [the Megillah]."[29] Rabbenu Simḥah (R. Simḥah ben Shmuel of Speyer, 12c., Germany) also states "and they [women] are not obligated to read [the Megillah] but only to hear."[30] Rabbenu Ḥannanel, Roke'aḥ, 'Ittur and Rabbenu Simḥah do not deal with whether women can fulfill the Megillah obligation for others. Ran, however, after presenting the view that women are only obligated to hear, states that women "fulfill the obligation [in Megillah] for other women, even though they do not fulfill the obligation for men."[31]

Accordingly, the Tosefta and the Bavli can be reconciled in the following fashion. The final phrase of the Tosefta is understood to mean that "women are exempt [from *reading* the Megillah]." As such, they cannot fulfill the obligation for men. However, according to this reading of the Tosefta, women are obligated to *hear* the Megillah and thus may read for other women. This, in fact, is the position of the Bahag according to Tosafot,[32] Rosh[33] (R. Asher ben Yeḥiel, 13c., Spain) and Ran.[34]

The Bavli can be explained in a similar fashion. The inclusion of women in Megillah does not refer to women reading the Megillah for men; rather it refers to women reading the Megillah for other women. This, in accordance with the opinion of R. Yehoshua ben Levi, that women are obligated—and this is what Tosafot adds—to *listen* to the reading of the Megillah.[35]

3. Blessing, "Lishmoa' " or " 'Al Mikra?"

Separate from the issue of whether women should read or hear the Megillah, is the question, which blessing should women recite? According to the school of Rashi, that women are obligated to read and can fulfill the obligation of men, it would seem that they would recite the blessing " *'al mikra Megillah*" for *reading* the Megillah.

Even according to those like *Semag* who declare that women cannot read for men because of external reasons, since they are fundamentally obligated in "*kri'ah*," when reading for women it would seem that they would still recite the blessing " *'al mikra Megillah.*"

The text of the *berakhah* becomes less clear according to the view of Tosafot and others who believe that women cannot read for men because they are obligated to *hear* Megillah, while men have the higher obligation of *reading.* On the one hand, it can be argued that if women are obligated to listen to the Megillah, they should recite the blessing of "*li-shmoa'*" when reading for other women. On the other hand, although the fulfillment of the *miẓvah* (*kiyyum ha-miẓvah*) is accomplished through *shmi'ah*, the reality is that this "*kiyyum*" can only be achieved through the act of reading. Hence " *'al mikra*" should still be recited.[36]

Ra'avyah (R. Eliezer ben Rabbenu Yoel Halevi, 12c., Germany) who is in agreement with the position that women are fundamentally obligated only in hearing Megillah, is the first Rishon to declare definitively that when reading for other women, a women must recite "*li-shmoa'*." This is the case, Ra'avyah adds, even ("*afilu*") when a woman reads for herself. One would have thought otherwise. It is one thing to recite "*li-shmoa'* " when others are listening. It is more difficult to say the blessing "*li-shmoa'*" when the only listener is the reader. Notwithstanding this concern, Ra'avyah writes, "And it seems to me that women recite the blessing of listening to the Megillah even if they read for themselves."[37]

This reading of Ra'avyah is supported by Mordekhai (R. Mordekhai ben Hillel, 13c., Germany). In explaining the Bavli and Tosefta as relating to a woman's obligation to hear the Megillah, Mordekhai explicitly states that women can "fulfill [the obligation] for other women like them." It is here that Mordekhai quotes Ra'avyah verbatim.[38]

III. *Shulḥan 'Arukh* and Rama

With this background, we can understand the different views on this issue as presented in the *Shulḥan 'Arukh* (R. Yosef Karo, 16c., Ereẓ Yisrael) and Rama (R. Moshe ben Yisrael Isserles, 16c., Poland). R. Yosef Karo writes, "All are obligated in the reading of the Megillah, men, women. . . . The reader and the one who listens to the reader fulfill their obligation with the proviso that the listener is on the same level of obligation as the reader. . . . *Ve-yesh omrim*, and there are those who say, that women cannot fulfill the obligation for men." The Rama adds, "*Ve-yesh omrim*, and there are those who say, if a woman reads for herself, she recites the blessing 'to hear the Megillah' (*li-shmoa'*) as she is not obligated in reading the Megillah."[39]

Based on our review of the Rishonim, the *Shulḥan 'Arukh* and Rama can be clearly understood. The first view of the Meḥaber is that of the school of Rashi, that women can read for men. The second view, the Meḥaber's "*ve-yesh omrim*" that women cannot read for men, is, according to *Magen Avraham* (R. Avraham Gombiner, 17c., Poland) referring to the school of *Semag*, that women cannot read for men because of external reasons.[40] Alternatively, Gaon of Vilna (R. Eliyahu of Vilna, 18c., Shklov) postulates that the Meḥaber's "*ve-yesh omrim*" is the view of Tosafot that women cannot read for men as women are obligated in "*shmi'ah*" while men are obligated in "*kri'ah*."[41]

According to Meḥaber's "*ve-yesh omrim*," it is unclear whether women would recite the blessing of "*kri'ah*" or "*shmi'ah*." It is here that Rama, in his "*ve-yesh omrim*," quotes Mordekhai who, in his commentary, had quoted Ra'avyah who said that when a woman reads the Megillah for other women, she would recite the blessing "*li-shmoa'*."[42] In fact, the language of Rama is almost identical with Mordekhai's quote of Ra'avyah. Note the similiarity: Mordekhai quoting Ra'avyah writes "*de-nashim mevarkhot 'al mishma' Megillah ve-afilu* (the Aramaic equivalent of *im*) *kar'u le-aẓman*," "women recite the blessing to hear Megillah and even if they read for themselves." Rama writes, "*Im ha-ishah kar'ah le-aẓmah, mevarekhet li-shmoa' Megillah*," "if a woman reads for herself she recites the blessing *li-shmoa' Megillah*." The major difference between the two formulations is that Rama inverts the sentence and skips the word "*ve-afilu*" when quoting Mordekhai in the name of Ra'avyah. But it is common to understand "*im*, if" as implicitly meaning "*ve-afilu im*, even if." In other words, not only when a woman reads for other women, but even if she reads for herself, the blessing of "*li-shmoa*'" is recited.

It is important to note that Rama, in his *Darkhei Moshe* commentary on the *Tur* (R. Ya'akov Ba'al ha-Turim, 14c., Spain), cites Mordekhai as supporting Bahag's ruling that women cannot fulfill the obligation for men.[43] It is, therefore, not suprising that Mordekhai is also cited in the brackets following the Rama's statement, indicating that Mordekhai was the source upon which Rama based his comment.[44]

IV. *AḤRONIM*

During the period of the late authorities (Aḥronim), both permissive and restrictive approaches took hold.

1. Permissive Approach

On the permissive side, some Aḥronim argued that the view of Rishonim that women cannot read for men because women are obligated to hear while men are obligated to read, may apply only to the day, not the night. This reasoning flows from various approaches used to understand the distinction between hearing and reading.

Some Aḥronim argue that hearing the Megillah is a function of the obligation to publicize the Purim reading, *pirsumei nisa*.[45] Here, women and men are equally obligated since *pirsumei nisa* applies equally to both. This is the obligation at night. Reading, however, is an added obligation during the day. While the nature of the added obligation is a matter of dispute, they have a common denominator—the exemption of women.

Marḥeshet suggests that the added obligation is linked to the *miẓvah* of reading Hallel; praise is, of course, due God on Purim.[46] Alternatively, *Ḥedvat Hashem* connects the reading of the Megillah to the *miẓvah* of remembering and obliterating Amalek since Haman was an Amalakite.[47] *Kehillat Ya'akov* raises the possibility that it is related to the *miẓvah* of *sho'alin ve-dorshin*, i.e., the *miẓvah* of Talmud Torah. In other words, the obligation to read the Megillah parallels and, indeed, intersects with the obligation to study the laws of Purim. While in the end he rejects this possibility, it remains worthy of discussion.[48] Let us now examine each of these positions.

Concerning the added dimension in Megillah to recite Hallel, *Marḥeshet* notes that "women are exempt from Hallel."[49] He then writes: "Even according to the view of Bahag, [the inability of women to be *moẓi* men] would only apply during the day [as they, unlike men, are exempt from Hallel]. But concerning the reading of the Megillah at night, at which time there is no obligation in Hallel as the obligation to recite Hallel only applies to the day . . . and the Megillah is read at night only for *pirsumei nisa*, women can fulfill the obligation for men, as their obligation is equal."[50]

Ḥedvat Hashem makes a similar comment concerning the connection between Megillah reading and Amalek. He cites *Marḥeshet* who argues that there is no obligation even for men to remember Amalek at night. This is based on the *Sefer ha-Ḥinukh*, who links going to war against Amalek to remembering Amalek.[51] Therefore, just as there is no *miẓvah* to destroy Amalek at night as there is no judgment then (*de-en danin ba-laylah*), so is there no *miẓvah* to mention Amalek at night. *Ḥedvat Hashem* then writes: "Therefore, concerning the [Megillah] reading at night, even men do not fulfill the *miẓvah* of remembering Amalek. Hence, men are also only obligated at night from the perspective of *shmi'ah* like women, and, therefore, at night women can be *moẓi* men as their obligation is equal."[52] During the day, however, a woman may not read the Megillah for men as reading it is a function of remembering Amalek. Since women, unlike men, are exempt from destroying Amalek, so are they exempt from remembering Amalek.[53]

The possibility raised by *Kehillat Ya'akov*, that Megillah includes the added dimension of Talmud Torah, is also mentioned by *Ḥedvat Hashem*. *Ḥedvat Hashem* explains that women may read the Megillah for men at night since ritualized forms of Talmud Torah are only applicable during the day. He writes: "From the perspective that everyone is obligated to read [the Megillah] in its proper time, [an obligation] which is based on our mandate [to be involved] in Talmud Torah, [it ought be remembered] that obligation only applies to the day, like the public reading of the Torah on every holiday which is limited to the day. It follows that when men read the Megillah at night, it is not a function of *sho'alin ve-dorshin*. Hence, for both [men and women] there is only the law of *pirsumei nisa*, and the obligation of men and women are equal, and they, therefore, can fulfill each others' obligation."[54]

Additionally, *Turei Even* (R. Aryeh Leib Gunzberg, 18c., Frankfurt on the Oder) introduces a new understanding of Bahag. The reason why women cannot read for men is not a function of *shmi'ah* and *kri'ah*, but rather it is because the source of their obligations are different. Women are obligated in Megillah *mi-de-rabbanan* since they too were part of the miracle.[55] Men, on the other hand, are obligated in Megillah *mi-divrei kabbalah*, in this case, from the Megillah itself. The status of obligation *mi-divrei kabbalah* is more than *mi-de-rabanan* although it is not quite on the level of a Biblical obligation.[56] Basing himself on *Turei Even*, *Ḥedvat Hashem* writes, "The upshot is, that at night women may fulfill a man's obligation, because at night they are both on the same level [of obligation] as even men are only obligated [to hear Megillah] rabbinically and are not obligated *mi-divrei kabbalah*. And when Bahag writes that a woman may not fulfill the obligation of a man, this applies only during the day when his obligation is greater."[57]

The distinction between day and night may resolve the contradiction between the Tosefta and the Bavli, as the Tosefta which states that a woman does not fulfill a man's obligation refers to the day, while the Bavli, which speaks of a woman being able to fulfill a man's obligation, refers to the night.[58]

2. *Restrictive Approach*

A more restrictive attitude also emerged amongst some Aḥronim. This attitude is found both within the position that women cannot read for men because of external reasons as well as the position that women cannot read for men because their level of obligation is less (*shmi'ah* vs. *kri'ah*).

Concerning the position that women cannot read for men because of external reasons, *Korban Netanel* (R. Netanel ben Naftali Ẓevi Weil, 17c., Germany) insists that Tosafot's understanding of

Bahag, that women cannot read for men because of *zila milta*, extends also to reading for women. In other words, not only is it *zila milta* if a woman reads for men, it is also *zila milta* if a woman reads for a number of other women. However, a woman reading for one woman is not *zila milta*.[59]

Concerning the position that women cannot read for men because their level of obligation is less, *Magen Avraham* quotes *Midrash ha-Ne'elam* on Rut (which is part of the *Zohar*) as stating that a woman cannot read the Megillah for women, and not even for herself.[60] *Ḥayyei Adam* (R. Avraham Danzig, late 18c., Vilna) disagrees, insisting that the correct reading of *Midrash ha-Ne'elam* on Rut indicates that a woman has a right to read for herself, but not for other women.[61]

Both the positions of *Korban Netanel* and *Midrash ha-Ne'elam*, as understood by *Magen Avraham* and *Ḥayyei Adam*, need further clarification.

Korban Netanel is difficult because the Tosafot which speaks of *zila milta* refers to the case of a woman leading *zimmun* or reading Megillah for men. Extending *zila milta* to a woman reading for other women is a forced reading of Tosafot.[62] Moreover, Bahag, which Tosafot sets out to explain, speaks of whether or not women can fulfill the Megillah obligation for men. In the words of *Ḥedvat Hashem*: "However, this view [*Korban Netanel*] is very difficult. Because Bahag, and, indeed, all Rishonim who quote Bahag only speak of a woman fulfilling the obligation for men [in Megillah], and not of women fulfilling the obligation [of Megillah] for other women. How then can Tosafot quote this law that women are unable to fulfill the obligation for other women [in Megillah] in the name of Bahag?"[63]

The restrictive explanation of *Midrash ha-Ne'elam* is similarly difficult since it runs contrary to the total text. *Midrash ha-Ne'elam* states: "And Rabbi Abba said, 'women . . . are obligated in the reading of Megillah. But they do not read for others (*le-aḥerim*).' "[64] From the context it seems clear that "*le-aḥerim*" means for men—coming as it does on the heels of the comment of the *Midrash ha-Ne'elam* that women should not recite Grace After Meals for men.[65] Additionally, the phrase in *Midrash ha-Ne'elam*, "*aval hen enan ko'rot le-aḥerim*," "but they do not read for others," could easily mean the following: "They, the women, do not read for others," that is, for men.[66] Finally, even if *Midrash ha-Ne'elam* presents a position that a woman cannot read for other women, it must be pointed out that this is a statement found in the *Zohar*, a non-halakhically binding text, one which runs contrary to the view of every Rishon.[67]

3. *Mishnah Brurah, 'Arukh ha-Shulḥan and other* Poskim

Notwithstanding these difficulties, *Mishnah Brurah* (R. Israel Meir ha-Kohen [Ḥafeẓ Ḥayyim], late 19c.-early 20c., Poland) utilizes these positions to explain the *yesh omrim* of the Meḥaber and the *yesh omrim* of the Rama. The *yesh omrim* of the Meḥaber denying a woman the right to read for men is, according to *Mishnah Brurah*, either based on *kevod ha-ẓibbur*[68] or on her lesser level of obligation, i.e. *shmi'ah* vs. *kri'ah.*[69] Either understanding of this denial, *Mishnah Brurah* argues, would even apply to a woman reading for one man.[70] *Mishnah Brurah* concludes his understanding of the *yesh omrim* of the Meḥaber by stating that a woman may read for "*ḥavertah*"—which, *Ḥafeẓ Ḥayyim* in his *Sha'ar ha-Ẓiyun* citing *Korban Netanel* explains to mean for one woman. Only in that case does *zila milta* not apply.[71]

Mishnah Brurah then explains Rama by first citing *Magen Avraham*'s understanding of the *Midrash ha-Ne'elam* that a woman should not even read for herself. He then continues, basing himself on *Ḥayyei Adam*'s understanding of the *Midrash ha-Ne'elam*, that if no man is there to read for her, a woman may read the Megillah for herself, reciting the blessing "*lishmoa' mikra Megillah.*"[72]

As we have already pointed out, explaining Meḥaber's *yesh omrim* with *Korban Netanel* is difficult because it would have the Meḥaber agree with a forced reading of Tosafot and Rosh. Indeed, R. Yosef Karo makes no mention of this forced ruling in his *Bet Yosef* commentary on the Tur.[73] Similarly, identifying Rama's position as being based on an understanding of the *Midrash ha-Ne'elam*, that a woman cannot read for other women, would have the Rama depending on a position found in the *Zohar* that seems to run contrary to every other Rishon.[74] In fact, Rama himself, in his *Darkhei Moshe*, states that a position of the *Zohar* should be given no greater halakhic weight than the *da'at yaḥid* of R. Shimon.[75] Rama goes on to cite Rabbi Yosef Karo who maintaines that we do not rule in accordance with the *Zohar* when it runs contrary to the way the talmudic text is generally understood.[76] It is, therefore, not surprising that Rama makes no mention of the *Midrash ha-Ne'elam* in discussing Megillah reading in his *Darkhei Mosheh.*[77]

'Arukh ha-Shulḥan (R. Yeḥiel Mikhel Epstein, 19c., Belorussia) explains the Meḥaber and Rama based upon the mainstream of the positions of the Rishonim. The second opinion of Meḥaber denying women the right to read for men is based, according to *'Arukh ha-*

Shulḥan, on *kavod ha-ẓibbur*. This would apply to women reading for men, not to women reading for women (even more than one woman). Rama, according to *'Arukh ha-Shulḥan*, then states that women cannot read for men because they are only obligated to hear while men are obligated to read. It is here that *'Arukh ha-Shulḥan* offers a novel interpretation of this view suggesting that women have a lesser *ḥiyyuv* because a woman's obligation in *pirsumei nisa* is less than that of a man. "However," *'Arukh ha-Shulḥan* concludes, "women can fulfill the obligation for other women since they are on the same level of obligation."[78]

Today there are authorities who object to a woman reading the Megillah for others. For example, Rabbi Hershel Schachter prohibits groups of women from hearing the Megillah from one another.[79] Other Torah scholars permit a woman to read the Megillah for other women.[80] For example, Rabbi Aharon Lichtenstein gave his imprimatur to such a reading at Midreshet Lindenbaum in Israel.[81]

In fact, Rabbi Ovadiah Yosef extends this right even to women reading the Megillah for men. He writes: "In truth, we follow the halakhah that even regarding reading the Megillah, women can fulfill the obligation of men. [This is] in accordance with the view of Rambam, Rashi, *Or Zarua'*. . . . And this is the decision of our teacher the *Shulḥan 'Arukh, Oraḥ Ḥayyim in the general opinion (stam)* he puts forth. Except that he concludes: 'And there are those who say that women cannot fulfill the obligation of their male counterparts.' And the principle is well known that when [*Shulḥan 'Arukh* presents two opinions,] a '*stam*' opinion and a '*yesh omrim*,' the law is like the '*stam*' view."[82]

V. MEGILLAH AND MINYAN

There is another issue that must be considered relative to a woman's right to read Megillah for someone else. Does Megillah reading require a minyan, and, if so, may women be counted in that minyan? Tangentially, does a group of women reading the Megillah run contrary to the preference that the Megillah be read in the largest assemblage possible—in the spirit of "*be-rov 'am hadrat melekh*?"

The Talmud (*Megillah* 5a) states: "Rav said: 'On the actual day of Purim, the Megillah may be read even by an individual, but on the alternative days [lit., not in its proper time][83] it should be read only in a company of ten.' Rav Assi, however, said: 'Whether on the actual day or on the alternative days, it should be read only in a company of ten.' In an actual case, Rav gave weight to the opinion of Rav Assi [and extended himself to assemble ten persons]."

Rif concludes: "Even though Rav gave weight to the view of R. Assi, we follow the view of Rav, because Rav Yoḥanan follows this position."[84] On the day of Purim, therefore, one may read the Megillah individually, although it is preferable that it be read with a minyan. On alternative days it should only be read in a company of ten.

Rabbenu Tam states that one need not pursue a minyan to read the Megillah even *le-khatḥilla*.[85] This applies to the fourteenth (or fifteenth), the day of Purim itself. However, Bahag concludes that the Megillah must always be read before ten people.[86] *Baḥ* notes that Bahag follows the view of Rav Assi that ten are required at all times, even *bi-de'avad*.[87]

Shulḥan 'Arukh concludes: "On the fourteenth or fifteenth day [the fifteenth is the proper time to read the Megillah in a city surrounded by walls from the time of Joshua], one must seek out ten [before whom the Megillah should be read], and if ten were not found, an individual may [nevertheless] read the Megillah."[88]

Assuming that women are obligated to read the Megillah, and that a minyan is necessary or at least preferable, the question is whether women may be counted toward such a minyan. There are three approaches to this question.[89]

The first approach clearly restricts participation in a minyan to men alone. The exclusion may be based on the talmudic statement (*Berakhot* 45b), "*ve-ha me'ah nashei kitrei gavrei damyan*," a hundred women are compared (from this legal perspective) to two men. Rashi understands this phrase to refer exclusively to the obligation of *zimmun*, the quorum needed to introduce the Grace After Meals. In his words: "They are not obligated to participate in *zimmun*, but if they wish they may."[90] Tosafot, on the other hand, associates the phrase with "*le-'inyan kibbuẓ tefillah u-le-'inyan kol davar she-be-'asarah*," indicating that women are not counted as part of a minyan for "public prayer and everything that requires ten." From the perspective of Tosafot, women are excluded, in all circumstances, from being counted into a minyan for prayer, or for that matter, for any other purpose that "requires ten" according to Jewish law.[91]

Beyond the legal exclusion of women from being counted for a minyan,[92] there emerged a school of thought which defined a minyan as a group of ten people united by a common obligation. From this perspective, there is no absolute declaration that women are necessarily ineligible for a minyan. Participants in a minyan must share a mutual obligation. If women share the obligation equally, they are counted; if not, they are excluded. Indeed, in matters concerning a minyan, Meiri points out: "There are those who say that in cases where women are equally obligated as men, they are counted toward the ten."[93]

From this perspective it would follow that if women are mandated to read the Megillah, they may be counted toward a Megillah minyan. So declares Meiri[94] and Ran. In the words of Ran: "How is it possible that women can fulfill the obligation of men to read the Megillah and not be counted with them as part of the [Megillah] minyan? Certainly they can be counted."[95]

Rama leaves the question of including women in the Megillah minyan unresolved as it would depend upon the degree of obligation that women have with respect to that *mizvah.* If a woman's obligation is on the same level as that of a man (i.e., *kri'ah*), they are counted into the minyan. If not (and their obligation is only *shmi'ah*), they may not be part of the minyan.[96]

Rabbi Aryeh Frimer suggests that there is a third approach to minyan. He writes: "It is necessary to differentiate between two types of minyanim. Normally, the Sages required ten male adults as a prerequisite for the performance of particular rituals, generally communal in nature. However, in certain cases, the minyan is not intrinsic to the performance of the *mizvah,* for the obligation is essentially the individual's. Rather, the minyan is needed only to give 'publicity' to the performance. In such a case, women are counted even if their obligation is not equivalent to that of men."[97]

Separate from the issue of whether women can be counted with men to make up a Megillah minyan is the question of whether women can make up the necessary quorum of ten by themselves for a women's Megillah reading. R. Ẓevi Pesaḥ Frank,[98] R. Yehudah Eliezer Waldenberg[99] and R. Ovadiah Yosef[100] agree that they can. For a women's Megillah minyan, women can be counted for one of two reasons: either because they are all on an equal level of obligation, or because the public reading of Megillah is based on the principle of *pirsumei nisa* where women can be equally included. In the words of Rabbi Ovadiah Yosef: "We reject that which R. Menasheh Klein wrote in *Mishneh Halakhot* against the custom of women to make a minyan for themselves to read the Megillah. His arguments are not clear. On the contrary, we should encourage such activities, provided the reader is an expert able to read correctly."[101]

VI. CONCLUSION

The issue of women reading Megillah for others touches the very core of the process of *pesak*. There has emerged in contemporary times a popular pattern of *pesak halakhah* which places almost exclusive reliance on the *Mishnah Brurah*. According to those who follow this position, women should not read Megillah even for other women.[102]

By contrast there is no Rishon who explicitly states that a woman may not read the Megillah for other women. Moreover, many Aḥronim support the position that women are permitted to read the Megillah for other women. This is not only the dominant position throughout Jewish history, but also the position in greatest conformity to the talmudic *sugya*, as we have seen.

Our analysis further indicates that while many authorities did not demand a minyan for Megillah reading (certainly when Megillah is read on Purim day), even if deemed necessary, women can make up that quorum for themselves.

The issue of women reading Megillah for men is more complex. Here, even the early authorities are divided. Some later authorities seem more inclined to permit this kind of reading at night rather than during the day.[103]

Whether women can be counted with men to make up a Megillah minyan—if a minyan for Megillah is necessary—is a subject of considerable debate. Of course, if ten men are present, there would be no need to even deal with the question, as a minyan would already be present.

It would be difficult to prohibit women's Megillah reading based on the *rov 'am* principle as there are countless examples of many Megillah readings sponsored by individual shuls. It is precisely because *rov 'am* is not mandatory that some *Poskim* have even suggested that women hear the Megillah at home, arguing that it is often difficult to hear the Megillah in the women's section as it is being read.[104]

While rabbis are within their right to rely on the minority opinion of halakhic authorities who prohibit women's Megillah reading, they fall short if, in this process, they do not give credence to those who, basing themselves on sources clearly rooted in Halakhah, permit a woman to read the Megillah for other women.[105]

It is important—especially at a time when *ahavat Yisrael* is so desperately needed—that every one involved in this intense debate realize that the Halakhah on this matter is not monolithic. Within clear guidelines there can often be two legitimate opposite opinions—and both may be correct in the spirit of "*elu ve-elu divrei Elokim ḥayyim*" (*'Eruvin* 13b). All sides in this debate should heed the words of Dr. David Berger: "Controversies over women's issues have lately created a particularly great danger of fragmentation, and we must beware of making disagreements which do not touch upon fundamentals of the faith the cause of schism within Modern Orthodoxy itself."[106]

One other point needs to be made. The argument that women asking to read Megillah are motivated by insincere feminist quests is particularly unfortunate.[107] Having met countless numbers of women in my synagogue, in my Torah classes at Stern College of Yeshiva University,[108] in our Torat Miriam fellowship, and in communities around the world who are seeking to participate in women's Megillah reading, I know first hand of their sincere motivation.

The right of women to read the Megillah has a clear basis in Halakhah. Their quest through this experience to reach higher religious levels of learning and spiritual striving is exemplary and should be applauded.

NOTES

Many thanks to the participants in MeORoT, the Modern Orthodox Rabbinic Training Fellowship and the Torat Miriam Fellowship for Women before whom I gave this shiur on Women and Megillah. Their probing questions and analysis helped shape this paper. Many thanks also to my associates Rabbi Barry Gelman and Rabbi Aaron Frank, as well as to the Rosh ha-Yeshivah of Yeshivat Chovevei Torah, Rabbi Dov Linzer, for their input. I am grateful as well to Rabbi Jacob J. Schacter for his invaluable suggestions as well as to Shimmie Kaminetsky for his help in the technical preparation of this article. And, of course, my gratitude to Rabbi Saul J. Berman, my colleague in MeORoT and Torat Miriam, for his insights and deep friendship.

1. In general, women can fulfill the obligation for men only if they share the same level of obligation. For example, since women and men are equally obligated to light Hanukkah candles, a woman may light Hanukkah candles for a man. See *Shulḥan 'Arukh, Oraḥ Ḥayyim* 675:3, and *Taz, ibid,* 675:4, s.v. *she-af hi ḥayyevet.*

2. I have not followed the common practice of translating *'avadim* as "slaves." The concept of slavery as understood in contemporary times is foreign to Jewish thought, and "slaves," therefore, would be a misleading and inappropriate English translation.

There are several terms in the Torah that have no suitable English equivalent. Such terms should not be translated. Leaving them in the original Hebrew makes the reader understand that a more detailed analysis of the word is necessary. See my "Women and Sifrei Torah," *Tradition* 20:2 (Summer 1982), 106–18, where the term "*tum'ah*" is also not translated for this reason.

3. *Or Zarua'*, *Hil. Megillah* 2:368.

4. *Bet ha-Beḥirah, Megillah* 4a. Meiri adds, "or from the Jerusalem Talmud." Meiri is here referring to the statement in the Jerusalem Talmud (*Megillah* 2:5) that R. Yehoshua b. Levi gathered his children and family together and read the Megillah for them. Some commentators suggest that this proves that women cannot read for others. However, argues Meiri, positions in the Bavli take precedence over those found in the Yerushalmi. It could also be added that it is not necessarily the case that the Jerusalem Talmud is positing that women cannot read for others, for it may simply be recording a particular incident where a man read for his children and family, not precluding the possibility of women reading for others as well. The statement of Bar Kapparah in the Jerusalem Talmud (*Megillah* 2:5) that one must read the Megillah before women and minors may mean that women are also obligated in Megillah.

5. Rashi, *'Arakhin* 3a, s.v. *la-atuyei.*

6. Rashba (R. Shlomo ben Avraham Ibn Adret, late 13c., Spain), *Megillah* 4a, presents a similar position. After quoting the Bavli as the source for the view that women are obligated to read the Megillah and can, therefore, fulfill the obligation for men, he quotes the Tosefta as the source supporting the position that women are obligated only to hear the Megillah and can therefore not fulfill the obligation for men. Rashba then declares that the Tosefta is an erroneous text (*shabeshta hi*). Hence, R. Ovadiah Yosef in *Sefer She'elot u-Teshuvot Yeḥaveh Da'at* 3:51, lists Rashba as supporting the position that women can fulfill the Megillah obligation for men.

7. *Sefer ha-Mikhtam, Megillah* 4a.

8. *Piskei ha-Rid, Megillah* 2:3; Riaz quoted in *Shiltei Gibborim* on R. Alfasi's commentary to *Megillah* 4a, n. 2.

9. *Nimukei Yosef, Megillah* 4a, s.v. *she-af,* 9a. *Sefer ha-Me'orot* (R. Meir ben Shimon mi-Narbonne ha-Me'ili, 13c., Provence), *Megillah* 4a, also states that women can read for men. However, in his commentary to *Megillah* 19a, he is more stringent.

Note also *Baḥ* (R. Yoel Sirkes, 16c., Poland) to *Tur Shulḥan 'Arukh, Oraḥ Ḥayyim* 689, s.v. *u-Ba'al ha-'Ittur katav,* who quotes the *'Ittur* (R. Yiẓh.ak ben Abba Mari, 12c., Provence) permitting women to read for men. However, a reading of the *'Ittur* indicates that women cannot read for men. See *'Aseret ha-Dibbrot, Hilkhot Megillah,* 110a, 113b.

10. Rambam, *Hil. Megillah* 1:1.

11. *Maggid Mishneh* in his commentary to Rambam, *ibid,* 1:2. See also *Shiltei Gibborim* to *Megillah* 4a, n. 2, who concurs.

12. *Sefer Yere'im, 'amud vav, issurim na'asim ve-adam na'aseh ra la-shamaim velo la-briyot,* p. 124a.

13. *Sefer ha-Manhig, Hilkhot Megillah, siman* 25–28, p. 249. *Sefer ha-Manhig* links these cases, as Esther in the Purim story and Yehudit in the Chanukkah story were each involved in bringing about the miracle.

14. *Shulḥan 'Arukh, Oraḥ Ḥayyim,* 675:3.

15. The position that women can fulfill the obligation of men is implicit in other Rishonim who do not distinguish between men and women in Megillah reading. See *Rif* (R. Alfasi, 11c., N. Africa), *Megillah* 4a. See also *Eẓ ha-Ḥayyim* by R. Ya'akov Ḥazzan mi-Lundritz (13c., England), *Hilkhot Megillah,* beginning of the second perek; *Perush Rabbenu Yehonatan me-Lunel* (12c., Provence), *Megillah* 2b; *Shibbolei ha-Leket* (R. Binyamin ben Avraham ha-Rofe, 13c., Italy), siman 195, p. 75.

16. *Sefer ha-Meorot, Megillah* 19b.

17. See *Orḥot Ḥayyim, Hilkhot Megillah u-Purim,* siman 2 and *Kol Bo* to *Megillah* 103. Cf. R. Ovadia Yosef, *Sefer She'elot u-Teshuvot Yeḥaveh Da'at* 3:51 who quotes *Ḥiddushei ha-Rashba, Berakhot* 24a, that "The law of *kol ishah ervah* only applies to songs or greetings of an endearing nature, but words alone (*kol devarim be-'alma*) are permitted." In a conversation I had with R. Ovadiah Yosef he told me that a woman reading the Megillah is not a violation of *kol ishah.* Also see R. Saul J. Ber-

man, "Kol Ishah," in *Rabbi Joseph H. Lookstein Memorial Volume*, ed. R. Leo Landman (New York, 1980), 45–66.

18. See also Auerbach's edition of *Sefer ha-Eshkol* (R. Avraham Av Bet-Din, 12c., Provence), *Hil. Ḥanukkah u-Purim*, siman 9, which also states that women may not read Megillah for men because of *kol ishah*. However, the Auerbach edition of the *'Ittur* is known to have questionable veracity. See Israel Ta-Shema, *R. Zeraḥyah ha-Levi Ba'al ha-Ma'or u-Veney Ḥugo* (Jerusalem, 1992), 40–41; see also Hanokh Albeck, in his introduction to *Sefer ha-Eshkol*. *Encyclopaedia Judaica* 2:147 concludes: "Although there are no grounds for accusing Auerbach of willfully tampering with the manuscript, the version of the Eshkol that Albeck had in hand is undoubtedly the authentic one."

19. *Tosafot, Sukkah* 38a, s.v. *be-emet amru*. This is the first of many different ways to understand the Bahag's position, as will be explained later on.

20. *Semag, Miẓvat 'Aseh* n. 4 of *Divrei Sofrim*.

21. *Ritva, Megillah* 4a, s.v. *ve-amar R. Yehoshua b. Levi*. Ritva states that if women read Megillah for men "it is not *kevod le-ẓibbur* and falls into the category of *me'erah* ('shame')." Note *Semak* (*Sefer Miẓvot Katan* of R. Isaac of Corbeil, 13c., France), Yom Shlishi, 299, who writes that while women are obligated to read Megillah, they cannot fulfill the obligation of men. However, *Semak* does not say which external reason prevents women from fulfilling the Megillah obligation for men.

22. See above, n. 20.

23. *Bet ha-Beḥirah, Megillah* 4a. Meiri argues that if the text reads "*nashim peturin*," women are exempt, why is there a need for the Tosefta to then say "*she-ein moẓi'in*," that they cannot fulfill the obligation [of others].

24. *Ḥiddushei ha-Rashba, Megillah* 4a.

25. *Ḥiddushei ha-Ran, Megillah* 4a.

26. See *Tosafot, 'Arakhin* 3a, s.v. *le-atuyei*.

27. Rabbenu Ḥannanel, *Megillah* 4:1, s.v. *ve-amar R. Yehoshua [ben Levi]*.

28. *Roke'ah., Hilkhot Purim*, n. 236.

29. *'Aseret ha-Dibrot, Hilkhot Megillah*, s.v. *mi kore*, p. 226.

30. Rabbenu Simḥah is quoted in *Haggahot Maimoniyot* to Rambam, *Hil. Megillah* 1:1. See also *Leket Yosher* (R. Yosef b. Moshe, 15c, Germany) (Jerusalem, 1964), 156. He argues that since women are only obligated in *shmi'ah*, they need not hear a clear enunciation of every letter of the Megillah, "*ḥitukh ha-otiyot*." It should be noted that in *Leket Yosher*, R. Yosef b. Moshe was presenting many of the customs and laws of R. Israel Isserlein, the *Terumat ha-Deshen* (15c., Germany).

31. *Ḥiddushei ha-Ran* to *Megillah* 4a, s.v. *nashim ḥayavot*. See Ran to Rif, *Megillah* 4a, who after quoting the Tosefta states that it is not correct, "*eno meḥaver*." In the end, however, Ran states, "It is proper to be concerned with his [Bahag] words and, therefore, be stringent." Here it appears that Ran is less enthusiastic in his support of Bahag, although he concludes that it is best to "be stringent."

32. *Tosafot, 'Arakhin* 3a, s.v. *le-atuyei*, writes that the Tosefta ends with the words "women . . . are exempt from reading Megillah." *Tosafot* then adds: "And Halakhot Gedolot [Bahag] adds, 'but they [the women] are obligated to hear.' "

It should be noted that the *Tosafot* in *Megillah* 4a, s.v. *nashim ḥayyavot be-mikra Megillah*, has an alternative version of the Tosefta that does not include the final phrase of "women are exempt." From *androginus*, however, one can deduce that women cannot read the Megillah for men. If an *androginus*, whose status is "female plus" cannot fulfill the reading obligation of a male, certainly a woman cannot. It follows that while women cannot read for men, they can read for other women as their obligation is the same, to *hear* the Megillah.

33. Rosh, *Megillah* 4a.

34. *Ḥiddushei ha-Ran, Megillah* 4a, s.v. *nashim ḥayyavot*.

35. Note *Shittah Mekubeẓet* (R. Beẓalel Ashkenazi, 16c., Erez. Yisrael), s.v. *Tosafot*

le-atuyei, who cites a text of the Bavli that reads "*le-atuyei mai? Le-atuyei katan.*" "What does the word *'ha-kol'* mean to include? It is meant to include a minor." Accordingly, the Bavli would not be in conflict with the Tosefta.

36. Perhaps this relates to the general question Rav Yosef Dov Soloveitchik, of blessed memory, often raised of whether the *nusaḥ ha-berakhah* describes the *ma'aseh ha-miẓvah* or the *kiyyum ha-miẓvah*.

37. Ra'avyah, *Masekhet Megillah*, n. 569. Ra'avyah also writes: "It is obvious (*davar pashut*) that women can read for themselves (*le-aẓman*)."

38. Mordekhai to *Megillah* 4a. It must be noted that many later Rishonim, mostly German, quoted both Bahag and Rashi without taking a position on the issue. For example, see Rosh (R. Asher ben Yeḥiel, 13c., Germany/Spain) to *Megillah* 4a; *Haggahot Maimoniyot* (R. Meir ben Yekutiel ha-Kohen, 13c., Germany) to Rambam, *Hil. Megillah* 1:1; *Sefer ha-Aguddah* (R. Alexandria Zusslan ha-Kohen, 14c., Germany) to *'Arakhin* 3a, s.v. *ha-kol*; *Ha-Agur* (R. Yaakov Landau, 15c., Germany), *Hil. Ḥannukah, siman* 43, p. 164; Rabbenu Yeruḥem (ben Meshulam, 14c., Northern France and later Spain—a major pupil of the Rosh whose roots were in Germany), *Toledot Adam ve-Ḥavah, Netiv 'Asiri, Ḥelek bet*, p. 63.

39. *Shulḥan 'Arukh, Oraḥ Ḥayyim* 689:1, 2. Note *Shakh* (R. Shabtai b. Meir ha-Kohen, 17c., *Moravia*), *Yoreh De'ah* 94:3, who rules that whenever *Shulḥan 'Arukh* quotes an opinion and then states "*yesh mi she-omer*," the Halakhhah always follows the first opinion. It is likely that this applies to "*yesh omrim*" as well.

40. *Magen Avraham* to *Shulḥan 'Arukh, Oraḥ Ḥayyim* 689:5 quotes the Re'em (R. Eliyahu ben Avraham Mizraḥi, 16c., Turkey) who argues that this would apply to a woman reading even for one man. The principle of *lo plug*, making no distinctions, applies in this case. Just as she cannot read for many men, she cannot read even for one man.

41. Gaon of Vilna, *Shulḥan 'Arukh, Orah. Ḥayyim* 689, s.v. *ve-yesh omrin she-ha-nashim*.

42. Having never seen Ra'avyah's commentary in the original, Rama quotes Mordekhai in Ra'avyah's name. From this perspective, the Rama is not offering a new opinion concerning a woman's reading Megillah for others. What he states is that if one follows the *yesh omrim*, the blessing *lishmoa'* should be recited.

43. See *Darkhei Moshe* to *Tur, Oraḥ Ḥayyim* 689:1. While *Darkhei Moshe* also cites *Rosh* and *Ran, Megillah* 4a, as supporting Bahag's view, it must be emphasized that these Rishonim make no reference to a woman's inability to read for other women.

44. See brackets at end of Rama to *Shulḥan 'Arukh, Oraḥ Ḥayyim* 689:2.

45. See, for example, *Avnei Nezer* (R. Avraham ben Zev Naḥum Bornstein, 19c., Germany), n. 511; *Marḥeshet* (R. Ḥanoch Eiges, 20c., Vilna), n. 22; *Kehillat Ya'akov* (R. Ya'akov Kanefsky, 20c., Israel), in his "Likutim" 5:50.

46. *Marḥeshet*, above. See also *Kehillat Ya'akov*, above. *Marḥeshet* quotes R. Naḥman's comment that "the reading of the Megillah is equivalent to Hallel" (*Megillah* 14a).

47. *Ḥedvat Hashem* (R. Shmuel Grunberger, 20c., United States), "*Be-'Inyanei Purim*," 5:3. See also *Marḥeshet* and *Avnei Nezer*, above.

48. *Kehillat Ya'akov*, above. When this chapter first appeared as an article in The Torah u-Madda Journal (1999), I mistakenly presented Kehillat Ya'akov's position as his conclusion. I am grateful to Rabbi Aaron Cohen for bringing this mistake to my attention.

49. The reason is because the recital of Hallel is a positive commandment fixed by time. See *Bi'ur Halakhah* to *Shulḥan 'Arukh, Oraḥ Ḥayyim* 422, s.v. *Hallel*, end, who concludes that although women are exempt from Hallel, they may recite Hallel with a *berakhah*. However, women from Sephardic communities recite Hallel without a berakhah. See Rabbi Dovid Auerbach (20c., Israel), *Halikhot Betah* 8:2, p. 54.

50. *Marḥeshet* 22:9. As pointed out in n. 46, *Marḥeshet* cites R. Naḥman's opinion

that reading the Megillah is equivalent to Hallel (*Megillah* 14a). Therefore, just as the obligation to recite Hallel applies only to the daytime, so the obligation to read the Megillah as Hallel applies only during the day.

Note '*Emek ha-Berakhah* who disagrees with *Marḥeshet*, claiming women are obligated in the recital of Hallel of Purim. He reasons that this Hallel is a spontaneous Hallel rather than the classic Hallel recited on Yom Tov concerning which women are exempt. Since women are equally obligated in Hallel on Purim, they may read Megillah for men during the day. See '*Emek ha-Berakhah, Hil. Keriyat ha-Megillah,* 3; see also *Ḥedvat Hashem*, above, for an extensive analysis of this position.

51. *Sefer ha-Ḥinukh* no. 603–605.
52. *Ḥedvat Hashem, "Be-'Inyanei Purim,"* 5:3.
53. See, for example, *Sefer ha-Ḥinukh* no. 603, who writes: "and this *miẓvah* (of remembering Amalek) applies . . . to men . . . and not women." There are authorities who maintain that women are obligated in *zekhirat 'Amalek*. See, for example, *Minḥat Ḥinukh* (R. Yosef Babad, 19c, Poland), *ibid*.
54. "*Be-'Inyanei Purim," Ḥedvat Hashem*, 6:2; see also "*Likkutim," Kehillat Ya'akov,* 5:50. Hedvat Hashem notes Kehillat Ya'akov's ultimate rejection of this view. Here again, I am grateful to Rabbi Aaron Cohen for bringing this to my attention.
55. Rashi, *Megillah* 4a, s.v. *she-af hen hayu be-oto ha-nes*, suggests that women were involved in the Purim miracle in the sense that Haman had decreed the murder of women as well as men (Esther 3:13). *Tosafot, Megillah* 4a, s.v. *she-af hen hayu be-oto ha-nes*, cites two positions: that of Rashbam, who states that the miracle of Purim was brought about because of the merit of Esther and the women of that time; and also the view of Rashi, with which *Tosafot* concurs.

Rashi and Rashbam (R. Shmuel ben Meir, 12c., France), *Pesaḥim* 108b, s.v. *she-af hen hayu be-oto ha-nes*, explain "*she-af*" to mean that the Purim miracle occurred as a result of righteous women, including Esther. *Tosafot, ibid.,* s.v. *hayu be-oto ha-nes*, citing a passage in the Yerushalmi, states that women were also included in Haman's decree of extinction.

56. *Turei Even, Megillah* 4a, s.v. *nashim ḥayyavot*. See also R. Daniel Shreiber, "Purim—A Halakhic Overview," '*Alei 'Eẓion* (Shevat 5757), 67.
57. "*Be-'Inyanei Purim," Ḥedvat Hashem* 4:8.

See *Or Same'aḥ, Hil. Megillah* 1:1, who argues that both men and women are obligated in Megillah *mi-divrei kabbalah*. However, men are obligated on a higher level as they are mandated to read the text from the scroll while women are only obligated to read it from any text, even by rote. Therefore, during the day when the *divrei kabbalah* obligation is operative, women cannot read for men. Rabbinically, however, both men and women are equally obligated to read the Megillah from a scroll. It would seem, therefore, that at night, when there is only a rabbinic obligation to read, women could do it for men.

Note also that *Ḥedvat Hashem* cites the opinion that [even at night] women cannot be *moẓi* men since their obligation is a double *de-rabbanan* (i.e. Megillah reading for a woman is *de-rabbanan*, based on *she-af hen hayu be-oto ha-nes*, and Megillah reading itself is a *de-rabbanan*), while a man's obligation is a single *de-rabbanan*, and one obligated in a two *de-rabbanan miẓvah* cannot fulfill the *miẓvah* for one obligated in a single *de-rabbanan. Ḥedvat Hashem*, however, notes the opinion that two *de-rabbanans* can be *moẓi* one *de-rabbanan*. See "*Be-'Inyanei Purim," Ḥedvat Hashem* 4:7.

58. See "*Be-'Inyanei Purim," Ḥedvat Hashem* 4:8; 6:2.
59. See *Korban Netanel*, n. 60 to Rosh on *Megillah, siman* 4.
60. *Magen Avraham* to *Shulḥan 'Arukh, Oraḥ Ḥayyim* 689:6. It is possible that *Magen Avraham* understands *Midrash ha-Ne'elam* on Rut to mean that women—even if only obligated in *shmi'ah*—must hear the Megillah from someone who is man-

dated in *kri'ah*. See *Midrash Rut ha-Ḥadash* (which is also called *Midrash ha-Ne'elam*), *Parshah gimmel*.

61. See "*Hilkhot Megillah,*" *Ḥayyei Adam* 155:11.

62. See *Tosafot* to *Sukkah* 38a, s.v. *be-emet amru*. There *Tosafot* asks, is not the Tosefta which states that women cannot fulfill the obligation of men in Grace After Meals proof that women are not obligated biblically (*mi-de-oraita*) in that *miẓvah*? To this *Tosafot* responds in his second answer that it is possible that women, like men, have a biblical obligation, but they cannot fulfill a man's obligation because of the external reason of *zila milta*. *Tosafot* notes that this is similar to Megillah where women may be on the same level of obligation as men but cannot read for them because of *zila milta*.

63. See "*Be-'Inyanei Purim,*" *Ḥedvat Hashem*, 4:8. Note also that *Korban Netanel* makes his point, about *Tosafot's* understanding of Bahag, on Rosh's comment that a woman can read "*le-ḥavertah*" (see Rosh, *Megillah* 4a, s.v. *amar R. Yehoshua b. Levi*). Rather than understand "*le-ḥavertah*" generically, *Korban Netanel* deduces from "*le-ḥavertah*" that a woman may read for one woman, but not for more than one, ie., a case which would be "*le-ḥaverotehen*." But Rosh writes "*le-ḥavertah*" in his analysis that women cannot read for men because their *ḥiyyuv* is less, ie., one of *shmi'ah* vs. *kri'ah*. To argue that the obligation of *shmi'ah* would only allow a woman to read for one woman but not more is extremely difficult.

Apparently, *Korban Netanel* understands the lesser obligation of *shmi'ah* as being a function of *zila milta*. In other words, the internal deficiency (*shmi'ah* vs. *kri'ah*) is caused by an external flaw (*zila milta*). Given this perspective of *Korban Netanel*, it seems that he did not see the *Tosafot ha-Rosh*, *Sukkah* 38a, s.v. *be-emet amru* (written by Rosh himself), who says that *zila milta* is confined to a woman reading for men. See R. Yehudah Herzl Henkin who makes this very point in *She'elot u-Teshuvot Benei Vanim* 2:10. Moreover, in the *Kiẓur Piskei ha-Rosh* (written by the son of the Rosh, R. Ya'akov b. Asher, 14 c., Germany/Spain; *Megillah* 1:4) which summarizes the rulings of the Rosh, it is clear that a woman can read for more than one woman.

64. *Midrash Rut ha-Ḥadash*, *Parshah gimmel*.

65. Rabbi Abba's comment follows the words: "We learnt, 'woe to a man whose wife or children say a blessing [Grace After Meals] for him.' "

66. Note a similar phrase in *Tosefta Megillah* 2:4, "*ve-en moẓi'in et ha-rabbim yedei ḥovatan,*" which means that [for Megillah reading] a woman cannot fulfill the obligation for men. Just as the word "*rabbim*" in the Tosefta refers to men, so could the word "*aḥerim*" in *Midrash ha-Ne'elam* refer to men.

Note also that Vilna Gaon in his commentary to *Shulḥan 'Arukh, Oraḥ Ḥayyim* 689:2, quotes the *Midrash ha-Ne'elam* in his discussion of the second view of the Meḥaber in which the Meḥaber states that women cannot fulfill the Megillah obligation of men. See *Biur Ha-Gra* to *Shulḥan 'Arukh, Oraḥ Ḥayyim* 689, s.v. *en moẓe'ot*.

See furthermore the Gaon's commentary to *Midrash Rut ha-Ḥadash* where it is not clear that he understands the text to mean that a woman cannot read for other women. When the Gra, commenting on the *Midrash Rut* writes, "*me-lashon zeh mashma' de-le-aẓman yekholim likrot,*" he may very well mean that from this formulation it would appear that a woman may read for other women. "*Le-aẓman*" does not mean "for herself" (in the singular), but rather "for themselves," that is, for other women.

67. The only deflection would be the forced reading of *Tosafot* in *Sukkah* 38a, s.v. *be-emet amru* and *Rosh* to *Megillah* 4a according to *Korban Netanel*.

68. This is the opinion of *Semag* quoted by *Magen Avraham* to *Shulḥan 'Arukh, Oraḥ Ḥayyim* 689:15. See *Sha'ar ha-Ẓiyun* to *Shulḥan 'Arukh, Oraḥ Ḥayyim* 689:13.

69. This is the opinion of *Tosafot* to '*Arakhin* 3a, s.v. *le-atuyei*, quoted by *Biur ha-Gra*, *Shulḥan 'Arukh, Oraḥ Ḥayyim* 689, s.v. *ve-yesh omrim she-ha-nashim*. See *Sha'ar ha-Ẓiyun* to *Shulḥan 'Arukh, Oraḥ Ḥayyim* 689:14.

70. *Mishnah Brurah* to *Shulḥan 'Arukh, Oraḥ Ḥayyim* 689:7. In the case of *kevod ha-ẓibbur*, the principle of *lo plug* is applied. If a woman cannot read for many men, she cannot read for even one man.

71. *Mishnah Brurah* 689:7; *Sha'ar ha-Ẓiyun* 689:15. Here, *Sha'ar ha-Ẓiyun* introduces *zila milta*, which *Mishnah Brurah* does not explicitly mention.

72. *Mishnah Brurah* 689:8. See also *Sha'ar ha-Ẓiyun*, n. 16 who disputes *Magen Avraham*'s reading of *Midrash ha-Ne'elam* that a woman cannot read for herself. Citing Gra's reading in the name of the *Zohar* of the *Midrash ha-Ne'elam*, and *Ḥayyei Adam*'s reading of the Midrash (*Hil. Megillah* 155:11), *Sha'ar ha-Ẓiyun* concludes that a woman can read for herself. Certainly this would be the case if there is no one else to read for her. Cf. above, n. 66.

73. See *Bet Yosef, Tur, Oraḥ Ḥayyim* 689.

74. Note also that although having taken a restrictive position in explaining Rama, *Sha'ar ha-Ẓiyun* states that the "first opinion [in Meḥaber] that women are obligated to read is the essential one (*'ikarit*)." See *Sha'ar ha-Ẓiyun* to *Shulḥan 'Arukh, Oraḥ Ḥayyim* 689:16.

75. *Darkhei Moshe, Yoreh De'ah* 65:12.

76. See *Bet Yosef, Tur Oraḥ Ḥayyim, siman* 25, s.v. *ve-yevarekh*. See also the following *poskim* who concur with this position: *She'elot u-Teshuvot Ḥakham Ẓevi* (R. Z.evi Ashkenazi, 17–18c.), no. 36, s.v. *ve-ẓarikh*; *She'ilat Ya'veẓ* (R. Yaakov Emden, 18c., Germany), 1:47; *Noda' bi-Yehudah* (R. Yeḥezkel Landau, 18c., Prague), *Mahadura Kama, Yoreh De'ah* no. 74, s.v. *u-me'atah*; *She'elot u-Teshuvot Ḥatam Sofer, Oraḥ Ḥayyim* no. 36; Rabbi Moshe Feinstein, *Iggrot Moshe, Oraḥ Ḥayyim*, 5:24; R. Ovadiah Yosef, *She'elot u-Teshuvot Yabia' Omer* 6, *Oraḥ Ḥayyim*, no. 2, s.v. *ve-'ad-ayin* and *Sefer She'elot u-Teshuvot Yeḥaveh Da'at*, 3:70, s.v. *amnam*.

77. See *Darkhei Moshe, Tur, Oraḥ Ḥayyim* 689:1.

78. *'Arukh ha-Shulḥan* to *Oraḥ Ḥayyim* 689:5.

79. See his "Ẓe'i Lakh be-'Ikvei ha-Ẓon," *Bet Yiẓḥak* 17 (5745), 118.

80. In recent years, great halakhists have been quoted on both sides of the issue. For an extensive list of the views of modern day posekim regarding this subject, see R. Aryeh Avraham Frimer and R. Dov Frimer, "Women's Prayer Services—Theory and Practice," *Tradition* 32:2 (Winter, 1998): nn. 44, 78, 79, 106, 220, 221.

81. Rabbi Lichtenstein asked that when Purim is a *nidḥeh* (pushed to another date), a woman should not read for other women.

82. R. Ovadiah Yosef, *Sefer She'elot u-Teshuvot Yeḥaveh Da'at* 3:51. See also R. Yiẓḥak Yosef (son of R. Ovadiah Yosef), *Sefer Yalkut Yosef, Hilkhot Mikra Megillah*, n. 12, who states that the essential view is that women can fulfill the Megillah obligation for men, but one should be stringent unless an urgent situation arises. See *Shakh* quoted above, n. 39.

83. See *Mishnah Megillah* 1:1.

84. Rif to *Megillah* 5a.

85. Rabbenu Tam as quoted in *Tur, Oraḥ Ḥayyim* 690. See *Tosafot, Megillah* 5a, s.v. *havah 'uvda*.

86. Quoted in *Tur, ibid.*

87. See *Baḥ* to *Tur, ibid*, s.v. *u-Bahag*.

88. *Shulḥan 'Arukh, Oraḥ Ḥayyim* 690:18.

89. For a general discussion of this subject, see *Women at Prayer* (Hoboken, 1990), 43–56.

90. Rashi, *Berakhot* 45b, s.v. *de-afilu me'ah ke-trei gavrei damyan*.

91. *Tosafot, ibid.*, s.v. *ve-ha me'ah nashei ke-trei gavrei damyan*.

92. See *Women at Prayer*, p. 46, n. 15.

93. *Bet ha-Beḥirah, Megillah* 5a. R. Aryeh Avraham Frimer, "Ma'amad ha-Ishah be-Halakhah—Nashim u-Minyan," *Or ha-Mizraḥ* 34 (Tishrei 5746), 69–86, suggests that this may be the position of Rashi recorded above. For Rashi, the absolute exclu-

sion relates only to *zimmun*. In all other areas, it would depend on the correlation principle. If women are equally obligated, they count toward the minyan; if not, they do not.

94. *Bet ha-Beḥirah, Berakhot* 47b.

95. Ran to *Megillah*, chap. 2, end, s.v. *ha-kol kesherim likrot ha-Megillah.*

96. See Rama to *Shulḥan 'Arukh, Oraḥ Ḥayyim* 690:18. From here there may be support for the position that Rama does not offer a definitive pesak concerning women reading Megillah for men (*Shulḥan 'Arukh, Oraḥ Ḥayyim* 689:2). If his position was that women cannot read for men (and, for that matter, for other women), he would unequivocally state that women cannot be counted in a Megillah minyan. This is true unless Rama's position is that the Megillah minyan is needed only for *pirsuma nisa*, in which case women can count even if they are not on the same level of obligation as men. See discussion of this Rama in *Women at Prayer*, p. 51, n. 30. See also *ibid*, pp. 53–56, where I argue that equality of obligation may be necessary even in a minyan needed for publicity (*pirsuma*).

97. See R. Aryeh Avraham Frimer (above, n. 93), p. 63. Still, in most cases of minyan needed for publicity (*pirsuma*), the connection between equality of obligation and the right to be counted among the ten is evident. See the examples cited in *Women at Prayer*, pp. 54–55.

98. R. Ẓevi Pesaḥ Frank, *Mikra'ei Kodesh: Hanukkah/Purim* (Jerusalem, 1982), 131–32, n. 29.

99. R. Eliezer Yehudah Waldenberg, *Ẓiẓ Eliezer* 13 (Jerusalem, 1985), p. 145, n. 73.

100. R. Ovadiah Yosef, *Yabia' Omer* 8 (Jerusalem, 1995), *Oraḥ Ḥayyim*, p. 246, n. 56.

101. *Ibid.* See also Joel B. Wolowelsky, *Women, Jewish Law, and Modernity*, (Hoboken, 1997), 94–98.

102. It is difficult to understand why *Magen Avraham*, *Ḥayyei Adam* and *Mishnah Brurah* disagreed with virtually every Rishon and were so restrictive. It should be noted that *Magen Avraham* whose view was adopted by *Ḥayyei Adam* and *Mishnah Brurah*, and, indeed, was the first to understand the Rama as being the position of the *Midrash ha-Ne'elam*, often quotes the *Zohar* as being the definitive *pesak*, even if it is contrary to the view of the poskim. See *Encyclopaedia Judaica* 7:776: "He [*Magen Avraham*] also thought highly of the *Zohar* and of the Kabbalists, R. Isaac Luria, and R. Isaiah Horowitz, occasionally accepting their decision against that of the codifiers." The position of *Korban Netanel* in his understanding of *zila milta*, as preventing a woman from reading the Megillah for other women, is equally difficult to understand. Perhaps the simple reality that women were not reading Megillah for others prompted the development of this more restrictive school.

103. It ought be pointed out that *Ḥedvat Hashem* and *Marḥeshet* quoted earlier were not necessarily offering a *pesak halakhah*. Rather, they were making a theoretical point in which they distinguished between Megillah reading at night and during the day.

104. See *Mishnah Brurah* to *Shulḥan 'Arukh, Oraḥ Ḥayyim* 689:1.

105. On January 14, 1997, the Vaad Harabonim of Queens issued a resolution prohibiting women Megillah readings, amongst other practices. In their statement they declared that "these practices are *'poreẓ geder bi-mesorat Yisrael.'* "

106. "The Sea Change in American Orthodox Judaism: A Symposium," *Tradition* 32:4 (Summer, 1998), 30.

107. See *Women at Prayer*, pp. 112–15.

108. In Purim of 5757–1997, 175 students (or almost twenty-five percent) of Stern College, Yeshiva University, petitioned to be able to have a women's Megillah reading.

Traditional Authorities and Sources Cited in This Book

Agur. Halakhic work by Rabbi Jacob Landau (Germany and Italy, 15th cent.).

Akedat Yiẓḥak. Commentary on Pentateuch by Rabbi Isaac Arama (Spain, 1420–1494).

Arukh ha-Shulḥan. Halakhic code by Rabbi Jehiel Michal Epstein (Belorussia, 1829–1908).

Ba'al ha-Ittur. Halakhic compendium by Rabbi Isaac ben Abba Mari of Marseilles (Provence and Spain, 1122–1193).

Ba'al ha-Ma'or. Halakhic work critical of Rif by Rabbi Zeraḥiah ben Isaac ha-Levi Gerondi (Provence, 12th cent.).

Ba'al Shem Ṭov. Rabbi Israel ben Eliezer (Russia, 1700–1760), rabbi and mystic; founder of the hasidic movement.

Ba'er Heitev. Commentary on *Shulḥan Arukh* by Rabbi Judah Ashkenazi (Germany and Poland, 18th cent.).

Baḥ (Bayit Ḥadash). Commentary on *Tur Shulḥan Arukh* by Rabbi Joel Sirkes (Poland, 1561–1640).

Be'er ha-Golah. Commentary on *Shulḥan Arukh* by Rabbi Moses Rivkes (Lithuania, 17th cent.).

Behag (Ba'al Halakhot Gedolot). Anonymous author of *Halakhot Gedolot*, a halakhic compendium dating from the gaonic period (8th–9th cent.).

Beit Yosef. Commentary on *Tur Shulḥan Arukh* by Rabbi Joseph Karo (Israel, 1488–1575).

Besamim Rosh. Written by Rabbi Saul Berlin (1740–1794) but attributed to Rosh (Germany and Spain, 1250–1327).

Be'ur ha-Gra. Commentary on *Shulḥan Arukh* by Rabbi Elijah ben Solomon (Lithuania, 1720–1797), also known as the Vilna Gaon.

Be'ur Halakhah. Halakhic work by Rabbi Israel Meir ha-Kohen (Lithuania, 1838–1933), also known as Ḥafeẓ Ḥayyim.

Binyamin Ze'ev. Responsa of Rabbi Benjamin Ze'ev ben Mattathias of Arta (Epirus, 16th cent.).

Dammesek Eliezer. Commentary on *Shulḥan Arukh* by Rabbi Eliezer Lipschutz (Poland, 18th cent.).

Divrei Ḥayyim. Halakhic works and hasidic discouses by Rabbi Ḥayyim Halberstam founder of the Zanz dynasty of hasidic leaders (Poland, 1792–1876).

Eliyahu Rabbah. Commentary on *Levush* by Rabbi Elijah Shapira (Bohemia, 1660–1712).

Gilyonei ha-Shas. Commentary on Talmud by Rabbi Joseph Engel (Poland, 1859–1920).

Gra. Ha-Gaon Rabbi Elijah ben Solomon Zalman (Lithuania, 1720–1797), also known as the Vilna Gaon.

Haggahot Asheri. Notes on Rosh's commentary on Talmud by Rabbi Israel of Krems (Austria, 14th cent.).

Haggahot ha-Gra. Notes on *Shulḥan Arukh* by Rabbi Elijah ben Solomon (Lithuania, 1720–1797), also known as the Vilna Gaon.

Haggahot Maimuniyyot. Commentary on *Mishneh Torah* by Rabbi Meir of Rothenburg (Germany, 1237–1299).

Haggahot Rabbi Akiva Eger. Notes on the *Shulḥan Arukh* by Rabbi Akiva Eger (Poland, 1761–1837).

Ḥayyei Adam. Halakhic work by Rabbi Abraham Danzig (Lithuania, 1748–1820).

Ḥida. Rabbi Ḥayyim Joseph David Azulai (Israel, 1724–1806). See also *Tuv Ayin.*

Ḥiddushei Batra. Commentary on the Talmud attributed to Rabbi Ḥayyim Altusky of Jerusalem.

Ḥiddushei Ran. Notes on *Sefer ha-Halakhot* by Rabbi Nissim Gerondi (Spain, 1310–1375).

Ḥiddushei Rav Ḥayyim ha-Levi. Commentary on Rambam's *Mishneh Torah* by Rabbi Ḥayyim ha-Levi Soloveichik (Lithuania, 1853–1918), grandfather of Rav Joseph B. Soloveitchik and Rav Aaron Soloveichik.

Iggerot ha-Re'ayah. Profound letters by Rabbi Abraham Isaac ha-Cohen Kook (1865–1935), first Ashkenazic Chief Rabbi of Israel.

Iggerot Mosheh. Responsa by Rav Moshe Feinstein (U.S., 1895–1986).

Issur ve-Heter. Responsa, etc. attributed to Rashi and compiled by his students.

Kaf ha-Ḥayyim. Commentary on *Shulḥan Arukh* by Rabbi Jacob Ḥayyim Sofer (Iraq, 20th cent.).

Keli Yakar. Commentary on Pentateuch by Rabbi Ephraim of Luntshits (Poland, 1550–1619).

Kenesset ha-Gedolah. Halakhic work by Rabbi Ḥayyim Benveniste (Turkey, 1603–1673).

Kerem Ẓevi. Responsa by Rabbi Samuel Turk (U.S., 20th cent.).

Keren Orah. Commentary on Talmud by Rabbi Isaac of Karlin (Lithuania, 1788–1851).

Kesef Mishneh. Commentary on *Mishneh Torah* by Rabbi Joseph Karo (Israel, 1488–1575).

Korban ha-Edah. Commentary on Jerusalem Talmud by Rabbi David Fraenkel (Germany, 18th cent.).

Koret ha-Berit. Commentary on *Shulḥan Arukh* by Rabbi Elia Posek (Russia, 20th cent.).

Leḥem Mishneh. Commentary on *Mishneh Torah* by Rabbi Abraham di Boton (Salonika, 1545–1588).

Levush. Halakhic code compiled by Rabbi Mordecai Jaffe (Poland, 1535–1612).

Levushei Serad. Commentary on *Shulḥan Arukh, Magen Avraham,* and *Taz* by Rabbi David Eyebeshuetz (Poland, 18th cent.).

Likkutei Halakhot. Commentary on sections of the Talmud by Rabbi Israel Meir ha-Kohen (Lithuania, 1838–1933), also known as Ḥafeẓ Ḥayyim.

Magen Avraham. Commentary on *Shulḥan Arukh* by Rabbi Abraham Gombiner (Poland, 1636–1683).

Magen Gibborim. Commentary on *Shulḥan Arukh* by Rabbi Mordecai Zev Ettinger (Poland, 1804–1863), in collaboration with his brother-in-law Joseph Saul ha-Levi Nathanson.

Maharsha. Moreinu ha-Rav Samuel Eliezer Edels (Poland, 1555–1631). Author of commentary on Tosafot.

Maḥazeh Eliyahu. Responsa of Rabbi Pesaḥ Eliyahu Falk (England, 20th cent.).

Maḥaẓit ha-Shekel. Commentary on *Shulḥan Arukh* by Rabbi Samuel Kolin (Germany, 1720–1806).

Maḥzor Vitry. Halakhic/liturgical work by Rabbi Simḥah ben Samuel of Vitry (France, 11th cent.).

Maimonides, Moses. See Rambam.

Margaliyyot ha-Yam. Commentary on Talmud by Rabbi Reuben Margaliot (Poland and Israel, 1889–1971).

Massekhet Soferim. Minor tractate of Talmud.

Megillat Esther. Defense of Rambam's *Sefer ha-Mitzvot* by Rabbi Isaac ben Eliezer De Leon (Spain and Italy, 16th cent.).

Meiri. Commentary on Talmud by Rabbi Menaḥem ha-Meiri (Provence, 1249–1316).

Menorat ha-Ma'or. Ethical work by Rabbi Isaac Aboab (Spain, 14th cent.).

Meshekh Ḥokhmah. Commentary on Pentateuch by Rabbi Meir Simḥah of Dvinsk (Latvia, 1843–1926).

Minḥat Ḥinnukh. Commentary on *Sefer ha-Ḥinnukh* by Rabbi Joseph Babad (Poland, 1800–1874).

Mishkenot Ya'akov. Responsa by Rabbi Jacob of Karlin (Lithuania, 1781–1844).

Mishnah Berurah. Commentary on *Shulḥan Arukh* by Rabbi Israel Meir ha-Kohen (Lithuania, 1838–1933), also known as Ḥafeẓ Ḥayyim.

Mishneh Torah (also known as *Yad ha-Ḥazakah*). Halakhic code compiled by Rabbi Moses Maimonides (Rambam) (Egypt, 1135–1204).

Mordekhai. Halakhic work by Rabbi Mordecai ben Hillel ha-Kohen (Germany, 1240–1298).

Moznayim la-Mishpat. Responsa by Rabbi Zalman Sorotzkin (Israel, 1881–1966).

Naḥalat Ya'akov. Responsa by Rabbi Jacob Lorberbaum (Poland, 1760–1832).

Naḥalat Ẓevi. Halakhic work by Rabbi Gedaliah Felder (Canada, 20th cent.).

Naḥmanides, Moses. See Ramban.

Or Same'aḥ. Commentary on *Mishneh Torah* by Rabbi Meir Simḥah of Dvinsk (Latvia, 1843–1926).

Or Zaru'a. Halakhic work by Rabbi Isaac of Vienna (Austria, 1180–1250).

Oẓar ha-Geonim. Compendium of gaonic responsa by Dr. Benjamin M. Lewin (Israel, 1879–1944).

Peri Ḥadash. Halakhic work critical of *Shulḥan Arukh* by Rabbi Hezekiah da Silva (Israel, 1659–1695).

Peri Megadim. Commentary on *Shulḥan Arukh* by Rabbi Joseph Teomim (Poland, 1727–1792).

Perishah. Commentary on *Tur Shulḥan Arukh* by Rabbi Joshua Falk (Poland, 1555–1614).

Perush ha-Mishnayot. Commentary on Mishnah by Rabbi Moses Maimonides (Rambam) (Egypt, 1135–1204).

Pitḥei Teshuvah. Commentary on *Shulḥan Arukh* by Rabbi Abraham Eisenstadt (Lithuania, 1813–1868).

Rabbenu Hai. Hai ben Sherira (Babylon, 939–1038), gaon of Pumbedita, author of responsa.

Rabbenu Jonah. Rabbi Jonah ben Abraham Gerondi. Talmudist, author, moralist, wrote commentary on Rif to Berakhot. (Spain, 1200–1263).

Rabbenu Simḥah. Rabbi Simḥah ben Samuel of Speyer (Germany, 12th–13th cent.), author of responsa.

Rabbenu Tam. Rabbi Jacob Tam (France, 1100–1171), one of the key Tosafot.

Radbaz. Rabbi David ben Solomon ibn Abi Zimra (Egypt, 1479–1530), author of responsa.

Rambam. Rabbi Moses ben Maimon (Maimonides) (Egypt, 1135–1204), philosopher, talmudist, and physician; author of *Mishneh Torah* (referred to in this volume as Rambam's *Code*), *Perush ha-Mishnayot, Sefer ha-Mizvot* (*Book of Commandments*), and *Moreh Nevukhim* (*Guide of the Perplexed*).

Ramban. Rabbi Moses ben Naḥman (Naḥmanides) (Spain, 1194–1270), philosopher and talmudist, author of numerous halakhic and talmudic works and of commentary on Pentateuch.

Ran. Rabbi Nissim of Gerondi (Spain, 1310–1375), see *Ḥiddushei Ran.*

Rashal. Rabbi Solomon Luria (Poland, 1510–1574), author of responsa and Talmudic commentaries.

Rashbam. Rabbi Samuel ben Meir (France, 1085–1174), author of commentary on Bible and parts of Talmud.

Rashi. Rabbi Solomon ben Isaac (France, 1040–1105). Foremost commentator on Bible and Talmud.

Rav Pe'alim. Responsa of Rabbi Joseph Ḥayyim ben Eliyahu (Iraq, 1835–1909).

Ravyah. Rabbi Eliezer ben Joel ha-Levi (Germany, 1140–1225), author of responsa.

Rema. Rabbi Moses Isserles (Poland, 1525–1572), author of *Mappah*, glosses to *Shulḥan Arukh* reflecting Ashkenazic practice.

Ri bereb Yehudah. One of the Tosafot.

Rif. Rabbi Isaac Alfasi (North Africa and Spain, 1013–1103), see *Sefer ha-Halakhot.*

Ritva. Rabbi Yom Tov Ishbili (Spain, 1250–1327), author of commentary on Talmud.

Rivash. Rabbi Isaac ben Sheset Perfet (North Africa, 1326–1408), author of responsa.

Rosh. Rabbi Asher ben Jehiel (Germany and Spain, 1250–1327) author of halakhic compilation on the Talmud.

Saadia Gaon. (Egypt, born 880), philosopher, talmudist, grammarian. Author of a liturgical handbook: *siddur.*

Sefer Abudarham. Halakhic commentary on prayer by Rabbi David ben Joseph Abudarham (Spain, 14th cent.).

Sefer Emek Berakhah. Responsa of Rabbi Aryeh Pomeranchik (Israel, 1908–1942).

Sefer ha-Berit. Work on circumcision by Rabbi Moshe Pirutinsky (U.S., 20th cent.).

Sefer ha-Eshkol. Halakhic code by Rabbi Abraham ben Isaac of Narbonne (Provence, 1110–1179).

Sefer ha-Halakhot. Halakhic discourses on the Talmud by Rabbi Isaac Alfasi (North Africa and Spain, 1013–1103).

Sefer ha-Ḥinnukh. Exposition of the 613 commandments by Rabbi Aaron ha-Levi of Barcelona (Spain, 14th cent.).

Sefer ha-Ikkarim. Religio-philosophical work by Rabbi Joseph Albo (Spain, 1380–1444).

Sefer ha-Masbir. Notes taken by a student on the classes of Rav Joseph Dov Soloveitchik. Analysed in *Ḥiddushei Batra.*

Sefer ha-Orah. Halakhic work by Rabbi Moses ben Rabbi Shemaiah (France, 12th cent.).

Sefer ha-Pardes. Anonymous halakhic work sometimes attributed to Rashi (France, 1040–1105).

Sefer Ḥasidim. Halakhic/philosophical work by Rabbi Judah he-Ḥasid (Judah the Pious) (Germany, 1150–1217).

Sefer Kuzari. Philosophical work by Rabbi Judah Halevi (Spain, 1080–1145).

Sefer Mayan Ganim. Responsa Rabbi Samuel ben Elḥanan Jacob Rakvalti (Italy, 16th cent.).

Semag (Sefer Mitzvot Gadol). Analysis of the 613 commandments by Rabbi Moses of Coucy (France, 13th cent.).

Seridei Eish. Responsa by Jehiel Jacob Weinberg (Germany and Switzerland, 1895–1966).

Sha'agat Aryeh. Responsa of Rabbi Aryeh Leib Gunzberg (Lithuania, 1695–1785).

Sha'ar ha-Zion. Notes by Rabbi Israel Meir ha-Kohen (Lithuania. 1838–1933), also known as Ḥafez Ḥayyim, to his *Mishnah Berurah.*

Shevut Ya'akov. Responsa of Rabbi Jacob Reicher (Poland, 18th cent.).

Shibbolei ha-Lekhet. Halakhic work by Rabbi Zedekiah ben Abraham Anav (Italy, 13th cent.).

Shulḥan Arukh. Preeminent code of Jewish law, divided into four parts, following the outline of the *Tur Shulḥan Arukh:* Oraḥ Ḥayyim—daily prayers, Sabbaths and festivals; Yoreh De'ah—dietary laws and other religious observances; Even ha-Ezer—family law and matters of personal status; Ḥoshen Mishpat—civil law. Compiled by Rabbi Joseph Karo (Spain and Israel, 1488–1575) and printed with Rema's glosses reflecting usages of Ashkenazic Jewry.

Shulḥan Arukh ha-Rav. Halakhic code by Rabbi Shneur Zalman of Lyady (Russia, 18th cent.), founder of Ḥabad Hassidism.

Sugah ba-Shoshanim. Halakhic work by Rabbi Eliyahu Shmuel Wind (Israel, 20th cent.).

Targum Yerushalmi (also known as Targum Jonathan ben Uzziel). Aramaic translation of Pentateuch (Israel, 7th–8th cent.).

Taz (*Turei Zahav*). Commentary on *Shulḥan Arukh* by Rabbi David ben Samuel ha-Levi (Poland, 1586–1667).

Teshuvah me-Ahavah. Responsa of Rabbi Eleazar Fleckeles (Bohemia, 1754–1826).

Tiferet Yisrael. Commentary on Mishnah by Rabbi Israel Lipschutz (Poland, 1782–1860).

Toledot Ya'akov. Responsa by Rabbi Jacob Zev Kahane.

Torah Temimah. Commentary on Pentateuch by Rabbi Barukh Epstein (Poland, 1860–1942).

Tosafot. Lit. "Additions." Comments on Talmud by students of Rashi and members of French and German yeshivot (12th–14th cent.).

Tosafot Rid. Commentary on Talmud by Rabbi Isaiah ben Mali di Trani (Italy, 1180–1260).

Tosafot Yom Tov. Commentary on Mishnah by Rabbi Yom Tov Lipmann Heller (Moravia, 1579–1654).

Tur Shulḥan Arukh (also known as *Arba'ah Turim*). Halakhic code compiled by Rabbi Jacob ben Asher (Germany and Spain, 1275–1340).

Tuv Ayin. Responsa of Rabbi Ḥayyim Joseph David Azulai (Israel, 1724–1806), also known as Ḥida.

Yabia Omer. Responsa of Rabbi Ovadiah Joseph (Israel, 20th cent.), former Sephardic Chief Rabbi.

Yad Eliyahu. Responsa of Rabbi Elijah Ragoler (Lithuania, 1794–1850).

Yaveẓ. Rabbi Jacob Emden (Germany, 1698–1776), author of commentary on Talmud, *Haggahot ve-Ḥiddushim.*

Yeḥaveh Da'at. Responsa of Rabbi Ovadiah Joseph (Israel, 20th cent.), former Sephardic Chief Rabbi.

Ẓlaḥ (Ẓiyyun le-Nefesh Ḥayyah). Commentary on Talmud by Rabbi Ezekiel Landau (Prague, 1713–1793).

Ẓiẓ Eliezer. Responsa by Rabbi Eliezer Waldenberg (Switzerland and Israel, 20th cent.).

Bibliography

Alpert, Rabbi Nissan, et al. "*Teshuvah be-Inyan Nashim be-Hakafot ve-khu.*" *Hadarom* 54 (Sivan, 5745): 49–50

Auerbach, Rabbi David. *Halikhot Beitah*. Jerusalem: Sha'arei Ziv, 5743.

Auman, Rabbi Kenneth. "Orthodoxy Requires Sage Discussion." *Shema*, 15/299, October 18, 1985. 145–146.

Barth, Dr. Aron. *The Modern Jew Faces Eternal Problems*. Jerusalem: World Zionist Organization, Religious Section of the Youth and Heḥalutz Department, 1956.

Berkovits, Rabbi Eliezer, *Women in Time and Torah*. Hoboken: Ktav Publishing House, 1990.

Berman, Rabbi Saul J. "Kol Ishah." In *Rabbi Joseph H. Lookstein Memorial Volume*, edited by Rabbi Leo Landman, pp. 45–66. New York: Ktav Publishing House, 1980.

———. "The Status of Women in Halakhic Judaism." *Tradition* 14, no. 2 (Fall 1973): 5–28.

Besdin, Rabbi Abraham R. *Reflections of the Rav: Lessons in Jewish Thought, Adapted from Lectures of Rabbi Joseph B. Soloveitchik*. Jerusalem: World Zionist Organization, Department for Torah Education and Culture in the Diaspora, 1979.

Bleich, Rabbi J. David. "Religious Experience? *tefillah betzibbur*?" *Shema*, 15/299, October 18, 1985. 146–149.

———. "Survey of Recent Halakhic Periodical Literature: Women in a *Minyan*?" *Tradition* 14, no. 2 (Fall 1973): 113–117.

———. "The Constitution and the Jewish Problem." *Shema*, 17/336, September 4, 1987: 123–26

Brama, Rabbi Beni. "*Kavim le-Shitato shel ha-Rav ha-Gaon Yosef Dov Soloveitchik be-Hanhagat Yeshivat Rambam*," in Amnon Shapira, *Teshuvah le-Ḥaverim ha-Shoalim al Ḥevra Me'urevet (Banim u-Banot) bi-Vnei Akiva be-Yamenu*. Jerusalem: Bnei Akiva, 57–59.

Bronspigel, Rabbi Abba. "Minyanim Meyuḥadim le-Nashim." *Hadarom*, no. 54 (Sivan 5745): 51–53.

De Sola Pool, Rabbi David. *The Kaddish*. New York: Bloch Publishing Co., 1929.

Elbogen, Ismar. *Ha-Tefillah be-Zibbur*. Israel: Dvir, 1972.

Ellison, Rabbi Elyakim. *Ha-Ishah ve-ha-Mitzvot*. Jerusalem: World Zionist Organization, Department for Torah Education and Culture in the Diaspora, 5735.

Elon, Dr. Menachem. *Ha-Mishpat ha-Ivri*. Jerusalem: Magnes Press, 5738.

Epstein, Rabbi Isidore. *The Faith of Judaism*. London: Soncino Press, 1954.

Feldman, Rabbi David M. "Women's Role and Jewish Law." *Conservative Judaism* 26, no. 4 (Summer 1972): 29–39.

Firer, Rabbi Ben Tzion. "*Be-Inyan Limud Torah le-Banot.*" *Noam* 3 (1966): 131–134.

Frimer, Rabbi Aryeh Avraham. "Ma'amad ha̤-Isha be-Halakhah—Nashim u-Minyan." *Or ha-Mizrach* 34 (Tishrei 5746): 69–86.

———. "Women and Minyan." *Tradition* 23, no. 4 (Summer 1988): 54–77.

Fuchs, Rabbi Yitzchak Ya'akov. *Ha-Tefillah be-Ẓibbur*. Jerusalem, 1978.

Henkin, Rabbi Yehudah Herzl. "Mahu Kevod ha-Ẓibbur?" *Hadarom*, no. 55 (Elul 5746): 33–41.

Hirsch, Rabbi Samson Raphael. *Horeb*. Translated by Dayan Dr. I. Grunfeld. London: Soncino Press, 1962.

———. *Commentary on the Bible*. London, 1963.

Kasdan, Rabbi Menachem M. "Are Women Obligated to Pray?" *Journal of Halakha and Contemporary Society* 1, no. 2 (Fall 1981).

———. "Hakhel." *Gesher* 4, no. 1 (1969): 70–80.

Kon, Abraham. *Prayer*. London: Soncino Press, 1971.

Krauss, Samuel. "The Jewish Rite of Covering the Head." *HUCA* 19 (1945–1946): 121–168.

Lamm, Rabbi Maurice. *The Jewish Way of Death and Mourning*. New York: Jonathan David, 1969.

Lamm, Rabbi Norman. *A Hedge of Roses*. New York: Feldheim, 1966.

———. "Separate Pews in the Synagogue: A Social and Psychological Approach." *Tradition* 1, no. 2 (Summer 1959): 141–164.

Leibowitz, Nehama. *Studies in the Book of Genesis*. Translated by Aryeh Newman. Jerusalem: World Zionist Organization, Department for Torah Education and Culture in the Dispora, 1972.

Lewin, Dr. B. *Ozar ha-Geonim*. Haifa, 1928.
Lichtenstein, Rabbi Aharon. "*Ba'ayot ha-Yesod be-Ḥinnukhah shel ha-Ishah*," in Ben-Zion Rosenfeld, ed. *Ha-Ishah ve-Ḥinnukhah*. Kfar Saḇa: Emunah, Ulpanat Bnei Akiva, 1980.
Meiselman, Rabbi Moshe. *Jewish Woman in Jewish Law*. New York: Ktav Publishing House, 1978.
Peli, Pinchas H. *On Repentance in the Thought and Oral Discourses of Rabbi Joseph B. Soloveitchik*. Jerusalem: Orot Publishing House, 1980.
Pianko, Arlene. "Women and the Shofar." *Tradition* 14, no. 4 (Fall 1974): 53–62.
Rackman, Rabbi Emanuel. *One Man's Judaism*. New York: Philosophical Library, 1970.
Riskin, Rabbi Shlomo. *Home Studies in Prayer*. New York: Yeshiva University Youth Bureau, 1967.
———. "Structure and Spontaneity in Prayer." *Judaism* 21, no. 3 (Summer 1972): 328–332.
Schachter, Rabbi Hershel. "Be-Inyanei Beit Knesset." *Or ha-Mizrach* 34 (Tishrei 5746): 54–67.
———. "Ẓe'i Lakh be-Ikvei ha-Ẓon." *Beit Yiẓḥak* 17 (5745): 118–134.
Silver, Arthur M. "May Women Be Taught Bible, Mishnah, and Talmud?" *Tradition* 17, no. 3 (Summer 1978): 74–85.
Slotki, Rev. Dr. I. W. *Soncino Commentary on First Kings*. London: Soncino Press, 1950.
Soloveichik, Rabbi Aharon. "The Attitude of Judaism Toward the Woman." In *Major Addresses Delivered at Midcontinent Conclave and National Leadership Conference, Union of Orthodox Jewish Congregations, (November 27–November 30, 1969)*, pp. 21–32. New York: UOJC, 1970.
———. "A Deeper Insight into the Miracle of Chanukah." *Ha-Mevaser* 3, no. 2 (Shevat 5725): 4.
Soloveitchik, Rav. Joseph B. "A Eulogy for the Talner Rabbi." In *Shiurei HaRav: A Conspectus of the Public Lectures of Rabbi Joseph B. Soloveitchik*, edited by Rabbi Joseph Epstein, pp. 18–26. New York: Tova Press, 1974.
———. "The Community." *Tradition* 17, no. 2 (Spring 1978): 7–24.
———. "The Lonely Man of Faith." *Tradition* 7, no. 2 (1965): 5–67.
Sorotzkin, Rabbi Zalman. *Moznayim la-Mishpat*. Jerusalem: 1968.
Sperber, Rabbi Dr. Daniel. *Minhagei Yisrael*. Jerusalem. Mosad HaRav Kook, 1989.

Stern, Rabbi Yeḥiel Mikhal. *Ḥiddushei ha-Ritva*. Jerusalem, Mosad Ha-Rav Kook, 1976.

Weiss, Rabbi Avraham, "Women and Sifrei Torah." *Tradition* 20, no. 2 (Summer 1982): 106–118.

Wolowelsky, Dr. Joel B. "Modern Orthodoxy and Women's Changing Self-Perception." *Tradition* 22, no. 1 (Spring 1986): 65–81.

Index

1. Biblical Passages

Genesis

1:27 — 1, 2
1:28 — 2n
2:7 — 2n
2:18 — 2n, 3, 4n
2:21–23 — 1
9:7 — 8n
18:28 — 46n
30:1 — 6, 7
31:1–2 — 6
42:5 — 38
49:1 — 33, 34n

Exodus

15:22 — 41
20:12 — 75n
23:25 — 14

Leviticus

15:16 — 87
15:16–18 — 86n
15:19 — 89
15:19–24 — 86n
18:5 — 52n
22:32 — 38, 43, 52n
25:46 — 40

Numbers

5:11–31 — 58
10:9 — 18
16:21 — 38, 43n

Deuteronomy

5:1 — 57, 64
6:4 — 33
6:4–9 — 102
6:7 — 23
11:13 — 13, 14
11:19 — 57
12:29–31 — 114
12:30 — 114
22:5 — 66n
31:10–12 — 34

Joshua

1:8 — 73

Judges

4–5 — 66

1 Kings

8:22–53 — 35
8:28 — 119

Isaiah

55:1 — 41
55:6 — 118

Jeremiah

23:13 — 58n
23:29 — 86

Ezekiel

11:16 — 35

Psalms

19:10 — 92
20:8 — 30
45:14 — 45n
68:27 — 39, 43n
69:14 — 119
145:16 — 30

Proverbs

8:12 — 58n

Job

36:5 — 39

Ecclesiastes

4:9–10 — 4

Esther

3:13 — 49n

2. Talmudic References

Mishnah

Berakhot

2:5 — 102n
3:3 — 23
5:1 — 101

Megillah

1:1 — 50n
1:3 — 41n
4:3 — 44n

Yevamot

6:6 — 8

Ketubbot

5:5 — 8

Sotah

3:4 58, 59
5:1 58n
9:15 91n

Sanhedrin

4:5 2

Avot (Ethics of the Fathers)

2:5 64

Tamid

5:1 36n

Zavim

5:12 94n

Yadayim

3:2 95n

Tosefta

Megillah

2:4 49
3:5 71

Bava Kamma

4:9 66n

Bavli

Berakhot

3a 37
4b 28
6a 119
7b–8a 119
8a 39
9b 101n
11b 72, 73
11b–12a 36
16a 102n
20a 23, 102n
20b 5n, 17n, 18n, 21n, 22n, 23, 50n, 69n, 88, 89
21a 19n
21b 38, 43
22a 85–86, 88
22b 87
26a 88, 101n
26b 20, 21
27b–28a 17n
30a 35n
30b 101, 103
30b–31a 30
33a 73n
34b 101, 104
45a 46n
45b 45, 47n, 70n, 71n
46a 72n
47b 40, 41, 43, 46n, 51
48a 46n

Shabbat

14a 95n
23a 5n

Eruvin

65a 103n

Pesaḥim

56a 33
91b 5n
108a–b 5n
108b 49

Yoma

70a 67

Sukkah

26b 86n, 93n
28a–b 5n
38a 5n, 19n, 70n

Rosh ha-Shanah

32b–33a 66, 73–74
33a 66, 73, 111n

Ta'anit

2a 13

Megillah

4a 5, 48, 49, 69
5a 47, 50
21b 41n, 76
23a 67, 69, 71n, 74n, 76n
23b 43
24b 67
32a 95n

Ḥagigah

3a 34n

Yevamot

61b 8
65b 8
109b 64

Ketubbot

7b 39n
8a 1
58b 9n
59b 8
61b 9n
105a 36

Sotah

20a 58
21b 58n
38 38n
39b 68
41a 34n
49a 29n

Gittin

38b 41n
60a 68, 82n

Kiddushin

29a 5, 14
29b 57
34a 5n
41a 8n
69a 88n

Bava Kamma

82a 41, 42, 87, 88n
82b 89

Bava Batra

19a–20b 86n

Sanhedrin

74a 52
74a–b 53
74b 38n, 43, 53
94b 66

Avodah Zarah

8a 21n

Soferim

13:8 81, 82n
18:4 78

Menahot

20b 117

Arakhin

2b–3a 48n

Tamid

32b 37

Yerushalmi

Berakhot

3:4 88n
4:1 21
5:1 118
7:3 38, 43

Megillah

3:1 36n
4:1 42

Shekalim

3:3 91n

Hagigah

1:1 34n

Ketubbot

13:1 36n

3. Names and Subjects

Abba Binyamin
  prayer in synagogue, 119, 120n
Abraham (patriarch)
  God of Abraham, 122
  introduced morning service, 20
Abudarham, R. David
  gender roles, 5, 6, 7
Adam and Eve, 1–3
Adda b. Abaha, R.
  devarim she-bi-kedushah, 38
Ahavah Rabbah, 26, 36
Ahavat Olam, 26
Akedat Yizhak
  women's roles, 6, 7
Akiva, R., 37
Aleinu, 29, 30
aliyot
  equality of obligation, 71, 75–77
  kevod zibbur, 67
  modesty, 70
  procedure at women's tefillah groups, 80–83, 107, 108, 110, 111n
  shame of ignorance, 68–70
  Torah blessings, 73, 74
  women and public Torah reading, 77–80
Alpert, Rabbi Nissan, xvi
Amidah, *See* Shemoneh Esreh
Arukh ha-Shulhan
  Birkhot ha-Shahar, 24
  Birkhot Shema, 27
  Pesukei de-Zimra, 25
  Shema, 24
  Shemoneh Esreh, 22
  Torah blessings, 74
  Women and public Torah reading, 78, 79
Aseret ha-Dibbrot, 36–37
Ashrei, 29–30
Auerbach, R. David
  Parashat Zakhor, 100
  prizutah, 54n
  Shema, 24
  women Torah reading, 79
Auman, R. Kenneth
  Rav Soloveitchik's view on women's tefillah groups, 107
avadim
  obligation to pray, 14
  to complete the ten, 40

ba'al keri
  reading and studying Torah, 86, 87, 89
  reciting prayers, 86–89
  wearing tefillin, 86n
Ba'al Shem Tov
  pathways to God are not identical, 123
Babylonian Exile
  history of prayer, 15, 33
  immersion, 87
Barekhu
  devarim she-bi-kedushah, 37, 80, 99
  minyan, 37, 44n, 46, 53, 80, 82
  in women's tefillah group, 55, 80, 100n, 111n
Barukh she-Amar, 25
Bat Mitzvah, xvn, 117
beged ish, 66n, 94n
Beit Yaakov
  tefillah groups for female students, 56
Ben Azzai
  Torah study for women, 58, 59

Berkovits, R. Eliezer
  minhag, 117, 118
Berman, R. Saul
  positive commandments fixed by time, 5n, 7n, 100n
  prayer, 44, 100n
  preference of the synagogue for prayer, 121n
  Rav Soloveitchik's view on women's tefillah groups, 107n
  subjective fulfillment of obligatory mitzvah, 100n
  Torah blessings when reading from the Torah scroll, 82n
  women's role, 10, 44n
Bernstein, R. Louis
  role of women, xv
Beruriah
  Torah study, 60, 66
Birkhat ha-Mazon, *See* Grace After Meals
Birkhot ha-Shaḥar, 24–25, 29, 80
Birkhot ha-Torah, *See* Torah blessings
Birkhot Shema, 26, 27, 29
Bitter waters, 58
Bleich, R. J. David
  Megillah, 51n
  minyan, 46n, 51n, 99
  public menorahs, 124n
  public prayer, 99
  Torah study, 83n
Breuer's
  tefillah groups for female students, 56n, 99
Bronspigel, R. Abba
  feminist movement, 112n
  minyan, 56n
  ona'ah bein adam le-ḥavero, 55n
  Rav Soloveitchik's and Rav Feinstein's views, 106n, 107n
  tefillah groups, xvin, 107n
  Torah reading, 77n
  women's role, xvin

Cantillation
  teaching women, 123n
Census
  women and minyan, 45n
Childbearing
  exemption of women, 8n
  secondary purpose, 6, 7
Christianity, influence of, 10–11
Circumcision
  minyan with women, 54, 55

Deborah
  judged Israel, 66
devarim she-bi-kedushah
  minyan, 37–39, 80
  obligation of women, 43, 46n, 55, 56, 100
  women's tefillah groups, 55–56, 80, 99, 107, 110, 111
Dietary Laws, 10

Eger, R. Akiva
  Pesukei de-Zimra, 26
Eleh Ezkerah, 81n
Eliezer, R.
  mitzvah de-rabbim shani, 40
  role of women, 8–9
  tiflut, 57–58, 59–61
Ellinson, R. Elyakim
  Torah study, 66n
Elon, Dr. Menachem
  minhag mevatel halakhah, 116n
erusin, 3n
Esther
  women's obligation in Megillah, 48, 49n
Eve
  creation of, 2n
  ezer ke-negdo, 3
  role of women, 6
eved
  complete the ten, 40
  obligation to pray, 14
ezer ke-negdo
  meaning of term, 3, 4n
Ezra the Scribe
  ba'al keri, 87
  Shemoneh Esreh, 15, 19
  Torah reading, 41, 42
ezrat nashim
  women carrying the Torah, 85, 112n

Feinstein, R. Moshe
  woman wearing tallit, 110
  women's tefillah groups, 108–110
Feminist movement, 112, 115
Firer, R. Ben Tzion
  Torah study, 62, 65
Five Roshei Yeshiva (Rabbis) from the faculty of Yeshiva University's Rabbi Isaac Elchanan Theological Seminary
  appeal to contemporary Torah scholars, 106n, 107n
  feminist movement, 112n, 114n
  statement on women's prayer groups,

hakafot and Megillah reading, xv, xvi
women and public Torah reading, 77n
women's minyan, 56n
ziyyuf ha-torah, 55n
Frimer, R. Aryeh Avraham
correlation principle, 47n
legal exclusion of women from minyan, 45n
pirsuma, 53–54, 55
women and minyan, 44n, 47
Fuchs, R. Yitzchak Ya'akov
praying in synagogue, 121
public prayer, 40–41, 121

Gender roles, 3–11, 44, 45, 79
Gerondi, R. Jonah
kavvanah, 103
Ge'ulah, 28
Gilyonei ha-Shas
Kiddush ha-Shem minyan, 53
Goren, R. Shlomo
women's tefillah groups, 110, 111n
Grace After Meals, 45, 69n, 70n–71n, 88, 96n

Ḥafeẓ Ḥayyim
Torah study, 62–63
Haftarah, 44n, 123n
Haggahot Asheri
Megillah minyan, 51n
hakafot, xvn, 85
Hakhel
description of, 34
hakhel and Torah study for women, 77, 78
obligation of women, 5n
Halevi, R. Judah
public prayer, 40
Halikhot Beitah
Shema, 24
Hallel
women reciting Hallel, 30
women reciting Hallel during the Seder, 5n
Ḥananya b. Teradyon, R., 81n, 82n
Hannah
model of prayer experience, 30
Ḥanukkah candles
kindling in synagogue in the presence of ten people, 54–55
obligation of women, 5n
women lighting Ḥanukkah candles for men, 49

Havdalah, 49n, 50n
Ḥayyei Adam
kavvanah, 102
Hebrew Institute of Riverdale, xvn
teaching trop, 123n
Henkin, R. Yehuda Herzl
feminist movement, 114
kol ishah, 70n
Megillah, 70n
Torah reading, 70n, 78n
Hertzfeld, Sharon
description of "tefillah for girls" at Rabbi Samson Raphael Hirsch (Breuer's), 56n
Ḥiddushei Rav Ḥayyim ha-Levi
kavvanah, 103, 104
Hirsch, R. Samson Raphael
kavod/kaved, 75n
tumah, 92n
Ḥiyya, R.
kavvanah, 101, 104
Home role of women
Jewish continuity, 10, 11
relationship to minyan, 44, 45
relationship to obligation to hear public Torah reading, 79
the only role, 5, 6
the primary role, 7–10
the secondary role, 6, 7
Huna b. R. Joshua, R.
kevod ẓibbur, 67

Individual and communal dialectic, 42
Isaac (patriarch)
God of Isaac, 122
introduced afternoon service, 20
Isaac, R.
synagogues in Babylon, 35
Israel, land of, 45n
Inheritance, 45n

Jacob (patriarch)
communal prayer, 33, 34
devarim she-bi-kedushah, 38
God of Jacob, 122
introduced evening service, 20
role of women, 6, 7
Jewish Theological Seminary, 113
Joseph (patriarch)
Kiddush Hashem, 52n
Joshua b. Levi, R.
kevod ẓibbur, 67
Megillah, 69
prayer, 16, 21

Judah b. Bathyra, R.
  tumah, 85–86, 87, 89, 90, 94

Kaddish
  devarim she-bi-kedushah, 37
  minyan, 37, 44n, 45–46, 53
  mourner's, 116
  in women's tefillah groups, 55, 99, 111
Karo, R. Joseph. *See Shulḥan Arukh*
Kasdan, R. Menachem
  hakhel, 34n
  private prayer, 31n
Kavvanah
  praying in the presence of God, 103, 104, 105
  preparing for prayer, 26
  to fulfill the mitzvah, 102, 103
  understanding words, 101, 102
  women's prayer groups, 100, 105, 106
Kedushah
  devarim she-bi-kedushah, 37
  minyan, 44n, 46, 53
  women's tefillah group, 55, 99, 111n
Keri'at Torah. *See* Torah reading
kevod ẓibbur
  cases, 67, 68
  definition, 75–77
  equality of obligation, 71–77
  modesty, 70
  relationship to *kavod*, 75–77
  shame of ignorance, 68, 69, 70
  Shulḥan Arukh, 77–78
Kiddush
  fulfill a man's obligation, 49n
  obligation of women, 5n
  Shabbat experience, 10
Kiddush ha-Shem
  minyan, 52–53
Klaperman, R. Gilbert
  role of women, xvn
kol ishah, 70n
Kon, R. Abraham
  synagogue, 35n
Kook, R. Avraham Yitzhak ha-Cohen
  Torah study, 60n
Korban Pesaḥ, 5n
Koret ha-Berit
  circumcision minyan, 55

La-Menaẓẓe'aḥ, 29, 30
Lamm, R. Norman
  mixed seating, 11n
  niddah and sanctity of time, 5n
  tumah, 92n
Leḥem Mishneh
  synagogue attendance, 120
Leibowitz, Nehama, 63
  role of women, 6–7
Lichtenstein, R. Aharon
  preference of the synogogue for prayer, 121
  Torah study, 63
Lincoln Square Synagogue
  teaching trop, 123n
Lubavitch
  lighting Shabbat candles, 116
  menorah on public property, 124n
  tefillah groups for female students, 56, 99
Lulav, 5n
Luzzatto, R. Moses Hayyim
  pathway to holiness, 91

Magen Avraham
  aliyot, 77–78
  Ge'ulah, 28
  kavvanah, 102
  prayer, 16
  Torah blessings, 25
  Torah reading, 77, 78
Magen Gibborim
  Shema, 23
Maimonides, R. Moses. *See* Rambam
Maimonides School
  Talmud study, 63
Male and female, creation of, 1–3
Margaliyyot ha-Yam
  Kiddush ha-Shem minyan, 53
Matzah, 5n
me'erah, 69, 70, 71n
Megillah reading
  me'erah, 69, 70
  obligation of women, 5n, 7, 48–49
  requirement of a minyan, 50
  women fulfilling obligation for men, 50, 51
  women's minyan xv, xvi, 48–51
Meiri, R. Menahem b. Solomon
  devarim she-bi-kedushah, 39
  women reading Megillah for men, 50
  women and minyan, 47
  women and public Torah reading, 76
Meiselman, R. Moshe
  Rav Soloveitchik's view on women's tefillah groups, 107
  public prayer, 79
  Torah blessing and reading, 107
Menstrual cycle. *See* Niddah

Mesillat Yesharim
pathway to holiness, 91
Minhag
anesthetic during circumcision, 117
approbation of scholars, 116, 117
bat mitzvah, 117
binding character as opposed to voluntary activity, 117
derived from non-committed circles, 116n
improper and insincere, 116
kaddish, 116
minhag mevatel halakhah, 116
new practice, 115, 116
prayer for Israel and its soldiers, 116
Shabbat candles, 116
"we never saw," 117, 118
wearing skullcaps, 116
Yizkor, 116
Minyan
asking pardon, 54
circumcision, 54, 55
communal prayer, 99
correlation principle, 46–53
devarim she-bi-kedushah, 37, 38, 43
Hanukkah candles, 54, 55
kiddush ha-Shem, 52–53
legal exclusion, 45–46
Megillah minyan, 48–51
onen, 48
pirsuma, 53–55
public Torah reading, 75–77
slaughterer unworthy, 54
tefillah be-ẓibbur, 43
women and minyan, 44–54
women's tefillah group not women's minyan, 55–56
women's tefillah groups, 80, 83, 111n
Mi-she-berakh le-Ẓahal, 116
Mishkenot Ya'akov
prayer in synagogue, 120
Mishnah Berurah
Birkhot ha-Shaḥar, 24
blessings before Shemoneh Esreh, 28n
devarim she-bi-kedushah, 37n, 46n
Ḥanukkah, 55n
havdalah, 50n
kavannah, 103n
Megillah, 49n, 50n
Musaf, 30n
onen, 48n
Pesukei de-Zimra, 26
public Torah reading, 78, 79
Shema, 23–24
Shemoneh Esreh, 22
Mitzvot
blessings for, 27, 66n, 74n, 94n, 111n
goal, 3n
marital obligations, 8–9, 10
Shema, 27
women's exemptions, 3, 5–6, 7, 23, 65–66, 74n, 94n, 99, 111n
Mixed seating, 11n
Musaf, 30

Nachmanides, R. Moses. *See* Ramban
Naḥalat Ẓevi
Shema, 23
Nathan, R.
prayer of the congregation, 39
niddah
awareness of sanctity of time, 5n
cleanliness, 93n, 94, 95, 96
contact with *Sefer Torah*, 85, 90, 91, 97
entering a synagogue, 90, 96, 97n
Ezra's *takkanah*, 88–89
looking at the *Sefer Torah*, 97n
mentioning the name of God, 90, 97
Rabbi Judah ben Bathyra's halakhah, 87

Omer, counting of, 5n
onen, 48
Or Zaru'a
niddah, 97

Papa, R.
Torah study, 64
Parashat Zakhor
women's obligation, 100n
Passover, 5n
Peri Megadim
Ge'ulah blessing, 28
Perishah
Talmud Torah, 60
periẓut,
Birkat ha-Mazon, 51n, 52n, 71n
desecration of the Sabbath, 54n
Megillah reading, 51n, 52n, 71n
Pesukei de-Zimra, 25–26, 29
Phinehas b. Jair, R.
pathway to holiness, 91
pirsuma
Megillah reading, 51n, 52n
pirsuma minyan, 53, 54, 55

Prayer
communal/public 33–42, 43–56, 79, 100
Hannah, 30–31
kavvanah, 100, 101–105, 106, 123–124
private, 13–31, 44
Rambam, 14–18, 20, 21, 101, 103, 104
Ramban, 18–19, 20, 21
Rav Soloveitchik, 19–21
synagogue, 35–36, 37, 96n, 99, 118–121
Temple, 36, 37
women's obligation: private prayer, 13–31; communal prayer, 43–56, 98, 105
(*see also names of prayers*)
Purim, 5n, 48, 51n, 70, 100n (*see* Megillah reading)

Rabbinical Council of America, xv, xvi
Rabinai
devarim she-bi-kedushah, 38
Rachel (matriarch)
role of women, 6, 7
Rackman, R. Emanuel
niddah and sanctity of time, 5n
Rambam
blessing for nonobligatory mitzvah, 66n, 74n, 94n, 111n
kavannah, 101, 103–105
Kiddush ha-Shem, 52n
marital obligations, 9
prayer: private, 14–18, 19–21, 22, 120; communal, 39, 119–120
Shema, 23, 86
synagogue attendance, 119–120
tefillin, 94n
Torah reading, 41–42
Torah scrolls, 86–87
Torah study, 59–61
transgression under duress, 53n
tumah, 86, 87, 89n
women and mitzvot, 5n, 14, 111n
Ramban
non-Jewish practices imitating, 114–115
prayer, 18–19, 20, 21, 22
Ran
daily prayer, 18n
Megillah minyan, 50, 51n, 52n
Rashi
devarim she-bi-kedushah, 40
imitating non-Jewish practices, 114–115
minyan, 45
prayer: private, 21, 22; communal, 40, 41
women and mitzvot, 21
Redemption, 28
Rema
kavvanah, 101, 102
Megillah, 50, 51n, 52n
niddah, 90–91, 93–96, 98
Shema, 23
tefillin, 94n
Torah scroll, 90, 93, 94
Torah study, 64
Responsa Mayan Ganim
Torah study, 61
Responsa Tuv Ayin
Torah study, 60
Rif
Shema, 23
Riskin, R. Shlomo
Rav Soloveitchik's view on women's tefillah groups, 107n
Shemoneh Esreh, 16n, 20n, 21n
structure and spontaneity in prayer, 20n, 21n
Ritva
kevod ẓibbur, 69
Megillah, 69
Torah reading, 70
Rivash
Torah reading, 69n
Rosh
devarim she-bi-kedushah, 40
public prayer, 40
Shema, 23
Rosh ha-Shanah, 93, 96n

Safra, R.
kavvanah, 101, 104
Schacter, R. Hershel
appeal to contemporary Torah scholars, 106, 107
devarim she-bi-kedushah, 99n
feminist movement, 112, 113, 114
incomplete fulfillment of prayer, 99n
minhag, 116, 117
minyan, 56n, 100n
Parashat Zakhor, 100n
public prayer, 99n
women and public Torah reading, 77n
women's prayer groups, xvin, 55n, 56n, 107n, 113, 116, 117
ziyyuf ha-Torah, 55n

Seder, 5n
Sefer ha-Berit
circumcision minyan, 54
Sefer Ḥasidim
Torah study, 64–65
Sefer Mitzvot Gadol
Torah study, 65
Sha'agat Aryeh
Ge'ulah, 28
Shabbat
candles, 116
declaring a slaughterer unworthy, 54
home aspects, 10
obligation of women, 50n
Shapiro, R. Avraham
women's prayer groups, 111, 112n
Shema
ba'al keri, 86, 88, 89n, 90
Ezra, 88, 89n, 90
Jacob and his sons, 33
kavvanah, 102, 103
minyan, 44n
Shulḥan Arukh, 23, 90
themes, 26–28
women, 5n, 21–24, 27, 47n
Shemoneh Esreh
ba'al keri, 90
history and function, 13, 15–16, 18–19, 22
kavvanah, 101–102, 103, 104, 105
minyan, 44n, 55
part of *hakhel*, 34
Rambam, 14–18, 19, 101, 103, 104, 105
Ramban, 18–19
relationship to Pesukei de-Zimra, 26
women, 16–17, 19, 25, 28, 55
Sherby, R. Louis, 108n
Sheshet, R.
kevod ẓibbur, 67
Shir shel Yom, 29, 30
Shofar, 5n
Shulḥan Arukh
aliyot, 77
kavvanah, 102
minyan, 45–46, 53
prayer, 17–18
Shema, 23, 90
synagogue attendance, 120
Torah blessings, 24, 80–81
tumah, 90, 91, 93–94
Shulḥan Arukh ha-Rav
tumah, 97
Sifrei Torah, *See* Torah scrolls
Simeon b. Gamliel, R.
forbade his wife to do work, 8–9
Simeon b. Lakish, R.
Jacob blessing his children, 33
Simḥat Torah, xv, 85
Simon, R.
devarim she-bi-kedushah, 38
Skullcaps
minhag of wearing, 116
Solomon
Temple dedication, 34–35
Soloveichik, R. Aharon
kavod/kaved, 75
Kiddush ha-Shem, 52n
tumah, 92
women and mitzvot, 3n, 5n
women's superiority to men, 2n–3n
Soloveitchik, R. Joseph B. (Yosef Dov)
Adam and Eve, 2n, 4n
ezer ke-negdo, 4n
kavvanah, 105
rationale of prayer, 19–20
women and Torah study, 63
women carrying Torah scroll, 112n
Sorotzkin, R. Zalman
Torah study, 62n
sotah, 58
Sperber, R. Daniel
minhagim, 116n
Sugah ba-Shoshanim
niddah touching Torah, 97
Sukkot
blessing, 72–73
dwelling in sukkah, 5n
hakhel, 34
Synagogues
kavvanah, 100, 119
mixed seating, 11n
niddah, 90–91, 93–94, 95, 96n
origin, 35–37
women's tefillah groups, 118, 122, 123

taharat ha-mishpaḥah, 10
Tallit
women wearing, 110
Tam, Rabbenu
blessings for non-obligatory mitzvah, 74n, 94n, 111n
private and comunal Torah study, 73–74
Tanḥum, R.
kevod ẓibbur, 67
Talmud Torah. *See* Torah study

tefillah be-makom ẓibbur, 120–121
tefillah be-ẓibbur
definition of, 39
female students in Yeshivot, 99, 100
greater efficacy, 39
preferable to private prayer?, 99, 100, 105, 106
rabbinical decree or an advantageous and good practice?, 40, 41
women in, 43–45, 46n, 100
Tefillah li-shelom ha-Medinah, 116
Tefillin, 5n, 66n, 93n, 94n
Tendler, R. Mordechai
Rav Feinstein's view on women's tefillah groups, 108, 109
Time
exemption of women from positive time bound commandments, 5–6
sanctity of, 5n
Torah blessings
at the Torah, 76
at women's tefillah groups, 80–83, 107, 108, 110, 111n
communal Torah blessings, 73–74
cover the entire day, 73
hakhel, 34
the blessings, 71–72
women's obligation, 24–25
Torah reading
history of communal Torah reading, 41–42
kevod ẓibbur, 68, 70, 71, 75–77
women, xvi, 56, 57, 76, 78, 79
Torah scrolls
women and *Sifre Torah*, 85–98
women reading from Torah scroll, 108
Torah study
at women's tefillah groups, 83n
distinction between private and communal Torah study, 79–80
encompasses all actions, 72–73
Torah blessings for, 25
women and Torah study, 57–66
Torah Temimah
Torah study, 61, 62
learn in order to do, 64
Tosafot
communal prayer, 41
women and minyan, 45
women and prayer, 22
Tur
synagogue attendance, 119
women and Torah study, 61

Ulla b. Rav
kevod ẓibbur, 67
U-Va le-Ẓion, 29, 30

Vilna Gaon
kavvanah, 102
Torah blessings, 25
women attending synagogue, 44

Weinberg, R. Jehiel Jacob
minhag, 117
Wind, R. Eliyahu Shmuel
niddah touching Torah, 97
Wise, Isaac Mayer
mixed seating, 11n
Wolowelsky, Dr. Joel B.
women and Torah study, 63n
Women's tefillah groups
conclusion, 123–124
debate in Rabbinical Council of America (RCA), xv–xvi
Hebrew Institute of Riverdale, xii
kavannah, 105–106
practices and procedures, 55, 56, 107, 108
proliferation of, xi
rabbinic views: critical, 55–56, 77–78, 83n, 99, 106, 112, 114, 115, 116; positive or neutral, 107, 108–110, 111, 112–115, 117–118
relation to synagogue, 118, 121
services for females in Yeshivot, 56
teaching trop, 123n
Torah blessings at women's tefillah groups, 80–83
touching the Torah, 85, 97–98

Yaveẓ
Torah reading, 68, 69
Yehai shemeh, 33–34
Yeshiva University
High School for Girls prayer services, 56, 99
statement of five rabbis on the faculty of Rabbi Isaac Elchanan Theological Seminary, xv, xxin
Torah study at Stern College, xii, 63
Yishtabbaḥ, 25
Yizkor, 116
Yom Kippur
Eleh Ezkerah, 81n
fasting, 5n
women attending services, 93

Yose, R.
  entering synagogue, 37
  studying but not observing Torah, 64
Yose bar Ḥanina, R.
  prayer instituted by the Patriarchs, 20, 21
Yoẓer ha-Me'orot
  individual obligation, 26
  said in Temple, 36

ẓarah
  definition as it relates to prayer, 19
ẓelem Elohim, 2
ẓeniut
  defining *kevod ẓibbur*, 70
zimmun, 45, 70n, 71n
ziyyuf ha-Torah, 55, 99n, 110
ẓiẓit
  beged ish, 66n, 94n
  exemption of women, 5n, 94n
  meaning of portion, 26
  ẓiẓit blessings, 74n, 94n